CONTEMPORARY
JAPAN

D0122020

A HISTORY OF THE CONTEMPORARY WORLD

General Editor: Keith Robbins

This series offers an historical perspective on the development of the contemporary world. Each of the books examines a particular region or a global theme as it has evolved in the recent past. The focus is primarily on the period since the 1980s but authors provide deeper context wherever necessary. While all the volumes offer an historical framework for analysis, the books are written for an interdisciplinary audience and assume no prior knowledge on the part of readers.

Published

Contemporary Japan
Jeff Kingston

In Preparation

Contemporary America
Michael Heale

Contemporary Latin America
Robert H Holden & Rina Villars

Contemporary South Asia
David Hall Matthews

Contemporary Africa
Tom Lodge

Contemporary China
Yongnian Zheng

CONTEMPORARY JAPAN

HISTORY, POLITICS, AND SOCIAL CHANGE SINCE THE 1980S

JEFF KINGSTON

WILEY-BLACKWELL

A John Wiley & Sons, Ltd., Publication

This edition first published 2011

Blackwell Publishing was acquired by John Wiley & Sons in February 2007. Blackwell's
publishing program has been merged with Wiley's global Scientific, Technical, and Medical
business to form Wiley-Blackwell.

Registered Office
John Wiley & Sons Ltd, The Atrium, Southern Gate, Chichester, West Sussex, PO19 8SQ,
United Kingdom

Editorial Offices
350 Main Street, Malden, MA 02148-5020, USA
9600 Garsington Road, Oxford, OX4 2DQ, UK
The Atrium, Southern Gate, Chichester, West Sussex, PO19 8SQ, UK

For details of our global editorial offices, for customer services, and for information about how
to apply for permission to reuse the copyright material in this book please see our website at
www.wiley.com/wiley-blackwell.

Library of Congress Cataloging-in-Publication Data

Kingston, Jeff, 1957–
  Contemporary Japan : history, politics and social change since the 1980s / Jeffrey Kingston.
      p. cm. – (History of the contemporary world)
  Includes bibliographical references and index.
  ISBN 978-1-4051-9194-4 (hardcover : alk. paper) – ISBN 978-1-4051-9193-7
(pbk. : alk. paper) 1. Japan–History–Heisei period, 1989– 2. Japan–Social
conditions–1989– 3. Japan–Economic conditions–1989– I. Title.
  DS891.K538 2011
  952.04–dc22

                          2010009774

A catalogue record for this book is available from the British Library.

Set in 10.5/13 pt Minion by Toppan Best-set Premedia Limited
Printed and bound in Malaysia by Vivar Printing Sdn Bhd

4   2011

Contents

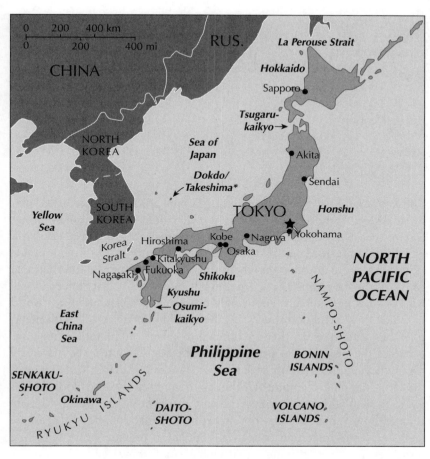

Map of Japan
*These are the Korean and Japanese names for this disputed territory

Series Editor's Preface

The contemporary world frequently presents a baffling spectacle: "new world orders" come and go; "clashes of civilizations" seem imminent if not actual; "peace dividends" appear easily to vanish into thin air; terrorism and "wars on terror" occupy the headlines. "Mature" states live alongside "failed" states in mutual apprehension. The "rules" of the international game, in these circumstances, are difficult to discern. What "international law" is, or is not, remains enduringly problematic. Certainly it is a world in which there are still frontiers, borders, and boundaries, but both metaphorically and in reality they are difficult to patrol and maintain. "Asylum" occupies the headlines as populations shift across continents, driven by fear. Other migrants simply seek a better standard of living. The organs of the "international community," though frequently invoked, look inadequate to deal with the myriad problems confronting the world. Climate change, however induced, is not susceptible to national control. Famine seems endemic in certain countries. Population pressures threaten finite resources. It is in this context that globalization, however understood, is both demonized and lauded.

Such a list of contemporary problems could be amplified in detail and almost indefinitely extended. It is a complex world, ripe for investigation in this ambitious new series of books. "Contemporary," of course, is always difficult to define. The focus in this series is on the evolution of the world since the 1980s. As time passes, and as the volumes appear, it no longer seems sensible to equate "the world since 1945" with "contemporary history." The legacy of the "Cold War" lingers on but it is emphatically "in the background." The fuzziness about "the 1980s" is deliberate. No single year ever carries the same significance across the globe. Authors are therefore establishing their own precise starting points, within the overall "contemporary" framework.

The series treats the history of particular regions, countries, or continents but does so in full awareness that such histories, for all their continuing distinctiveness, can only rarely be considered apart from the history of the world as a whole. Economic, demographic, environmental, and religious issues transcend state, regional, or continental boundaries. Just as the world itself struggles to reconcile diversity and individuality with unity and common purpose, so do the authors of these volumes. The concept is challenging. Authors have been selected who sit loosely on their disciplinary identity – whether that be as historians, political scientists, or students of international relations. The task is to integrate as many aspects of contemporary life as possible in an accessible manner.

This volume on Japan rises to the challenge. The country's history conspicuously illustrates the interactions that have been alluded to. The first half of the twentieth century saw its engagement with "the world" collapse in catastrophe. The country started thereafter on its "new beginning" under outside direction. Yet its proud and self-contained past still continued to send somewhat ambivalent messages into a Japan which proceeded to make itself a "modern miracle." This account, however, is no bland narrative of a "success story." It is, rather, an account of decades in which the reconciliations – economic, cultural, demographic, political – which appeared to have been solid achievements all began to unravel. It is this process of renewed self-examination, visible across so many areas of both private and public life, which this book treats as an interconnected whole. There can be no better example, to begin this series, of a country seeking anxiously both to adjust and to retain its own culture and identity in a changing world.

Keith Robbins

Acknowledgments

I would like to thank the following people for their assistance, comments, advice, inspiration and encouragement with all the usual caveats about absolving them of responsibility for what I have written: Jake Adelstein, Hideaki Asahi, Michael and Marie-Therese Barrett, Tom Boardman, Mary Brinton, Roland Buerk, David Campbell, John Campbell, Christian Caryl, Kyle Cleveland, Florian Coulmas, Lucy Craft, Gerald Curtis, Greg Davis, Phil Deans, Mure Dickie, Alexis Dudden, Robert Dujarric, Bill Emmott, Martin Fackler, Malcolm Foster, Howard French, John Glionna, Roger Goodman, Mariko Hashioka, Laura Hein, Ektarina Hertog, Steve Hesse, Peter Hill, Kaori Hitomi, Jun Honna, Andrew Horvat, Tin Tin Htun, Hiroshi Ishida, Makoto Ishida, Velisarios Kattoulas, David Leheny, Bertil Lintner, Atsushi Maki, Gavan McCormack, David McNeill, Johnny Miller, Sebastian Moffett, Jack Mosher, Mariko Nagai, Chika Nakayama, Atsushi Ogata, Akihiro Ogawa, Robert Orr, David Pilling, Lawrence Repeta, Donald Richie, Ken Ruoff, Sven Saaler, Richard Samuels, Murray and Jenny Sayle, Fritz Schmitz, Miki Seko, Mark Selden, Sawako Shirahase, David Slater, Emi Sumitomo, Ayumi Suzuki, Yuki Tanaka, Kazuhiko Togo, Henry Tricks, Gabrielle Vogt, Yoshibumi Wakamiya, Shinya Watanabe, Robert Whiting, Charles Worthen, Hyun Sook Yun, Dominique Ziegler, and many others who know who you are. Also I wish to express thanks to the people at Wiley who took on this project and ensured its smooth sailing, especially Tessa Harvey, Keith Robbins, Tom Bates, Gillian Kane, Sarah Dancy, and Brian Goodale.

Finally, my deep gratitude to Machiko Osawa, who contributed greatly to this book and, along with our dogs Rhubarb and Goro, listened patiently and kept me in good spirits.

Please note that in Japan, Japanese names begin with the family name, but here are cited according to Western convention: given name followed by surname.

Part I
Introduction

Chapter 1

Transformations After World War II

Japan's recovery from the war devastation that left its cities and factories in ruins was surprisingly rapid, but nobody in the late 1940s could have foreseen that its economy would one day become the second largest in the world. In the aftermath of defeat, Japanese experienced unprecedented socio-economic upheaval during what has to be regarded as one of the world's great success stories in the second half of the twentieth century. Japan was reconstituted during the US Occupation (1945–52), generated an economic miracle in the late 1950s and 1960s, weathered the oil shocks in the 1970s, and saw an extraordinary asset bubble burst at the end of the 1980s, setting the stage for the Lost Decade of the 1990s. This was a time of one-party democracy under the Liberal Democratic Party (LDP) that ruled Japan as a partner of the bureaucracy and big business in what is known as Japan, Inc. or the Iron Triangle. It was also a time when the long shadows of wartime deprivation and dislocation shaped a national consensus prioritizing stability, security, and policies aimed at minimizing risk.

In post-WWII Japan, there was massive migration from rural areas to the cities, pulled by the lure of jobs and pushed by the limited opportunities of small-scale farming. The ensuing growth of cities, with housing developments, train lines, and highways, created a mass commuting culture with a rhythm very distinct from traditional rural life. The salaryman lifestyle became iconic, a way of life rooted in the breadwinner model, with a work-driven husband, a full-time housewife, and at least two children, usually living with some of their grandparents. Signs of growing affluence became more conspicuous in an expanding middle class. Women were nominally freed from patriarchy with the abolition of the *ie* (patrilineal family) system, and gained the right to vote and other constitutional guarantees, but in the workforce they remained largely marginalized. The rapid growth of the 1960s did not generate large income disparities as was common in Western industrialized societies, and the relatively egalitarian distribution combined with job security strengthened social cohesion and a sense of shared destinies. This social capital remains one of the foundations and strengths of post-WWII Japan, but is under threat due to widening income disparities.

The spread of mass media, especially television, helped nurture a strong sense of nation even as overt displays of nationalism remained taboo, tainted by war. Emperor Hirohito was transformed from a wartime leader into an avuncular and soft-spoken symbol of the nation. Japan was visibly welcomed back into the community of nations at the 1964 Tokyo Olympics, a sign that it had been rehabilitated under the auspices of US hegemony.

While neighbors may have found the continuing presence of the US military reassuring, Japanese remained divided and ambivalent about this encroachment on their sovereignty. Mass demonstrations against renewal of the US–Japan Security Treaty in 1960 revealed a surprising depth of anger, not only directed against Washington. Prime Minister Nobusuke Kishi, who negotiated the renewal, was a suspected Class-A war criminal, one of those senior leaders deemed responsible for orchestrating Japan's military rampage through Asia 1931–45. He was never indicted, and was released from prison for reasons that remain unclear given his culpable record in Manchuria and later as the wartime Minister of Commerce and Industry. Many Japanese, with the horrors of the war fresh in their memories, deeply resented Kishi's rise to premier through backroom political maneuvering; he represented an unacceptable link to a thoroughly discredited past. In those days, nobody was trying to glorify or justify Japan's wartime exploits as some do now, and anyone associated with Japanese militarism was *persona non grata*, making it especially galling that such a key figure in the wartime cabinet was suddenly the leader of a country that was trying to reinvent itself by repudiating such continuities.

Occupation 1945–52

Allied in name, but an American show in practice, the Supreme Commander of the Allied Powers (SCAP, a term often used to refer more generally to the Occupation authorities) was personified in the larger-than-life, dominating presence of General Douglas MacArthur. General Headquarters (GHQ), the administration under SCAP, governed indirectly through the existing Japanese bureaucracy; this was a significant contrast to the situation in a divided Germany where the Allied powers ruled directly.

The US presided over Japan in the aftermath of war in order to demilitarize and democratize its former enemy.[1] SCAP acted on the perception that the military had derailed democracy and hijacked the nation into war, and that the high concentration of political and economic power made Japan vulnerable to such a scenario. With Germany and the two world wars it precipitated in mind, the US sought to inoculate Japan from a militarist revival. Thus, SCAP focused on eliminating the military and dispersing political and economic power more widely.

Demilitarizing Japan started with demobilizing the troops, confiscating their weapons, and eliminating military institutions. This was followed up by a ban on war, and the means to wage it, in Article 9 of the Constitution authored by SCAP and adopted by Japan in 1947. Martial arts were also banned and SCAP authorities censored the media and films in clumsy efforts to stifle non-existent militaristic sentiments. People were war weary and the military was widely blamed for the destruction and suffering the Japanese people endured.

The war in the Pacific (1941–5), inflamed by racial prejudice and fears, was a "war without mercy."[2] Given the extent of excesses and atrocities committed by Japan, the US, and its allies, the mutual accommodations and relative beneficence of the Occupation are striking. The arrival of the Americans sparked fears of retribution, and soon after the surrender the Japanese authorities were already recruiting women to provide sexual services to the troops. Throughout the Occupation, American troops did commit serious crimes against the civilian population, including murder, rape, and assault, but not on the scale that many Japanese had feared, knowing as they did how the Imperial Armed Forces operated in the territories it occupied.

In late 1945 and early 1946, the Americans helped avert a famine by bringing in food supplies. They were also importing all sorts of commodities that were illicitly diverted to the thriving black markets where almost anything was available for a price. Soldiers used their PX (Post Exchange, a store operated by the military) privileges to advantage, discovering just how valuable nylon stockings, among other sundries, could be in a barter economy. Rationing was in force, but few people survived without supplementing their diet by other means. Those without enough money for black-market purchases traveled to the countryside where they would barter kimonos or other valuables for rice and vegetables. Making their way back home on crowded trains, they took pains to evade police who often confiscated the food they were bringing back to their families.

Japan in the early postwar years was not the relatively crime-free haven it has become, and violence was common. There were bloody gang wars and turf battles between Japanese mobsters and rivals from Korea and Taiwan, a legacy of empire. Demobilized soldiers had useful skills and few options, providing the yakuza (organized crime) with a large pool of potential recruits. Prostitution flourished because many women had few other ways to support themselves and their families. Nonetheless, there were recriminations against these so-called *pan-pan* girls brazenly soliciting GIs, attractive because they were flush with cash and had access to the prized goods available at the PX. Drug use was also at epidemic proportions as many people had addictions to amphetamines which they had developed during the war as soldiers or factory workers. In the hard scrabble for survival, theft and robbery were common crimes of desperation.

Unions flourished under SCAP because it released union organizers held in prison during the war years and because of labor reforms that made it easier to organize workers. SCAP believed that strong unions would help spread political power more widely and strengthen democracy. Harsh working and living conditions, along with wages that failed to keep up with galloping inflation, also helped unions grow increasingly powerful. When SCAP banned a general strike in early 1947, unions felt betrayed while companies understood that the authorities would tolerate union busting tactics. Management targeted union members with the help of mobsters, undermining the yakuza's self-styled image as protectors of the weak and vulnerable. Workers came to understand that joining the moderate company-sponsored unions and renouncing membership of the more radical unions was their best, or at least safest, option, providing valuable context for understanding how labor relations became harmonious as Japan made the transition to high-speed economic growth in the late 1950s.

In 1946, SCAP convened the International Military Tribunal for the Far East (IMTFE), prosecuting 28 high-level leaders deemed most responsible for orchestrating the war, the so-called Class-A war criminals that were charged with crimes against peace. Emperor Hirohito was notable for his absence, disappointing US allies such as the UK and Australia who demanded he be held accountable. This also disappointed many Japanese who felt that the war was fought in his name and mourned the loss of some 2.1 million soldiers who died at his behest in addition to some 800,000 civilian wartime deaths. At the very least, some thought, Hirohito should have abdicated to show contrition and take responsibility for the devastation Japanese suffered as a result of the government's reckless aggression.

The Imperial Household Agency, with the connivance of SCAP, reinvented Emperor Hirohito as a powerless figurehead in wartime Japan who was out of the loop, misled and manipulated by the military leaders, and fearful of a coup should he intervene.[3] This was the script for the IMTFE, and the orthodox narrative that prevailed until Hirohito's death in 1989. During the trial, the Class-A war criminals were coached to avoid implicating Hirohito. At one critical juncture when General Hideki Tojo slipped up, the court was recessed and he was reminded of his lines. When the session resumed, the court record was erased and Tojo, a loyal and willing scapegoat, insulated Hirohito from guilt by assuming all responsibility.

The US decided that Emperor Hirohito was more valuable alive promoting constitutional democracy than as a martyr for the right wing to rally around. Instead of feeling the hangman's noose, he renounced his divinity and became a model constitutional monarch. Throughout the Occupation he lent his support to SCAP democratization efforts while also serving as a reassuring symbol of nation and continuity amidst hardship and upheaval. By not prosecuting Hirohito, however, the US complicated the issue of war responsibility. Japan has often been criticized for not assuming that burden; but if the man in whose name the war was fought was not held accountable and was depicted as a victim of militarist hotheads, why should anyone assume war responsibility?

The legal proceedings of the IMTFE were deeply flawed and the defendants did not receive a fair trial; guilty verdicts were preordained. In addition, Allied war crimes went unexamined and unpunished, leading many observers to dismiss the whole spectacle as "victor's justice." Since then, right-wingers in Japan have harped on the very real flaws of the trial in a bid to exonerate Japan of the serious war crimes it committed.

There were profound inconsistencies in the Occupation, most prominently the decreeing of democracy without consulting the people. SCAP wrote Japan's Constitution, one with a distinctly foreign flavor, and established the ground rules for democracy, rendering it a top-down, rather than grassroots, initiative. Potential political candidates who were blacklisted by SCAP had no recourse. The media, considered a vital element of democratization by SCAP, was routinely censored, ensuring no criticism of SCAP and no delving into the atomic bombings. SCAP also nurtured a vibrant union movement to strengthen democracy by spreading political power more widely, and then stood by and watched Japanese companies crush it through violent means.

There was a limited reckoning for war crimes, but overall there were considerable continuities bridging wartime and postwar Japan. Aside from letting Hirohito off the hook, the US made common cause with the conservative political elite who ran Japan during the war years. Most of Japan's bureaucracy was left intact aside from some purges of top-level officials. The *zaibatsu*, family-owned industrial conglomerates that dominated the Japanese economy during the war years, were initially targeted for dissolution; they were blamed for aiding and abetting the government's imperial expansion. However, they were restructured rather than dissolved. Under "new management," these corporations remain prominent in the contemporary Japanese economy, including such familiar names as Mitsui, Mitsubishi, and Sumitomo among others.

The "reverse course" began in 1947, when the Cold War with the Soviet Union was heating up. Prior to this shift in Occupation policies, the US and SCAP sought to punish and reform Japan while cultivating democracy. After 1947, the US backtracked on many of these reform initiatives, abandoned punitive policies, and emphasized economic recovery. In the context of the Cold War, Japan was a designated showcase for the superiority of the US system and that meant, above all, reviving the Japanese economy. At the time, there was growing left-wing political influence in Japan and it was hoped that improved living standards and working conditions would stem what seemed an alarming development. Economic recovery held the added attraction of promoting Japanese self-reliance and weaning it from US subsidies. There was to be no Marshall Plan as in Europe because there was little support in the US for such largesse towards Japan.

Due to the nature of SCAP's indirect rule through Japanese institutions, it is important to acknowledge the significant influence of Japanese officials over the pace and scope of Occupation-era reforms. They were not merely passive junior partners carrying out orders from on high; they played a key role in shaping the agenda and realizing it. There was considerable scope for stonewalling, foot-dragging, and diluting or reinterpreting initiatives, and much leeway for Japanese officials to exploit new opportunities to implement their own long-standing agendas such as land reform.

Perhaps the most profound transformation unleashed under the auspices of SCAP was land reform. As with all SCAP reforms, it was implemented through the Japanese government by Japanese officials with considerable discretionary authority in translating directives into realities on the ground. This massive agrarian reform helped tenant farmers, tilling the soil under unfavorable conditions, to become owners of the land they cultivated. Land reform was aimed at breaking the monopoly over economic and political power enjoyed by the rural gentry, thereby weakening a class seen to have supported Japanese militarism. It also undercut the influence of left-wing political groups in the countryside since land reform had been one of their more appealing pledges. Farm output increased as a result of this reform, as farmers who own their land and retain the fruits of their labor work the land more intensively. Aside from boosting Japan's food availability and self-sufficiency, this meant that many rural households that previously lived a barely subsistence lifestyle, burdened with heavy debts, were suddenly and dramatically lifted out of poverty. This created a virtuous economic cycle. The owner-farmers became a new large middle class of consumers buying the output from Japan's reviving factories that were rapidly increased their workforces, thereby absorbing rural surplus labor. Those remaining in the countryside were better off as small parcels of land had to support fewer people. Moreover, this growing middle class of owner-cultivators became loyal supporters of the LDP, helping to keep it in power.

Politics

In the post-WWII era, the most striking political development was extended one-party rule by the LDP since it was formed in 1955.[4] The party was a merger of conservative parties responding to growing support for the Japan Socialist Party (JSP). These were the two main contenders in this era, but it was an unequal contest.

Japan's one-party democracy was called the 1955 system, one that was sustained by powerful conservative support. Big business and the bureaucracy favored the LDP and its conservative agenda. This provided the LDP with generous campaign funding and opportunities to wield its influence to cultivate and sustain loyal constituencies. LDP candidates enjoyed the advantages of incumbency and once elected usually retained their seats and often kept them in the family, passing them on to sons. Porkbarrel projects became a mainstay of party support as public works contracts were doled out to favored construction companies, a generosity that was reciprocated. Aside from ensuring a steady flow of projects to their districts, politicians relied on support organizations (*koenkai*) to raise money and serve as a conduit for favors and patronage.

The LDP emphasized pragmatism, downplaying ideological issues in the wake of the 1960 mass demonstrations while delivering rapid economic growth and a doubling of incomes, giving people a reason to support it despite misgivings about systemic corruption. The LDP was the junior partner to the bureaucracy in policy-making, perhaps reassuring voters that responsible and competent technocrats were in charge rather than unsavory politicians. It succeeded in convincing voters that it was more capable than the opposition to manage the economy and maintain good relations with the US vital to Japan's security. It also adopted the popular three non-nuclear principles and eased anxieties about Japan's incremental rearmament by informally limiting defense spending to 1 percent of GDP. The LDP was skillful at reinventing itself, responding to political challenges by adopting opposition proposals and policies such as the ambitious environmental legislation implemented at the outset of the 1970s. In this sense, political competition pushed the LDP to adopt more socially progressive policies than it might otherwise have done. Negotiating with the US for the reversion of Okinawa in 1972 also demonstrated that it could effectively champion national interests and stand up to the US.

There have been few LDP leaders untainted by money politics, but this never seemed to matter to enough voters to make a difference. Neither did media exposés of mob ties. And it was only in the 1990s that rumors of CIA funding were proven true. Like the Christian Democrats in Italy, the LDP stayed in power so long because it was deft at co-opting, ruthless in political infighting, and savvy in the ways of channeling money. But the LDP grew increasingly sclerotic and discredited by the prolonged recession of the Lost Decade and its failed attempts to revive the economy, setting the stage for its ouster from power in 2009.

Foreign Policy

The security alliance with the US has been a divisive political issue, one that created a clear distinction between the LDP and the JSP. The JSP favored ending it, ousting the US from its bases in Japan, and embracing unilateral pacifism as outlined in Article 9 of the Constitution. It stressed that Japan should be neutral in the Cold War and that the alliance, and ongoing US military presence, exposed Japan to unnecessary risks. The mass demonstrations in 1960 against renewing the security treaty were a show of force by the left, tapping into popular misgivings about the alliance. These apprehensions grew during the Vietnam War as the US used its bases in Japan in support of the war and also purchased war-related material from Japanese producers, including napalm. The Vietnam War was embarrassing to Japan's political elite because Japan was in the uncomfortable position of aiding a war against fellow Asians.

During the Korean War (1950–3), US bases in Japan played an important role in the conflict while the Japanese economy was revived by large-scale, war-related procurements. PM Shigeru Yoshida called the Korean War a "gift from the gods" because American purchases jolted the economy out of recession. He brushed off US demands that Japan rearm, emphasizing that Japan could not afford to do so without threatening its economic recovery. This rare instance of Japan standing up to Washington is known as the Yoshida doctrine.

In 1952 the US Occupation ended on terms negotiated in the San Francisco Peace Treaty of 1951. Japan agreed that the US could maintain bases in Japan and also retain control over Okinawa (a group of islands lying to the southwest of the Japanese archipelago) where most of its bases were located. It also negotiated reparations agreements in the 1950s with most of the Southeast Asian nations it occupied during the war (Burma, Indonesia, Vietnam, and the Philippines), involving export credits that helped Japanese firms establish markets for Japanese goods in these countries. By the mid-1950s there were signs of a deal with the Soviet Union on the disputed northern islands off the coast of Hokkaido, but Tokyo killed the deal by suddenly raising its demands. The Soviets occupied these islands in the waning days of the war and have kept them ever since. For the US, such a deal was undesirable because it would have improved the Soviet image, undermined US Cold War propaganda and lessened Moscow's tensions with Tokyo.

Normalization of relations with South Korea in 1965 was a significant effort by Japan to overcome smoldering hostility stemming from its brutal colonial rule in Korea between 1910 and 1945. Normalization was a necessary but insufficient step to turn the page on the past; tensions between the two nations over their shared and traumatic past are never far below the surface, occasionally erupting over history textbooks or territorial disputes. Japan paid the South Korean government $800 million in grants and soft loans as compensation and in return Seoul renounced all further individual or government claims. The South Korean government also assumed responsibility for compensating Korean victims of Japanese colonial rule from the funds Japan provided. Aside from small token payments, however, most of the money went to building infrastructure. Since the South Korean government released the original normalization documents in 2005, old wounds have reopened and the issue of compensation claims remains controversial and unresolved.

Japan normalized relations with China in 1972, following Washington's lead. The US decision to reverse its long-standing Cold War policy of isolating China and pretending that Taiwan was the legitimate government came as a complete surprise to Japan, one of the two Nixon shocks that raised questions about Washington's reliability. Tokyo was unhappy that it had not been consulted or informed beforehand, underscoring the fundamental inequality of the alliance.[5]

Normalization of ties with China led to the Treaty of Peace and Friendship in 1978. From this beginning there have been belated efforts to atone for the massive destruction Japan's Imperial Armed Forces inflicted over wide areas of China. China renounced claims to reparations and war damages; however, beginning in 1979, Japan responded with a sustained large-scale development aid program involving mostly loans but also grants, technical cooperation, and training programs. Numerous infrastructure projects ranging from highways and railways to seaports, airports, and power stations were funded by the Japanese government and have played a critical role in facilitating China's rapid economic rise. These massive amounts of economic and technical assistance are the functional equivalent of reparations without the associated political and historical baggage. They have not dissipated popular animosity in China directed towards Japan, and to some extent are accepted with minimal gratitude as a down payment on what China is owed for Japan's past sins. These projects, however, have cemented strong economic ties, nurturing a booming market for Japan's exports while creating a low-cost production site.

In 1974 when PM Tanaka toured Southeast Asia, the government was shocked by anti-Japanese demonstrations. In response it unveiled what it called "heart-to-heart" diplomacy, engaging in sustained soft-power efforts to enhance cultural and student exchanges, bolstered by sharp increases in official development assistance (ODA). Japan has wielded its economic resources and technical prowess effectively since the 1970s to gain influence, heal wounds, and promote economic development throughout Asia.

Tokyo has been reluctant to use ODA as an overt political weapon to pressure foreign governments, but like other nations it has leveraged ODA to its economic benefit by tying aid to Japanese-provided goods and services. Its politically neutral approach to ODA meant that it provided crucial support to repressive regimes such as Burma under Ne Win, the Philippines under Marcos, and Indonesia under Suharto. The emphasis on loans for mega-infrastructure projects was also mortgaging poor countries' futures even as Japan knew that officials involved were lining their pockets. However, as Washington emphasized burden sharing and ratcheted up pressure on Japan to assume greater international responsibilities commensurate with its economic status, Japan responded generously to Asia's huge development needs. By 1989, just as the economic bubble was peaking, Japan also emerged as the world's largest donor of ODA.

Economy

After WWII, Japan's economic prospects were grim. Intense aerial bombing had leveled many of its factories, it was short of capital and resources, and it was an international pariah whose products were generally unwelcome in overseas markets save one. The US played a crucial role in Japan's recovery through emergency assistance, the land reform, taming hyperinflation, setting a low exchange rate for the yen (JPY360 = $1) favorable for exports, and jumpstarting growth with massive Korean War procurements. More importantly it kept the wartime bureaucracy largely intact and preserved the so-called "1940 system" that conferred extraordinary discretionary powers on it. This system emerged from the exigencies of mobilizing and maximizing all resources in support of the war effort. In the post-WWII era, the new goals were recovery, development, and growth. Japan's capitalist model, thus, was a hybrid, planned economy with considerable flexibility to respond to market signals. The Japanese government proved adept at combining its sweeping regulatory and informal powers with targeted subsidies and predatory trading policies to produce the economic miracle of sustained high growth in GDP that lasted from 1955 to 1973, a period when GDP per worker quadrupled.[6] This vaunted industrial policy would not have been possible, however, without favored access to the US market and favorable terms for licensing US technologies. The US also promoted Japan's readmission to international commerce by sponsoring its admission to the General Agreement on Tariffs and Trade (GATT) in 1963 and facilitating loans from international financial institutions.

The family-owned *zaibatsu* conglomerates reemerged in the post-Occupation era as *keiretsu*, bank-centered industrial groups. The Bank of

Japan provided these banks easy access to cheap credit, and they lent it to *keiretsu* family companies on favorable terms, helping them borrow beyond their means and make the investments they needed to boost productivity and capacity. The *keiretsu* fostered vertical and horizontal integration across a wide range of industries and sealed close ties through extensive cross-share holding of stocks, serving to block foreign penetration of the Japanese economy. Tight controls over allocation of the foreign exchange necessary to pay for imports (the yen was not used in international commerce) enabled the government to screen and prioritize imports while also insulating the domestic economy from foreign competition.

The 1960s boom resulted from massive infrastructure projects, tax cuts, low interest rates, and trade liberalization combined with growing global markets for Japan's exports. In 1960 PM Hayato Ikeda (1960–4) promised a doubling of incomes and the government delivered, exceeding that target in less than a decade. With astonishing speed, Japan went from a manufacturer of cheap, low-quality products to an exporter of high-quality goods making significant inroads in overseas markets, sparking trade disputes by the end of the 1960s. These economic tensions flared for most of the rest of the twentieth century, generating political problems that undermined bilateral ties with the US.

In order to manage these political tensions, the US and Japan negotiated a series of agreements aimed at managing trade and lowering trade imbalances, but Japan's trade surplus with the US grew apace. There was a strong conviction in the US and Europe that Japan was a neo-mercantilist state engaged in unfair trading practices that boosted exports while limiting imports through a combination of government regulations, subsidies, and non-tariff barriers. Essentially, Japan's trading partners attributed its success to "cheating" and unfair advantages. In Japan, these accusations were seen as unfair and as reflecting an unwillingness to accept that Japan had become more competitive because of its innovations, superior products, and business acumen.

In 1985, in response to growing political problems associated with global trade imbalances, the G7 (Group of Seven leading industrialized nations) negotiated the Plaza Accords. As a result, the yen was allowed to appreciate dramatically, a policy aimed at raising the price of Japanese exports and lowering the price of its imports, thereby encouraging a market correction in trade imbalances. Economic theory anticipated such an outcome, but markets and consumers had other ideas. Japan's trade surpluses continued to rise and in 1987, when stock markets around the world collapsed, it was the only economy that kept steaming along. This kept pressure on the government to maintain monetary easing policies aimed at boosting growth to pull other economies out of recession, in essence throwing fuel onto an already overheating economy.

Following the Plaza Accords, the Japanese bubble in asset prices (land and stocks) began to rise, pumped up by growing trade surpluses and the government's decision to maintain low interest rates.[7] Companies and banks were eagerly bidding up the prices of land and stocks because there were few attractive investment alternatives. Prices soared because there was too much money chasing too few assets and there was a collective hysteria that accompanies all bubbles throughout history. Reason is suspended in the face of dazzling price appreciation as everyone piles in simultaneously, more worried about missing out on the quick gains than the consequences of the inevitable downward spiral. Awash in cash, companies invested heavily in expanding capacity and speculating in land and stocks.

Japan's bubble was extraordinary. Between 1985 and 1989 the stock market average tripled while the urban land price index quadrupled. In 1989, concerned about the inflationary impact of these frothy asset markets, the government popped the bubble by ratcheting up interest rates. The ensuing collapse ushered in the Lost Decade of the 1990s.

In order to understand why Japan's economic malaise has lasted as long as it has, it is important to appreciate the underlying problems that were obscured by the asset bubble. The government-directed system that revived Japan's economy and led to the economic miracle was suited to the tasks of recovery and high growth, but was less suited to the dynamics of a mature economy. Regulations and practices that revived Japan began to exact a cost on efficiency and productivity, beginning in the 1970s.

The oil shocks of the 1970s hit the Japanese economy hard because it relied extensively on imported energy and had many energy-intensive heavy industries and petroleum-processing industries built on the assumption of low oil prices. Oil prices suddenly spiked fourfold in 1974 following an oil embargo and production cuts initiated by the Organization of Petroleum Exporting Countries (OPEC) in 1973, followed by a second oil shock in 1979–80. Japan's growth abated to an average of 3 percent of GDP between 1973 and 1990, down from an average of 8.4 percent in the 1960s.

Richard Katz argues that the government's response mitigated the immediate impact of the oil shocks but, in postponing the reckoning and delaying needed adjustments, made the remedies more painful.[8] Rising wages and increased competition from South Korea and Taiwan were already undermining Japan's competitiveness before the oil shocks. In adjusting to higher oil prices and to avoid bankruptcies and job losses, the government encouraged companies in designated "sunset" industries to form recession cartels, allowing them to set prices and allocate market share. The government also provided subsidies to these firms, part of a larger strategy of protecting jobs. Katz argues that by insulating these industries from market forces, the government stifled gains in productivity, subsidized inefficiency, raised input costs for all producers, misallocated resources into industries with dim prospects, and created an unsustainable economy.

By 1990, Japan had caught up dramatically with other global economies, and its most famous exporting firms boasted high productivity, but overall productivity remained well behind other advanced industrialized economies. By 1990, real GDP per worker in Japan had tripled since 1960, but it ranked only 17 out of the top 23 global economies, still one-third less than the US and lagging even Spain. The domestic sectors of the economy did not have the high productivity of the export sectors honed through international competition. These domestic industries, largely protected from such competition, were grossly inefficient, explaining why Japan's overall productivity ranked only ninth among the eleven largest economies in the early 1990s.[9]

Thus, when we consider the reasons for prolonged economic recession in the Lost Decade, it is important to bear in mind that Japan entered the 1990s with accumulating fundamental problems separate from the asset price bubble. The response of Japan, Inc. to the twin oil shocks in the 1970s postponed and deepened the economic reckoning, lowering productivity and misallocating resources. When the economic boom at the end of the 1980s receded, the vulnerabilities and flaws of the Japanese economic model became more apparent. As we shall see, the government's poor handling of the economic crisis in the 1990s amplified the underlying problems while prolonging the bubble-induced hangover.

Heisei Transformations

In the coming chapters we examine the changes and continuities in Japan since the Heisei era began in 1989.[10] This has been a period of incremental and gradual transformation as the ways and means of Japan, Inc. have faded. Government, business, and bureaucratic actors still cling to past practices, but as these methods, inclinations, and policies have been discredited, and no longer seem adequate to the tasks at hand, they are being abandoned incrementally. Japan's enormous problems stemming from the Lost Decade are driving this process, and here we analyze the consequences.

One major theme addressed in the coming chapters is increasing risk in a society that is risk averse and has long tried to minimize and mitigate risk. In contemporary Japan, many influential advocates in the Iron Triangle believe that introducing risk through market-oriented, structural reforms involving deregulation and privatization is the cure for ongoing economic stagnation and low growth in productivity. These advocates believe Japan's economic problems are due in significant ways to muting of market forces and minimization of risk, and argue that the nation's prospects are dire if it fails to embrace sweeping reforms that boost productivity and change the inefficient way companies do business and the government runs the economy.

It is not obvious to many Japanese, however, that less government intervention, reduced social welfare spending, and the unshackling of businesses from regulations that protect workers' rights will achieve these goals. Rising risk has caused a reassessment of the relationship between citizens and the state and between workers and employers. As the state and employers shift the burdens of risk increasingly onto families and individuals by emphasizing *jiko sekinin* (self-responsibility), they are challenging long-established patterns of trust, dependency, reciprocity, and security.[11] The "outsourcing" of security, trimming of the safety net, and heightening of risks for individuals and their families have gained momentum in Heisei Japan, a trend that once enjoyed what seemed unassailable legitimacy under the ideology of self-responsibility.

However, as we see in the coming chapters, there has been a public backlash indicting such measures and criticizing the consequences of *jiko sekinin*. Public discourse shifted rapidly in the first decade of the twenty-first century from lionizing the mantra of deregulation and privatization to focusing on growing disparities, poverty, marginalized youth, unstable jobs and families, and the emergence of a society of "winners" and "losers." Several sweeping reform initiatives were introduced by the LDP, but the promised gains have not materialized. Many households suffered significant declines in income and security as wages, bonuses, and overtime pay fell and unemployment rose to 5.7 percent by mid-2009, a startling figure for a nation famous for lifetime employment and paternalistic employers.

The 2008 subprime loan crisis that swept through global markets caused considerable and lingering economic dislocation, driving many firms into bankruptcy and leaving many more teetering at the edge of the abyss.

In these circumstances, many of Japan's export-oriented companies faced severe contractions in overseas demand, with overall exports dropping by a devastating 33 percent in 2009 alone. Firms took advantage of liberalized employment rules to shed more than 240,000 non-regular workers in the year following October 2008. While this may be unremarkable in the US, it was shocking in Japan where the implicit social contract is based on secure jobs and paternalistic employers. In public discourse, this mass firing of workers was viewed as heartless and unacceptable, and was depicted as such in the mass media and in political campaigning. There is a consensus among ordinary Japanese, as evident in the ouster of the LDP in the 2009 parliamentary elections, that deregulation, market-oriented reforms, and rising risk are the culprits in widening income disparities and fading job security – unwelcome trends that challenge egalitarian ideals and national identity in a risk-averse society.

Japanese, like almost everyone else, seek security and avoid risk. The Japanese economy may have soared like a Phoenix from the ashes of war devastation, but the Japan, Inc. paradigm was shaped by the deprivation, anxieties, and uncertainties those ashes represented. Post-WWII Japan has been built on predictable economic, employment, and social systems that emphasize security and insulate people from risk. For example, the convoy banking system embraced by the government was based on the principle that all boats go at the pace of the slowest for collective security, meaning that the efficiency and profits of industry leaders are mobilized or sacrificed to help the weakest. But the high costs of the convoy system make it a heavy burden and so now the government is backing away from it, becoming less interventionist and opening space for greater risk. The high-profile bankruptcy of Japan Airlines in 2010 is a sign of the times. Reduced government intervention is one of many major changes in the rules of the game that many observers credit with creating a nation of winners and losers.

In the first decade of the twenty-first century, the emergence of a society with identifiable winners and losers became the controversial focus of heated political debate because it is contrary to Japanese preferences and inclinations. The emphasis on group mentality, collective identity, and egalitarianism in Japan has shaped attitudes and expectations that are threatened by risk and its divisive and uneven consequences. The neo-liberal market-oriented reforms of PM Junichiro Koizumi (2001–6) promoting deregulation and privatization have produced a powerful backlash and are blamed for widening disparities, increased vulnerability, and an inadequate social safety net (various social welfare programs aimed at keeping households from slipping below the poverty line). For most Japanese, this is not the Japan they want or identify with.

There is no deep yearning for a return to the unviable and discredited practices of Japan, Inc., but there is a palpable longing for the safety and security conferred by that system. People understand that change is inevitable, and that revitalizing Japan entails accommodating, at least to some degree, greater risk and market forces, but they also want a transformation that provides a reassuring sense of security along with tangible benefits. As the economic crisis intensified in 2009, the people repudiated the LDP and Koizumi's reform agenda, drawn to the Democratic Party of Japan's (DPJ) promise of a more fraternal society and its plans to roll back many of these reforms. The LDP's failure to manage risk and deal with its consequences was its undoing. Striking a balance between the risks unleashed by reform and the need for security is an ongoing challenge. People are willing to make sacrifices for reforms they can believe in, but they also want an adequate safety net to mitigate the dislocation and protect the most vulnerable.

The coming chapters assess the various risks and responses to them in contemporary Japan. It is not just Japan's economy and companies, and not only its values and identity, which are at risk. Greater risk is transforming employment relationships, the family, and perceptions of people towards the government and employers. The risks of the past haunting Japan in the present are one factor driving attempts at reconciliation with regional neighbors over the colonial and wartime past, while risks to a national identity rooted in patriotism push in the other direction. The security risks posed by North Korea and China weigh heavily on Japan, forcing a rethink of national security policies that raise other concerns about the risks to Article 9 represented by those who seek to revise the Constitution. The risks of economic stagnation, growing disparities, and unemployment are a driving force behind political reform as people respond to the implications for the family, job security, and retirement. The risks of rapid aging, depopulation, and a shrinking labor force are compelling a reappraisal of pensions, medical care, and immigration. For most Japanese, the evident benefits of and need for immigration are overshadowed by the perceived risks that it generates. The growing presence of foreigners in Japan is generally unwelcome and seen as a risk not only in terms of crime rates, but also to a national identity rooted in a sense of homogeneity. Global warming and the risks of environmental catastrophe are driving Japan's bold environmental initiatives.

Amazingly, at the beginning of the Heisei era, before the Lost Decade suddenly shook things up, none of these risks were apparent. In a surprisingly short period of time Japanese have had to confront this daunting array of risks for which they were largely unprepared. The social malaise that envelops twenty-first-century Japan, thus, is not just about the economy; people are feeling greater uncertainty and apprehension, and have little hope for the future.

Japan may be a less risky society than many others, but by its own standards, the sudden sharp rise in risk has shaken society and generated considerable anxieties. Risk is a threat to social cohesion and national identity because it appears to be spread much more unevenly than in the past, challenging egalitarian ideals that are the bond that binds. Japan has enjoyed a strong sense of social cohesion because most people thought they were in the same boat, rowing more or less at the same pace in the same direction. Now people realize more than ever that this is a myth and are unhappy that people are riding in boats of different qualities, at different speeds, heading in different directions. Managing this risk, and restoring a sense of shared destinies, is the great challenge facing Heisei Japan.

The other major theme that reverberates across these pages is the ongoing quiet transformation of Japan. Contemporary Japan is remarkably different from the Japan that existed at the outset of the Heisei era in 1989. All societies change, but the pace and scope of change in Japan has been staggering and deeply unsettling in many ways for its citizens. This is a time of transition from the Japan, Inc. system to an unknown destination through uncharted waters. Many of the profound changes in Japan go largely unnoticed because this transformation is gradual and incremental, being built brick by brick, law by law, through regulation and deregulation. Each initiative taken on its own seems of little import, but when placed in the larger mosaic of reform, the shape of this sweeping transformation emerges, clarified by the passage of time. Reforms involving the judiciary, government transparency, and civil society do not make for immediate and obvious change, but viewed cumulatively over two decades, the transformation has been astounding.

The coming chapters, nonetheless, paint a bleak portrait of contemporary Japan. There is no escaping the massive challenges facing the nation and the probability that some of these will remain impervious to reforms and policy initiatives. Most Japanese are pessimistic about the future for very good reasons. While not dismissing such concerns, I believe that Japan faces a difficult transition but not a catastrophic one. Reforms will not "solve" Japan's problems, but they can mitigate their consequences. Pragmatic adjustments and compromise reforms are more likely than dramatic policy shifts, but probably will have only a limited impact on addressing the many issues raised in coming pages. Muddling through is probably the best case scenario, one in which the government plays a far more significant role in providing social welfare services and acts to manage the consequences of higher risk. Paradoxically, the government remit in contemporary Japan extends much further into individual, family, work, and community problems than in the recent past despite *jiko sekinin*, and precisely at a time when there is a profound crisis in the government's credibility. This makes partnering with civil society organizations all the more imperative because they can serve as an effective bridge between the government and communities and deliver expanded social welfare services more efficiently and cheaply than the bureaucracy. Whether the government can measure up to expectations to intervene in an intelligent, timely, and effective manner is an open question, but the odds improve to the extent that government agencies involve civil society organizations in shaping policies and implementing them.

One of the more important and unexpected changes in contemporary Japan is the landslide victory of the DPJ in the 2009 elections that ended the LDP's long-standing political dominance. This is a promising development for Japan, bringing fresh thinking to Japan's considerable problems. Even with new leadership and greater commitment to reform, Japan faces a difficult transition while climbing out of the deep hole dug by the LDP in its half-century of rule. The DPJ's emphasis on shifting spending from large public works projects to social welfare programs is expanding the safety net and easing the consequences of recession and rapid aging. Its agenda of taming the bureaucracy while harnessing the dynamism of civil society organizations offers glimmers of hope, but translating these laudable goals into tangible gains will prove frustrating and incremental rather than a magic wand of onward and upward transformation.

In the coming pages we focus on what has been happening in Japan since 1989 when the Cold War ended, the Japanese economic bubble burst, and Emperor Hirohito died. In the next chapter we limn the socioeconomic consequences and policy lessons of the Lost Decade of the 1990s. In the second section we focus on the risks and challenges facing contemporary Japan, and what they portend, by exploring demographic trends, families in crisis, and fading job security. The third section considers political developments and the implications for governance, security policy, immigration, and regional reconciliation over history. The fourth section examines two traditional institutions – the imperial family and the yakuza – and how they are evolving and responding to new risks and challenges in the twenty-first century. Finally, a postscript discusses Japan's prospects and identifies six key policy areas for measuring progress.

Chapter 2

The Lost Decade

Japan's Lost Decade began in the early 1990s, but the grip of economic stagnation has persisted for two decades and there are few signs it will dissipate anytime soon. Everything seems to have gone wrong simultaneously in the Heisei era (since 1989), a reign name that has become synonymous with prolonged malaise. This tumultuous period began with a bang as the asset bubble of the 1980s suddenly burst, banks were buried under bad loans, and the economy imploded, while unemployment, suicides, divorce, and domestic violence soared. With the misery index rising, the swaggering self-confidence of the 1980s gave way to sweeping anxieties that extend well beyond the economy. Japan, Inc. lost credibility as the media drew back the curtains on the seamy ways and means of the system and the leaders who ran it. These changing perceptions go to the core of Japan's transformation, subverting long-standing relations based on trust between people and government and with their employers. People came to understand that the bureaucrats who guided the economic miracle made a series of colossal mistakes leading to the Lost Decade and in dealing with its consequences. They also now understand the limits of employer paternalism and to what extent a succession of political leaders has failed the test of leadership, perhaps with the exception of Prime Minister Junichiro Koizumi (2001–6). He was an uncharacteristically bold leader by Japanese standards, but is blamed by many for amplifying disparities, increasing risk, and trimming the social safety net just as more people needed it.

Economy Implodes

Much was lost in the Lost Decade beyond the usual economic indicators, but it is important to grasp the depth and shock of the economic crisis.

The short-lived bubble economy at the end of the 1980s was a period of collective hysteria, a crazy time of frothy fortunes, pie-in-the-sky projects, and lavish living that suddenly evaporated. The impact of the crash of the stock market and land prices has had profound consequences, hammering banks, businesses, investors, borrowers, customers, and employees. The implosion of asset prices in the early 1990s erased about $16 trillion in wealth, equivalent to three times the size of Japan's GDP. As of 2010, the stock market average and land prices still hover close to the lows of the early 1990s, down two-thirds from the peak in 1989. This financial tsunami swept through the entire economy, leaving a swathe of destruction in its wake.

The Lost Decade is very much a story about how businessmen, policy-makers, regulators, and investors reconsidered the norms and verities of Japan, Inc. and began the process of retooling economic institutions, practices, and patterns to revive the economy. For some observers, it is also a story of lost opportunities to implement even more sweeping reforms. Instead of a big bang, Japan adopted measured and incremental reforms, deregulating and privatizing on a piecemeal basis. For others, it was a time of betrayal when the implicit social contract was sundered, creating a society of winners and losers.

Shunning mass redundancies, companies largely kept faith with their regular workers, offering some early retirement while reducing overtime pay and bonuses. The 1990s was a period when the baby boom generation (1947–9), some 7 million strong, were moving up the corporate hierarchy and thus becoming more expensive due to the seniority wage system. This bulge at the top came at a time when companies were feeling the pinch of the economic crisis, putting a premium on cost-cutting measures. In order to subsidize the high wages of core workers, Japanese firms have increasingly relied on non-regular workers (part-time, temporary, dispatched, contract workers) who are usually paid much less and have little job security.[1] This situation puts even more pressure on the shrinking corps of full-time workers, forcing them to work extremely long hours that interfere with their family lives, one of the factors contributing to Japan's low birthrate.

Lessons from Japan

The financial crisis that brought the global economy to its knees in 2008, known in Japan as the "Lehman shock," led to renewed interest in how the

Japanese government handled the Lost Decade. Why did the bursting of the bubble lead to more than a decade of stagnation? It is no surprise that bubbles burst – they have done so repeatedly since the Dutch tulip mania of the seventeenth century – but what combination of misguided policies and folly sustained the hangover for so long? Clearly there are many differences, the most prominent being that the more recent crisis was global and systemic while Japan's was largely domestic. Another major difference is that Japan's leaders dithered for a decade, failing to act with dispatch, hoping that the downturn would be short-lived and recovery would solve the problems of massive bad debts.

Indeed, until the end of the 1990s the government concealed the extent of loan defaults, fearing that realistic accounting would send markets into a tailspin. There was also hope that economic conditions would improve and that, with an upturn in the business cycle, bankers and lenders would be able to work their way out of the mess. However, business conditions remained depressed and the bad loan problems festered. The government decided it could no longer stand by while the nation's entire financial system teetered on the edge of insolvency, and thus put it on life support by easing monetary policy and injecting funds into troubled institutions.

Japan's economy has suffered from prolonged deflation for two decades despite various attempts to jolt it out of its torpor. With the banks overwhelmed by non-performing loans and collateral values evaporating, the government forced rescue mergers between them without addressing the underlying problems. So the bad debts festered while the government leaned on banks to continue lending to zombie companies (bankrupt and uncompetitive firms) so they would not go bankrupt. This policy of keeping insolvent businesses afloat proved an expensive and ill-considered gamble. Temporizing in this way held grave consequences for the economy, squandering resources and adding to deflationary pressures as zombie firms had incentives to lower prices just to maintain enough cash flow to service interest payments. This deflationary spiral made it difficult for all firms since they also had to lower prices, but could not make a profit by doing so. So propping up the zombie companies, by allowing them to continue borrowing even though their prospects of repaying debts were remote, ended up weakening all companies, especially those focused on the stagnant domestic market. This policy also saddled banks with more non-performing loans.

In hindsight, the height of folly came in 1997 when the government decided to raise taxes in order to rein in growing budget deficits and restore fiscal discipline. This initiative stifled a fragile recovery and banks were in worse shape than ever. Even with low interest rates, they could not entice corporations to borrow, as the economy was mired in what is called the liquidity trap.

Richard Koo calls this the balance sheet recession.[2] He argues that the massive fall in asset prices in the 1990s led healthy companies to repay loans and minimize debt in order to restore their credit ratings. When companies do this collectively to burnish their balance sheets, demand for loans dries up, putting banks in a difficult situation while the economy overall suffers from over-saving by the private sector. Koo argues that the Japanese government had the right idea with massive fiscal stimulus packages aimed at stimulating consumption, but erred in reducing such stimulus too soon. Koo argues that the zigzagging between fiscal stimulus and austerity prolonged the recession.

In the late 1990s, following the tax hike debacle, the government tried more fiscal stimulus, massively expanding budgets for public works construction projects. While this did lead to roads and bridges to nowhere, and the other pathologies of the construction state, it also put money in consumers' pockets and boosted demand.[3] However, incipient recovery was nipped in the bud in 2001 when the government tightened interest rates and fiscal policy. With the economy slipping back into recession, and the US reeling from the dot.com crash, the government aggressively adopted quantitative easing, an aggressive monetary stimulus based on zero interest rates and buying back government bonds (*rinban*). This policy lasted until 2006 and is credited by some with sustaining the longest period of uninterrupted economic expansion in the post-WWII era. Economic growth averaged a modest 2 percent and seemed sustainable until the government took its foot off the pedal, ending its zero-interest and *rinban* policies simultaneously.

Critics of quantitative easing say that the recovery had more to do with booming Chinese demand while deflationary pressures were "solved" by higher oil prices. When the experiment began, there were no major liquidity problems in Japan and corporations had cash on hand to self-finance expansion. Banks had already been cured through capital injections, loan writedowns, and government guarantees. The downside of quantitative easing was a destabilizing of the bond market and thus the entire financial system.

The lessons from Japan's botched policy-making during the Lost Decade emphasize the need for governments to act quickly to underwrite systemic financial risks by recapitalizing banks, guaranteeing bank deposits, and forcing banks to fully disclose and write down bad assets. The lessons also suggest the need to sustain high levels of fiscal stimulus, erring on the side of too much for too long. Many economists also think there is still much work to be done on restructuring business in Japan to boost productivity, because government monetary policies have insulated firms from pressures that would force more extensive restructuring.

Another sobering lesson from Japan's Lost Decade is that the economic problems have persisted much longer than anyone imagined – two decades and counting. The Japanese people have endured tough times with great fortitude and considerable patience. Unpopular taxpayer-funded bailouts of the banks restored stability to a wobbly financial system, but at the expense of public confidence in the credibility of government leaders and bankers. The human toll has been enormous. Layoffs and unemployment have been relatively limited, but the malaise can be measured by other means. Many families took on massive mortgages, only to see the value of their property plummet. This phenomenon of negative equity has helped depress consumption as families minimize their spending. Too many fathers commit suicide so that their families can collect on life insurance policies. The growing numbers of homeless men living rough also reveal a stunning degree of hardship in what is known as an affluent country. So too does the shift of many young women into the sex industry and the rise in juvenile delinquency. Widening disparities are disturbing in a society with an identity rooted in egalitarian ideals; younger workers are being disproportionately shunned to the margins of the labor market where wages and job security are low. The Japanese have been remarkably stoical in coping with these problems, but social cohesion is at risk.

Media Awakens

During the Lost Decade, the Japanese media has played a key role in promoting greater transparency and accountability. It is often criticized for being a snoozy watchdog on a short leash, but since the outset of the Heisei era the media has been aggressive in exposing a series of scandals involving bureaucrats and politicians that have helped citizens more closely monitor government. In this sense, it has played a pivotal role in changing the way citizens view the powers that be and made them less trusting. It has also forced the nation to shed an orchestrated innocence concerning its wartime past and the torments it inflicted on the rest of Asia. It is during the Heisei era that Japanese have learned much more about the wartime Showa era (1926–89), and the media has propelled and shaped this education, forcing people to reassess a past that reverberates throughout Japan and in the region.[4]

As citizens have rallied to protest government policies and negligence, the media has given them a voice and invaluable support. On issues ranging from food safety and information disclosure to corruption and privacy protection, the media has done a reasonably good job of holding the government accountable. The *kisha* club system, a cartel giving mainstream domestic media privileged access to official sources, continues to stifle and influence news coverage, although the Democratic Party of Japan (DPJ) promises to reform this system. Despite considerable self-censorship, however, the media has grown feistier and less beholden and is the leading user of the freedom of information laws that have helped expose wrongdoing at all levels of government.

The media has also shone a light on the harsh consequences of the Lost Decade and abuse of power. The *kakusa shakai* (society of disparities), domestic violence, child abuse, suicide, working poor, mobster influence, systemic corruption among bureaucrats and politicians, human trafficking, and many other previously taboo topics are now openly discussed. These problems are not new, but during the Lost Decade the shackles and blinders have loosened considerably. What was largely ignored is now the subject of public debate, policy initiatives, legal reforms, and increasing accountability.

Time of Reckoning

In 1995, the Kobe earthquake and the subsequent gassing of Tokyo commuters by religious fanatics had repercussions beyond the toll of victims. The earthquake highlighted the government's woeful preparations for a natural disaster that all Japanese are supposed to be prepared for, while the terrorist attacks in Tokyo's subways heightened a sense of insecurity and concerns that the government was not able to protect its citizens.

The Great Hanshin–Awaji Earthquake struck Kobe on January 17, 1995, devastating the city and raising questions about construction safety standards and the government's disaster relief preparations. The earthquake registered 7.2 on the Richter scale, causing 6,200 deaths and an estimated

$100 billion in damages. About one-third of Kobe was partially or completely destroyed and thousands of families were displaced from their ruined homes.

The inept and slow response of both the municipal and central governments took the nation by surprise. Incredibly, the city had no contingency disaster plan and there were no prearrangements for emergency relief centers. Offers of assistance by foreign relief agencies and US military forces stationed in Japan were spurned, and the nation's Self-Defense Forces (SDF) waited in nearby barracks for a call that was inexplicably delayed in coming. Inadequate relief efforts left a lasting impression on a nation that had assumed government officials knew best. Nobody could overlook the fact that bureaucratic negligence and rigidity amplified the consequences of this natural disaster, further undermining the waning credibility of government institutions. What could be more damning, and embarrassing, than the yakuza opening the first soup kitchens for survivors? Perhaps reports that the prime minister first learned about the disaster while listening to the news.

In response to the earthquake, over 1 million student volunteers poured into Kobe from all over the country. This response reaffirmed that a sense of community is alive and well in Japan. The volunteers' goodwill and enthusiasm stood in stark contrast to the bureaucrats' lackluster response. Japanese non-profit organizations (NPOs) helped coordinate these volunteer efforts and played a crucial role in providing relief for devastated communities. The media featured the critical role of NPOs in mitigating the consequences of the earthquake, drawing a sharp contrast with government bungling. This generated public support for NPOs and, as a direct result of the Kobe earthquake, the government passed an NPO law in 1998 aimed at facilitating their operations and tapping their potential. Since then, civil society organizations have mushroomed despite shortcomings in the law and government policies that leave NPOs short of funds and professional staff.

Two months after the earthquake, the Japanese were shaken by another traumatic event. On March 20, 1995, members of the Aum Shinrikyo (Supreme Truth Sect) released sarin gas in Tokyo's metro, killing 13 people and causing a further 6,252 commuters to fall ill. This brazen attack on commuters sent shockwaves throughout the archipelago, stirring anxieties about what might follow. It turns out that there were earlier indications of what the cult was up to and missed opportunities to apprehend them before the subway attack, stirring anger against the authorities. Yet again, the government had failed to secure the safety of the people and found itself in the dock alongside the cultists, accused of dereliction of duty.

Following the arrest of Aum's top leaders, the nation put itself on the analyst's couch, asking why this tragedy had happened. What was attractive about the cult and its teachings? How did Shoko Asahara, the leader, command such blind devotion and loyalty that otherwise ordinary people would become terrorists at his bidding? The frenzied media coverage of Aum mesmerized audiences obsessed with working out why talented young men and women decided to join a cult and participate in terrorist actions against fellow Japanese. Was this a backlash against excessive social pressures to conform and succeed? Were they lured with promises of power and authority that young people are routinely denied in the seniority-based hierarchy of Japanese corporations? Some analysts suggested they were reacting against the materialism and spiritual void that permeate contemporary Japan. Yet, none of these explanations seem fully convincing and the mystery of Aum continues to haunt the Japanese.

The Japanese sense of security was shattered by this cataclysmic attack on society, generating apprehension about what else may be lurking beneath the surface of reassuring appearances. Even though Aum leaders have been sentenced to death, hanging them will not erase lingering fears that the authorities will be any more effective in preventing similar tragedies. This crisis of credibility haunts the government and makes regaining the public's trust as important as it is difficult.

Untrustworthy

Before the cascade of revelations about wrongdoing and folly in the higher echelons of government throughout the 1990s, Japan's bureaucrats enjoyed a good reputation. They were the best and the brightest after all, graduates of the elite universities who had overseen the economic miracle and raised living standards dramatically in the post-WWII era. But in the 1990s, the more people read about bureaucrats wining, dining, and living the high life at taxpayers' expense, the less they respected government officials. They also read about elaborate scams by bureaucrats to falsely claim expenses for trips they never took and accumulate slush funds for discretionary spending. In addition, there were high-profile cases of embezzlement and misappropriation of funds. Ethical questions were also raised by officials being treated by corporate executives from industries under their purview to expensive gifts, golfing outings, and unseemly visits to *nopan shabushabu* – dubious dining establishments featuring simmered beef, mirrored floors, and young women wearing short skirts without underwear.

For all of these reasons, citizens have deep misgivings about the practice of *amakudari* (descent from heaven). This system involves retiring bureaucrats securing post-retirement sinecures at companies they previously supervised in carrying out their official duties. This conflict of interest raises suspicions that officials exercise their authority and discretionary powers with an eye towards currying favor and landing a lucrative job at firms they have been dealing with. *Amakudari* is a notorious hotbed of corruption that costs taxpayers considerable sums in subsidies and inflated government contracts. The crusade against *amakudari* has a long and checkered history dating back to the 1970s, but has not prevailed because of lax enforcement.

It is a sign of the times that during the 2009 election campaign the DPJ struck a chord with voters by running against the bureaucrats. The DPJ promised to seize policy-making power from the mandarins on behalf of the people and, in doing so, reform fundamentally how the nation is governed. The DPJ also promised to curb *amakudari* and to cut state funding for the quasi-state enterprises where many bureaucrats are employed after retiring. It may have more success in taming the bureaucracy because, unlike the LDP, it seems to have the political will to follow through on its crusade. However, bureaucrats are tested infighters and taking away their prerogatives and diminishing their influence will be no easy task.

Transparency

During the Lost Decade the people have confronted the lapses of the elite and the fundamental flaws of a system no longer capable of meeting the challenges facing the nation. Japan, Inc. ran out of gas and from the 1990s there have been concerted efforts to rectify the evident problems, expand the scope of reforms and reinvent Japan. In a process involving ordinary citizens and NPOs, but also including reformist elements in business, the bureaucracy, and politics, Japan has responded in innovative ways to many of its problems.

Given the questionable conduct by the men charged with running government, it is not surprising that so many citizens came to support information disclosure legislation. Knowing a little about official shenanigans underscored how important it is to more closely monitor the government. Citizen support for transparency gained momentum throughout the 1990s, and by 1997 every prefecture and major town passed freedom of information legislation. Spurred by this grassroots rebellion against opaque government, the national government also passed information disclosure legislation in 1999 that was implemented in 2001.

Although the law now facilitates information disclosure, government officials controlling the information do not readily comply with the spirit of transparency. Habits and inclinations change slowly and thus, in many cases, requestors find that official responses to their requests for information are dilatory or incomplete. What has been surprising is the courts' strong support for information disclosure, ruling against the state in the majority of cases.[5] The judiciary is holding the government accountable according to the rule of law and denying unreasonable exclusions, deletions, omissions, and non-compliance. Promoting transparency is still a work in progress, and remains in the early stages of that process, but there have been enormous advances in two decades and what was thought impossible is now happening. The government is divulging much more about the way it governs and officials now are exercising their authority knowing that their decisions are far more open to scrutiny than ever before.

A more vigilant citizenry, organizing themselves in a mushrooming network of NPOs, is increasingly mobilizing popular and media support to transform transparency from an accepted principle into a standard practice of good governance. It is these efforts to recast and rejuvenate civil society, as the following example from Gifu Prefecture demonstrates, that are propelling and shaping Japan's ongoing transformation.

In June 2004, the Supreme Court nullified a 1998 decision by the governor of Gifu Prefecture to deny public access to environmental impact assessments related to a controversial road project. Surprisingly, the Supreme Court overturned earlier district (1999) and high court (2000) rulings in favor of the government. This ruling creates a precedent that supports citizens groups' efforts throughout Japan to gain greater access to documents used in preparing environmental impact assessments, even if they are deemed unofficial. In mandating public disclosure of such information, the Supreme Court has made it more difficult for officials to skew assessments in favor of construction projects.

Living, Nature, Life, and People Network, a Gifu-based citizens group, had requested documents used by the government in preparing a preliminary environmental impact assessment concerning the proposed Tokai Loop Highway in 1996. The governor refused to release these documents, arguing that they were not public information and as such not subject to information disclosure. The Supreme Court ruled that the prefecture was in violation of its own information disclosure law and rejected the prefecture's argument that the documents in question are covered by legal guidelines for withholding information. This ruling is consistent with the judiciary's relatively strong support for information disclosure in lawsuits nationwide that is supporting transparency and accountability.

This is an astonishing case for a number of reasons, illustrating how the NPOs, information disclosure, and a feistier media and judiciary are mutually reinforcing forces for reform. Dedicated citizens in a small NPO with few resources persisted in their fight for transparency and were able to halt construction of a major public works project involving powerful vested interests in government and industry. The case in Gifu demonstrates that citizens are gaining momentum to protect the environment and bolster the rule of law while affirming the principle of transparency. The DPJ supports this trend and is aggressively downsizing the construction state, canceling two major dam projects in its first month in office and serving notice on many more public works projects as it cuts wasteful spending. It pledges to prioritize social welfare spending over public works, and in its 2010 budget for the first time the allocations for social services represented more than one-half of the entire budget while public works spending was slashed by 18 percent.

The barriers to manipulating information and skirting disclosure ordinances are not insurmountable, but such behavior now carries the risk of judicial sanction and public ire. It was during the 1990s that citizens groups gathered information about bureaucrats' systemic misuse of public funds for lavish wining and dining, leisure outings, and claiming expenses for non-existent business trips at a time when ordinary citizens were feeling the pain of recession and declining incomes. Such misappropriations were widespread throughout government offices in Japan, and so routine that there were standard (but not very effective, as it turns out) procedures for obscuring this illicit spending. Information disclosure exposed this malfeasance and underscored the important role NPOs can play in promoting transparency and accountability. This is a trend supporting good governance at the behest of the people, marking a significant step in reinventing Japan, where the opinions and welfare of citizens are becoming more important.

Disparities

The *kakusa shakai* (society of disparities) is prominent in contemporary public discourse and is one of the most profound consequences of the Lost Decade. During the post-WWII era, social cohesion was maintained by a collective belief in everyone sharing the same fate and enjoying similar lifestyles. This myth of social solidarity was expressed most prominently in annual government surveys in which some 90 percent of the Japanese saw themselves as members of the middle class. Certainly the government and media helped orchestrate this comforting sense of belonging, and over-stated the egalitarian outcomes of the economic miracle. But this myth had broad appeal and was implicit in the social contract, bestowing legitimacy on the Japan, Inc. model.

From the 1980s, inequality has been increasing in Japan. According to the OECD, Japan's Gini coefficient, a measure of income inequality, rose 13 percent between the mid-1980s and 2000 compared to an OECD average of 7 percent.[6] During this same period, the proportion of the Japanese population living in absolute poverty grew 5 percent; strikingly, the only OECD member to record an increase in absolute poverty. Since 2000, the relative poverty rate, defined as less than one-half the median household disposable income, has exceeded 15 percent, again above the OECD average of 10 percent. What seems clear is that those at the lower end of the income distribution are falling further behind. The power of the egalitarian myth, however, ensured that growing inequality remained largely ignored until the twenty-first century because it was a social taboo, one that threatened to undermine the credibility of the status quo. The Lost Decade, however, exposed the problems, excesses, and venality of this status quo. As people lost faith in the system they began to scrutinize it more critically. Growing gaps in income and wealth drew more media coverage, sparking a deep sense of betrayal among many Japanese. Thus when speaking of what was lost in the Lost Decade, it is important not to overlook the loss of faith in the system and those respon-sible for it.

Many observers with their own agendas have rushed to pin the blame for Japan's growing income gap on Prime Minister Koizumi and his neo-liberal economic policies of deregulation, market liberalization, and priva-tization. The main problem with this argument is that the growing income divide was already evident well before he took office in 2001, meaning that his policies could not be the main causal factor. As the OECD notes, "The trends in inequality and poverty ... should not be attributed to the policies of the current government, which took office in 2001, but instead reflect more long-run developments."

Clearly, one of these developments is the aging of Japan's population. This has played a role in the widening income gap as the effects of individual human capital investment grow more pronounced over time; university and high-school graduates' salaries start at roughly similar levels, but wage gaps widen throughout a career. As the baby boom generation has moved up through the corporate hierarchy, this trend has been amplified. In addition, because the degree of income inequality among those over age 65 is higher than the average, as they grow in proportion to the total population, disparities are more evident.

A more important factor in the growing divide, however, is growing wage differentials between regular full-time workers and non-regular workers and the swelling ranks of the latter since the 1980s. As of 2008, non-regular workers account for 34.1 percent of the workforce, up from 20 percent in 1992 and 16.4 percent in 1985. Between 1992 and 2002, the number of full-time workers declined by 3.5 million while the number of non-regular workers increased by 5.67 million. As the OECD notes:

> While population ageing has played a role, there has also been a marked rise in inequality among the 18 to 65 age group as a result of the increasing variance in wages. This trend cannot be explained by differences in the earnings of full-time employees, which have narrowed in recent years. Instead, the greater dispersion of market income is due to the increasing proportion of non-regular workers – primarily part-time employees – who are paid only 40% as much per hour as full-time employees. The growing dualism in the labour market thus creates serious equity issues, which are exacerbated by the limited mobility between the regular and irregular segments of the labour market.[7]

In addition, disparities have grown because social spending outlays on the working-age population are small compared to the elderly, while low-income households receive little support.

The sudden surge in numbers of non-regular workers is due to companies cutting costs as they adjusted to deep recession and heightened global competition during the Lost Decade. This shift in employment patterns was facilitated by incremental deregulation of the labor market by the government beginning in 1998 under PM Keizo Obuchi (1998–2000). In 2004, under PM Koizumi, the government deregulated manufacturing jobs, allowing companies to hire contingent non-regular workers indirectly through staffing agencies with no job security and low wages. This policy placed large numbers of manufacturing workers at risk. The folly of this progressive shredding of job protections became apparent over 2008–9 as companies fired nearly a quarter of a million of these workers in response to the global economic crisis.

Aside from sundering the myth of the middle class, and forcing society to contemplate the implications of growing disparities, the growth of non-regular employment has had profound social consequences. In a society where the lifetime employment ideal involves a full-time job at the same company for an entire career, the sudden shift to contingent employment for so many workers has had serious repercussions that we cannot yet fully understand. These marginalized workers are mostly young and their prospects are bleak. Very few will make the transition to regular employment and many face a tough future eking it out. Their lack of status, stable income, and confidence about the future means many will not marry and have children. These children of the Lost Decade are the unfortunate generation, one without much of a stake in the existing system.

There are no panaceas, but the DPJ government and society understand that they cannot ignore the problems and consequences of treating so many of Japan's youth as disposable commodities. Japan's social cohesion is at risk because the LDP government embraced more market-oriented policies that are increasing disparities. Advocates of such policies within Japan insist they are necessary to make Japan more competitive and promote economic growth, but the consequences of doing so without modifying social welfare policies have put more people at risk. The DPJ won a landslide victory in 2009 in large part because the public soured on neo-liberal reforms and the LDP did not prepare for the foreseeable consequences. The task ahead is to balance the imperatives of economic restructuring and raising productivity with social welfare reforms aimed at mitigating the consequences.

Japan's Quiet Transformation

Japan's quiet transformation involves a series of reforms that considered on their own seem of little consequence, but taken together are generating sweeping change that until the DPJ's 2009 victory has drawn little media attention.[8] Key legislative building blocks of the quiet transformation are in place and now it is a question of building on this foundation. The NPO legislation (1998), national information disclosure legislation (1999), and an ambitious array of judicial reforms adopted in 2002 are strengthening Japan's civil society while promoting greater transparency and accountability. The growing numbers of lawyers, the changes in their legal education, speedier trials, an intellectual property rights court, and a lay judge system, in addition to other judicial reforms, are transforming and strengthening the shift from the *rule by law* to the *rule of law* in Japan. The DPJ aims to strengthen this trend by curbing the autonomous, discretionary powers of the bureaucracy that have driven the rule by law.

Despite these encouraging developments, reform never happens as quickly or as comprehensively as advocates wish, and it is a slow process with setbacks along the way that make people question whether reform is happening or only an illusion. Much depends on continued public activism, civil society organizations, the media, and the choices and policies of government, business, and politicians. The reform process has renewed momentum under the DPJ, but can easily be derailed.

Heisei Japan has been a period of transition in which subtle changes coexist with prominent continuities. There is a lag between reform initiatives and substantive consequences, just as there are gaps between intentions and results. Reform is not a linear process, onward and upward, in Japan, relying more on pragmatic compromises and fine-tuning than shock therapy and sweeping measures. Yet, Japan in 2010 is very different from the way it was in 1990; from a historical perspective 20 years is but a brief moment, but during these fleeting two decades many of the seemingly ineradicable verities, assumptions, and practices of Japan have been unalterably transformed.

The reinvention of Japan is a work in progress. The responses to those problems are reshaping existing institutions, practices, and attitudes in powerful ways. There are four main factors driving this process:

1 discrediting of Japan, Inc. during the Lost Decade;
2 staggering fiscal problems;
3 the demographic time bomb;
4 global norming as Japan tries to become more competitive economically and improve governance by adopting policies and practices that have worked elsewhere.

The Lost Decade has been a time of remarkable transformation, involving a recasting of the norms, values, and assumptions of society. It is not what remains to be done, but the magnitude of what has already been achieved that provides the most accurate barometer of change in contemporary Japan and its future prospects. During the Heisei era, Japanese people, organizations, and policy-makers are responding to various challenges in thoughtful, significant, and diverse ways that are facilitating significant social, economic, political, and cultural change. This has been an unsettling era, leaving many Japanese ambivalent about, or resistant to, reform. Some still cling to old norms even as they fade away and offer no solutions or viable alternatives. The Lost Decade malaise, a massive public debt to GDP ratio of 200 percent, and the rapid aging of society, however, are generating a sense of looming catastrophe that is forcing reconsideration of the existing paradigm. The changes limned above and in the coming pages are happening because there is a consensus that Japan must reinvent itself even if there are differences on how to proceed and where to go.

During the Heisei era, ongoing incremental social and cultural transformations are being negotiated and contested. It has been a revealing time of adversity and adaptation that is defining the nation and shaping its prospects. Emerging from the devastation of war, stability and security have been key priorities in Japan. The introduction of greater risk in a society that has emphasized minimizing and mitigating risk is a defining legacy of the Lost Decade. As we examine in coming chapters, the social consequences of this heightened risk have been enormous and in some cases devastating. Many Japanese believe that the greatest fundamental risk to Japan's future is the demographic time bomb, the subject of our next chapter.

Part II
Risk and Consequences

Chapter 3

Defusing the Demographic Time Bomb

The key elements of the demographic time bomb include Japanese having fewer children, the graying of the baby boom cohort (1947–9), and the elderly living longer. This potential crisis generates considerable media coverage and a cascade of attention grabbing statistics. For example, from 1988 to 2007 the number of Japan's over-65-year-olds doubled and they now constitute nearly one-quarter of the total population, a figure projected to reach more than 40 percent by 2055. Adding to the prevailing sense of malaise, since 2007 Japan's population is slowly declining. The nexus of low fertility, depopulation, and aging is creating a sense of urgency and anxiety about how to mitigate the consequences of these trends for the nation's future.[1] The implications are enormous, ranging from pensions and elderly care to a shrinking labor force, economic stagnation, family patterns, and social cohesion.

Japan is one of the most rapidly aging societies in the world. As of 2009, 23 percent of the population, numbering 29 million, is over 65 years old compared to about 13 percent in the US. More than 10 percent of the population is over age 75, while children constitute only 13 percent of the population. There are so many centenarians – 40,000 as of 2009, up fourfold from 10,000 in 1999 – that the government has cut back on congratulatory payments and reduced the silver content of commemorative sake cups from 94 g to a frugal 63 g. This is a symbolic contribution to the government's sweeping plans to slash the soaring medical care and social welfare costs of the elderly.

Based on current trends, by 2040 the elderly (over 65) will outnumber the young by four to one. More importantly, the number of workers supporting each retiree is shrinking from 10 in 1950 to 3.6 in 2000 and 1.9 by 2025, and there are fewer replacements in sight. According to the National Institute of Population and Social Security Research, by 2055

Japan's population will shrink 30 percent to 90 million, the same as in 1955 when the vaunted economic miracle of high growth began. The implications this time, however, do not look so rosy in terms of social policy, tax burdens, the economy, politics, and immigration. Opinions about the likely consequences vary widely, ranging from doomsday scenarios to society coping as it pragmatically improvises.

Consequences

The cataclysm view emphasizes the grim economic consequences of an aging society. Fewer babies today mean fewer consumers, workers, and taxpayers tomorrow, translating into economic decline. The bulge of retirees at the top will depend on the taxes and premiums of fewer workers to fund their pensions, medical care, and other social programs targeting the elderly. The surge in demand for elderly care is also overwhelming existing capacity, pushing up government spending on medical care and pulling many productive workers, mostly women, from the workforce to care for aging relatives. Declining tax revenues means that the government will have to raise taxes, take on even more debt – the public debt is 200 percent of GDP as of 2010, by far the highest in the OECD – and initiate significant cuts in benefits that will challenge existing priorities and set the stage for divisive political battles. As the workforce ages, productivity gains are at risk as older workers are thought less adept at new technologies. They are also more expensive due to the seniority wage system, not quite the "more for less" ratio companies have in mind. Moreover, in a nation eager to nurture entrepreneurship and creativity, the elderly are not seen as risk takers or innovators. They are, however, politically powerful with a high voting rate (80 percent), roughly double that of younger Japanese, meaning they can push their agenda at the polls in ways that slow reforms necessary and beneficial for society, but threatening to their interests. In addition, the growing number of retirees is also increasing poverty as pensions prove inadequate and people live longer than they anticipated when they were saving for retirement, putting added pressure on social services. Taken overall, these aging-related costs suggest a dismal future for Japan.

The time bomb is certainly ticking away, warning that consequences are at hand, but in many respects Japan has already been adjusting incrementally to a graying society and managing to cope. Since the beginning of the Heisei era, the government has initiated a series of policy reforms aimed at coping with the rapid aging of society. These reforms target the urgent problems of pensions, elderly care, and medical care costs. To be sure, the government is racing to catch up to various aspects of this unfolding aging crisis, and will continue to frustrate critics, but in terms of what governments around the world are doing and the scale of the problems, Japan is not necessarily in such dire straits.

The alarmists also overlook the potential contributions of senior citizens. Many seniors in Japan continue working after retirement on reduced salaries because firms value their skills. The average mandatory retirement age has progressively climbed from age 55 to age 65, but some experts now suggest raising this to age 70 in light of improved longevity and health.

It may come as a surprise to some readers that many senior citizens in Japan actually want to keep working, not only out of economic necessity, but also reflecting the deeply ingrained work ethic and the meaning and focus it gives their lives. Staying active also staves off psychological and physical health problems while enabling seniors to contribute to society. It also reduces stress on their wives who have grown accustomed to their infrequent presence at home and often suffer from depression and stress-related illnesses when their husbands retire and are suddenly constantly around and very demanding. Other retirees are finding fulfillment in volunteer work in civil society organizations and community projects, while some are even going overseas in support of Japanese development initiatives under the auspices of the Japan Overseas Volunteer Corps. And, retirees are a growing consumer market for niche products and services catering to their needs, spawning silver businesses ranging from leisure and education to healthcare and housing.

As John Campbell and Naoki Ikegami remind us, the impact of a shrinking population and aging are gradual and predictable and thus eminently manageable.[2] Associated costs are growing modestly – less than 2 percent per year – meaning they are not insurmountable and that reforms need not be as drastic as doomsday predictions forecast.[3] There is an ongoing adjustment of policies and institutions in Japan driven by perceptions about what needs to be done, suggesting that fears about the consequences of inaction or the need for a big bang are overstated.

It is also important to view the aging of the labor force in a wider perspective. As firms look to hire workers from a shrinking labor pool, they are hiring more women. As women upgrade their professional skills, and firms and the government belatedly adopt more family-friendly policies that enable them to maintain careers while raising families, the overall economy stands to benefit while households can enjoy the security and opportunities of two-income households. In addition, in wading through the welter of statistics, it is worth bearing in mind that current demographic trends are subject to unforeseen changes the further into the future they are extrapolated.

Baby Drought

Japanese women are bearing fewer children and postponing or refraining from marriage. From a high of 4.3 babies in 1947, the total fertility rate – the average number of babies a woman will bear – dropped to a record low 1.29 in 2003, well below the number of babies needed (2.07) to maintain the current population. Since then the fertility rate has stabilized at about 1.37, but surveys indicate that even if people are able to have all the children they desire, the maximum fertility rate would climb only to 1.75.

As of 2009, the number of children younger than 15 fell to about 17 million, only 13 percent of the nation's 127 million people. Japan now has the lowest percentage of children among 31 major countries, trailing even Germany and Italy. In the US and South Korea, by comparison, children constitute 20 and 17 percent of the respective populations. One major factor is the low level of family-related social spending as a percentage of GDP in Japan, 0.75 percent as of 2003 compared to 2.01 percent in Germany, 2.93 percent in the UK, and 3.02 percent in France.

Women are having fewer children mostly because it is very difficult to combine work with child rearing in Japan. As a result, many working women are delaying or forgoing marriage altogether, while a growing number of those who marry choose not to have children. As attitudes and social norms have changed, and lifestyles diversify, getting married and having children is no longer the default option it once was. Women who are now enjoying greater social and economic freedom wonder if having kids is really what they want, and consider carefully what they stand to lose by raising a family, especially given that their husbands (and their employers) continue to shift most of the child-rearing burden on them.

Belatedly, firms and the government are implementing family-friendly policies aimed at providing the types of support women need to continue working while raising families, but these programs lag in comparison to most other OECD nations. However, the main reason why dual-earner couples face immense difficulties raising children is the long hours they must commit to their jobs.[4] There are few signs that firms are adopting flexible work options that would make achieving work–life balance more feasible. Moreover, the government has not given firms sufficient incentives to do so and also has not invested enough resources in creating a family-friendly social infrastructure, a neglect that forces many women to make a choice between careers or motherhood. Unlike in other leading industrialized nations, for women in Japan, careers and children are far too much of an either/or situation.

In 55 percent of married households, both spouses are working, marking a huge shift from the breadwinner model featuring a full-time housewife at home. In such two-income households, the lack of support from government and firms, combined with the absence of either spouse's parents, makes childcare a critical issue. Women cite the lack of childcare as one of the main reasons they are not having children. In some areas there are long waiting lists to get into public daycare programs, while private options are expensive and usually have inferior facilities. Nationwide, as of 2009, there are 40,000 children on the waiting lists of authorized daycare centers – this in a country where the government constantly harps on the importance of boosting the birthrate. Mothers and fathers can take childcare leave, with their jobs guaranteed, but they lose 40 percent of their income during their 14 weeks of paid leave.

For Japan, growing risk and instability in the job market are translating into fewer children. For non-regular workers with limited incomes and tenuous job security, getting married and having children is beyond reach, seen as something only people with "normal" lives and regular jobs can aspire to. Given that one-third of the entire workforce, mostly young workers in their prime, is engaged on these anxiety-inducing terms, the implications for the birthrate are quite serious.

In Japan, 62 percent of women drop out of the workforce when they have their first child, partly due to difficulties in securing daycare, but also due to a desire by young mothers, reflecting prevailing values and norms, to raise their children for the first 3 years of their lives. These women do not have the flexible work options available to working women in many European countries that enable them to work reduced schedules, telecommute from home, or share jobs that make it much easier to balance work and family responsibilities. The problem is that it is extremely difficult for these women who quit their jobs to return to the workforce to similar full-time positions. This is primarily a problem of rigid corporate employment practices that emphasize continuous tenure and limited mid-career recruitment. It is also a reflection of gender discrimination that relegates working mothers to the labor force periphery; regular workers work regular hours according to employment practices that suit married male workers who have a wife at home to take care of family responsibilities. Gender assumptions of employers are evident in the very common *tanshin funin* system that involves dispatching male workers to a firm's distant branch offices for a few years, living separately from their wife and any children who remain at home. There is an implicit assumption that the wife will take care of all household matters without any support from their husbands, including childcare, making it difficult for these wives to work full-time.

Women who need flexible work schedules to manage family responsibilities can only work part-time because there are no provisions for regular workers that take account of women's lifecycle needs. There is also a daycare Catch-22 situation: in order to take on a full-time job, mothers have to line up childcare beforehand, but in Japan's public system it is difficult to secure a slot unless one is already working full-time and is given priority. Thus, aspiring "mother returners" who are not employed but want to reenter the labor market are given low priority for childcare, making it difficult for them to get a job except as a part-timer where wages and job security are low. Thus, once a woman drops out of the workforce to raise a child, this Catch-22 situation hampers her return to a rewarding career and shunts her into part-time work. This helps explain why more than 50 percent of employed women are non-regular workers.

When women are contemplating having a child, they are aware that this very probably means ending their careers unless they are public sector employees or professionals (lawyers, doctors, architects, etc.) who have credentials that give them privileged career tracks not subject to corporate human resource managers. Less privileged and credentialed women know very well that returning to work will mean a huge drop in pay, status, and responsibilities. They also know from the mass media that raising and educating children are very expensive. Thus, the opportunity costs of abandoned careers, estimated at $1.5 million lost earnings for college-educated women, combined with the high price of raising and educating children, a minimum of $300,000, deter many women from giving birth, especially given how hard it can be to secure convenient and reasonably priced childcare.

The lack of childcare is not a new problem, but even as women opt to have fewer babies the government has not been able to keep up with demand. There is a maldistribution of public daycare facilities: in many rural areas, where it is difficult for women to find jobs, daycare is plentiful; while in urban areas, where women can secure full-time jobs more easily, there is not enough. Given very strict regulations and high standards about the quality and space of the facilities, expanding public daycare is an expensive undertaking, especially in the cities where it is most needed. Attempts to promote private sector daycare have not worked well because regulations are understandably strict, but make the costs of doing business, and the fees for users, very high. In 2001, the central government revised the Child Welfare Law to encourage municipalities to privatize their daycare operations. NPOs and for-profit companies can now bid to manage what had been public facilities and trim costs by hiring non-regular, non-unionized staff. However, parents prefer public daycare because it is heavily subsidized, providing excellent care for very reasonable fees. In this context, private facilities have a hard time competing and are not affordable for many households. The major advantages that private facilities have are longer and more flexible hours – public facilities require set dropoff and pickup times that are generally inconvenient for working people – and convenient locations chosen by the customer.

The DPJ-led government is trying to help ease the financial burden of raising children by introducing free schooling and providing a child-rearing allowance from 2010, but until women are able to better balance their career and family responsibilities, such inducements are unlikely to have a dramatic impact.

Growing Old

Wandering in the countryside, it is easy to see spry octogenarians hoeing, planting, weeding, harvesting, and hauling. When asked about the secret of longevity, one improbably vigorous 100-year-old said hard work and a large glass of sake at night keeps him going. In cities, the elderly gather in the morning in local parks for group calisthenics synchronized by the commands of NHK's popular morning radio program. They also volunteer in neighborhood patrols and as school crossing guards. Today's older Japanese have had tough lives and generally have healthy lifestyles, staying active, eating well, and following doctor's orders. There is universal medical insurance in Japan, meaning that people have regular checkups and access to decent healthcare at low cost. As the OECD notes, "Japan's health-care system stands out as one of the best in the world in a number of respects, including access, effectiveness and efficiency."[5] The World Health Organization also notes that Japanese enjoy good health for longer than everyone else in the world.

Getting old, however, is not what it used to be. Overall life expectancy in Japan as of 2009 is one of the highest in the world, at 86.05 years for women and 79.29 for men, compared to 81.3 and 76.23 in the UK. Amazingly, back in 1935 average life expectancy in Japan was only 45, rising to 60 by 1950 and climbing ever since. Healthy diets have helped, but the relatively healthy old age enjoyed by Japanese is not just a taste for tofu. There is a high level of literacy and so people are very aware about health issues, while medical screening is extensive and medical services are delivered in a timely manner at a very reasonable cost.

Officials have also stepped up programs that encourage the elderly to stay active and working. The government has been gradually extending the retirement age, and town offices provide a range of programs for the elderly ranging from continuing education to volunteer work. The nanny state is also setting guidelines and targets for healthier living, including reduction of sodium in the diet, encouraging regular exercise, and conducting early intervention screening. In Japan, such public health campaigns are effective, at least for the elderly who have time to worry about such things and are more accustomed to deferring to the state. Another factor is the contentment of elderly Japanese who maintain strong community ties and active social networks.

The smoking, eating, and drinking habits of middle-aged and younger Japanese raise serious concerns, however, about future trends. The popularity and ubiquity of McDonald's in Japan, and a raft of competitors spewing out similarly unhealthy food, are not a good sign. The fast food, convenience store lifestyle has taken root in Japan and young people often turn up their noses at the healthy fare of their elders. As a result, the country faces the new health threats of an affluent society hooked on Marlboros and Big Macs.

Top of the list are lung cancer and diabetes. Stomach cancer was the most common cause of cancer deaths 20 years ago, but has declined significantly as a result of improvements in diet, screening, and treatment. These days, lung cancer is the leading cause of death in a country where the government has a 50 percent stake in Japan Tobacco, a former state monopoly privatized in 1985, that controls about two-thirds of the Japanese market.[6] Compounding the moral hazard, cigarette taxes are a significant source of government revenues.[7] The government's vested interest in promoting tobacco sales means it has not been very aggressive in tackling smoking-induced cancer, estimated at 90,000 cases a year, representing 20 percent of all cancers in Japan as of 2004. Warning labels are relatively small and mild while prices are one-third levels in the US. Overall about 25 percent of the population smokes and nearly 40 percent of adult males are smokers compared to 24 percent in the US. In recent years, TV no longer carries cigarette ads and smokers face greater restrictions on where they smoke, but they still enjoy considerable freedom that subjects many others to second-hand smoke. The Health Promotion Law of 2002 stipulates that managers of public places must make efforts to "prevent passive smoking," but there is no punishment for non-compliance.

Lifestyle diseases such as diabetes, heart disease, and high blood pressure are soaring because of growing consumption of fattier, high-cholesterol foods and a more sedentary lifestyle causing steady increases in body mass index (BMI). In response, the government has launched a major campaign to reduce BMI, setting strict guidelines, mandatory "flab checks," and waist measuring in annual health exams for those 40 and older, and threatening penalties for companies with overweight employees. Some 13 million Japanese suffer from what is known as "metabo" (metabolic syndrome, i.e. overweight) and 14 million are at risk. But the guidelines for determining metabo are extreme and only about 3 percent of Japanese are actually obese, the lowest in the OECD, compared to 30 percent of Americans.

Managing Crisis

The government projects that social security spending will reach JPY41,000 billion ($430 billion) by 2015, up an eye-popping 42 percent from 2006. Scary numbers along these lines are regularly invoked to create a sense of crisis that justifies and propels reforms. Certainly, Japan does face urgent problems in coping with the aging society, but its relatively good track record in dealing with an explosion in the numbers of elderly since the 1980s suggests that it is equal to the task. Frequent adjustments and fine-tuning combined with some recent sweeping reforms signal that the situation is not nearly as grim as the unnerving statistics and gloomy headlines suggest.

Medical care costs in Japan are massive and growing, but incremental, biennial adjustments of fee schedules for medical services and products under the national health scheme have contained costs despite rapid aging and soaring demand for medical services.[8] Since demographic change is predictable, the government can adjust public policy and individuals' choices in ways that maintain a balance between revenues and expenditures while ensuring access to good medical services.

Japan spends less than half per capita of what the US does on healthcare, but by most measures Japanese are considerably healthier. Good health is due mostly to lifestyle (and far lower levels of violence than in the US), but it is also a reflection of widely available, high-quality healthcare. Between 1980 and 2003, while the proportion of the over-65 population rose from 9 to 19 percent, total health spending rose from 7 to 8 percent of GDP. During the same period, the elderly population in the US rose from 11 to 12 percent while healthcare spending nearly doubled from 9 to 17 percent of GDP. Japan's growth rate in health spending was a modest 4 percent per annum in the 1990s.[9]

Significant medical reforms have been implemented in recent years that are aimed at raising revenues and containing costs. These efforts are typical of how the government is trying to ensure a sustainable system by balancing revenues and expenditures. Naturally, efforts to restrict services, pare choices, and increase co-payments by the elderly provoke a strong negative reaction, and there have been many missteps, but the government has maintained a highly egalitarian medical care system based on need while shifting more of the burden on those who can afford to pay.

The Long-Term-Care Insurance System (Kaigo Hoken Seido) introduced in 2000 (revised in 2009) requires all Japanese employees over age 40 to pay premiums for nursing insurance and provides nursing services and daycare for everyone who needs care.[10] This constitutes the third pillar in Japan's social security system, along with basic healthcare insurance and pensions.

There are options for services in the home and at local facilities that are determined in consultation with local care managers based on national long-term care (LTC) criteria. The LTC criteria are subject to periodic reforms aimed at reducing nursing care expenses and increasing co-payments. This ongoing rationing of services makes budgetary sense, but sparks controversy in a country with mandated universal medical coverage and expectations that access to services should be based entirely on perceived need. For the most needy in terms of ability to pay and health problems, the system delivers high-quality services at low cost, but for others, services are being scaled back and costs are rising.

As the government tightens eligibility criteria for levels of LTC service to rein in soaring costs, it is encountering stiff resistance. Naturally, the public is angry about reduced benefits while out-of-pocket costs are increasing, essentially delivering less for more. This pressure is politically useful to lobby for increasing revenues by lowering the age for mandatory nursing care insurance premiums. Currently, these premiums cover about one-half of LTC costs, with the remainder coming from central and local government coffers. Given the fiscal crisis enveloping government at all levels, the temptation to cover more LTC costs by future beneficiaries is irresistible. Providing medical services to the swelling ranks of elderly is also invoked to press for increases in the relatively regressive consumption tax.

Controversially, in 2005 the government announced a drastic series of cuts in the number of long-term care beds in hospitals.[11] These LTC beds, according to the plan, are restricted to patients who require a high level of medical care. Those who do not have acute conditions are being transferred to their homes where they can receive nursing services or placed in assisted living facilities. Many geriatric patients have been "warehoused" in hospitals on a long-term basis (more than 6 months) even though they do not have acute conditions requiring such relatively intensive and expensive care.[12] The government sees this as a misallocation of limited resources that could be more effectively deployed elsewhere. To facilitate the transition away from LTC beds, the government seeks to shift patients to subsidized nursing home facilities that provide an assisted living environment, but there is an acute shortage of capacity and significant regional disparities in availability. In the meantime, many patients needing care somewhere in between home nursing and hospitalization are not well served.

In another sweeping reform, in 2008 the government introduced a new medical care system for people over age 75, termed "later stage seniors," shifting 13 million people from their existing national healthcare plan. The previous system was managed by 1,800 municipal governments and now is managed by 47 prefectural-based regional organizations. For most people, the shift did not entail any significant changes in their premiums or level of service. Under this system, most 75+ people retained a co-payment of 10 percent, but this can reach a maximum of 30 percent for those earning more than JPY5.2 million on a means-tested scale. This ceiling is the typical co-payment rate in the Japanese health system for everyone else.

While there are compelling reasons behind this spate of reforms, ones that belie the popular perception of policy paralysis, there are serious problems with rationing of services. For example, the government faces a huge challenge in establishing enough assisted living facilities, especially for those without sufficient financial resources. In addition, in-home care may not be a good substitute for institutionalization in many cases, especially if the household is unable to provide sufficient caregiving or pay for supplementary assistance. In many cases the elderly are caring for their ailing spouses (*roro kaigo*, elderly caring for elderly) and they often need more support than the care manager assigns them.

Japan's medical care system also faces an acute shortage of doctors, nurses, and caregivers, especially in rural areas. There are 270,000 doctors in Japan – at 2 per 1,000 population the lowest ratio in the G8 and the third to last in the 30-member OECD. To reach the OECD average, Japan needs 140,000 more doctors, representing more than a 50 percent increase.

Fewer doctors and more patients needing more medical care mean brief visits and little interaction between patient and doctor. In addition, fees are regulated and low, putting pressure on physicians to process a high volume of patients and also over-prescribe drugs since they can boost their incomes by selling them. The large number of consultations per doctor also translates into very long working hours, a serious issue that deters many from considering such a career. In addition, waiting rooms are crowded, often meaning lengthy waits for consultations.

Aside from an overall lack of doctors, there are acute shortages in certain fields such as obstetrics and gynecology – odd given the government's avowed aim of raising the birthrate. Cutbacks and consolidation of services have been especially felt in rural areas where few people are dispersed over wide areas. Delivering adequate care to such communities is never easy, but is exacerbated by deteriorating local finances and the preference of doctors to live and practice in urban areas where they can work in better equipped medical facilities and enjoy raising families with access to better schools and urban amenities. Progress towards meeting the ambitious targets of the central government's elderly care plans varies widely by region because many cash-strapped local authorities lack sufficient resources. Making do with less, however, is placing heavy burdens on families that are on the front line in providing care for elderly relatives.

Caregiving

Japanese policy is consistent with global trends away from institutionalization towards greater emphasis on home- and community-based care. The guiding principle of these new plans is to encourage older people to live with a minimum of dislocation and a maximum of independence for as long as possible. Many elderly Japanese want to live independently at home if at all possible and 93 percent of people aged 65 and over do so. With declining government support, however, combined with rising demand for such services and a shortage of professional caregivers, families are in crisis, in many cases overburdened and overwhelmed by their caregiving obligations.

Traditional values emphasizing family-based care confront dramatic transformations in the family involving residential and women's employment patterns. In 1980 the proportion of elderly people living with a child was 70 percent, but by 2006 this proportion had declined to 44 percent and it continues to recede.[13] While this is high compared to Western countries, Japanese observe and benchmark trends in terms of what is going on in their own society and older Japanese find this a troubling sign of changing family values. Despite the value society places on grandparents living with their children and grandchildren, the number of households including three generations is 3.53 million, accounting for only 18.3 percent of all households, as of 2007. The proportion of elderly living only with a spouse nearly doubled from 20 percent in 1980 to 37 percent by 2007, while those living alone increased from 9 to 16 percent in the same period. These figures highlight one of the major flaws in relying so extensively on family-based care. Many elderly can't or won't rely on their extended families; more are dependent on spouses who are also elderly; and quite a few elderly are all on their own.

Urban real-estate prices and cramped housing make three-generation households increasingly impractical, while increased women's labor force participation limits their role as family caregivers unless they give up their jobs. Family values and norms are changing due to demographic transitions, making institutional living arrangements for elderly citizens away from their families more socially acceptable. There remains, however, a strong inclination to rely on the family for caregiving as much as possible, with women accounting for 85 percent of all caregivers. Some 35 percent of these women caregivers report giving up their job in order to nurse ailing elderly relatives. They are both obliged and inclined, by rearing and social expectations, to take on this burdensome task. But many are getting too old for the job.

About one-half of family caregivers are age 60 or over, meaning that much of elderly care is in the hands of the elderly. The LTC plan is aimed at providing nursing support for these primary caregivers depending on the care manager's assessment of need, periodically adjusted according to changes in the patient's condition. Even though this is a godsend to families enduring what the media dubs "nursing hell," many of the caregivers are themselves frail and even with nursing assistance are pushed beyond their limits, taking a toll on their health and reducing their capacity for caregiving. Moreover, changing norms, expectations, employment patterns, and gender roles are undermining this family-based caregiving model and it is unlikely that younger women will take on these tasks in the future to the same degree as their mothers and grandmothers have.

The government's current family-based caregiving model with supplementary professional support cannot last given trends in the familial support ratio, defined as the number of females age 40–59 to the total population age 65–84.[14] This model puts primary responsibility on relatives, assisted to varying degrees by professional caregivers. Given that primary caregivers are usually women relatives, the declining number of middle-aged women combined with the rapid growth in the over-65-year-old population suggests some clear implications for home-based, family-provided caregiving. In 1990 the familial support ratio was 1.3, declining dramatically to 0.65 in 2010, and the future demographic potential for familial support is not promising. There are already increasing numbers of households without any caregivers; wife caregivers largely outlive their husbands, but as these widows grow frail they often do not have a relative to rely on. For them, at some point, assisted living and other institutional arrangements are necessary.

Large increases in the number of professional caregivers can make a difference, but their responsibilities will increase to the extent that families lack the capacity to help themselves. More intensive professional caregiving at home will be costly and require even larger numbers of professionals. Japan already has some 9 million elderly enrolled in community-based adult daycare programs, and those receiving nursing care at home are projected to rise from 4.1 million in 2004 to 6.4 million by 2014. This includes elderly suffering from senile dementia, rising from an estimated 1 million in 1990 to a projected 2.62 million by 2015. As the 7 million baby boomers begin entering their 70s from 2017, demand for nursing care services, along with assisted living facilities, will subsequently skyrocket.

As of 2008 there were 1.3 million nursing care assistants in Japan and the number of jobs in this sector is now expanding by some 14 percent per annum. The government predicts shortages of workers due to the difficulties of recruiting and retaining qualified workers. One reason is that few people want to work as care assistants. Caregiving is what most Japanese consider an undesirable 3K job (*kitanai, kitsui, kiken*: dirty, difficult, and dangerous). Pay is low, working conditions are demanding, and turnover is very high in this low-status job. Low pay is a major problem as the average monthly pay of a licensed care worker is only 60 percent of the average for all industries. The low wages and hard work help explain why there is such a high turnover rate.

In 2008, the ratio of job offers to job seekers in caregiving was 2.58, but by mid-2009, amidst the recession, this ratio improved to 1.28. This is the "silver lining" to the economic crisis, highlighting the greater desperation of households facing a tight job market, declining job security, and a 20 percent drop in their disposable income over the previous decade. However, retaining these workers and recruiting sufficient numbers of new workers will prove difficult as long as wages remain so low.

Japan pays its garbage collectors reasonably well, offering benefits and job security, and has no problem hiring and retaining enough workers for a job most people don't want to do. Tackling the shortage of nurses and caregivers is not merely a matter of improving wages and benefits, offering job security, and investing in their training, but such measures would help. However, given the government's emphasis on cost-cutting, and low industry margins, prospects for significant improvements along these lines appear limited.

Clearly, Japan faces an acute shortage of nurses and caregivers, but has not enacted policies that would address this problem effectively. With 1.3 million employed nurses, Japan faces an urgent need for 40,000 more nurses just to mitigate current levels of understaffing, while more than 60 percent of elderly care institutions do not have enough caregivers. In this situation, it makes sense to consider tapping foreign labor.

Could the answer come from overseas? Perhaps, but there is a tight global market for nurses and caregivers as aging societies elsewhere are also competing for the same limited pool of professionals and offer a better deal than Japan. The difficulties of mastering written Japanese, stringent qualification exams, and the distinct possibility of being sent home for failure to pass exams that even many Japanese can't pass will hamper Japan's efforts to recruit and retain sufficient numbers of foreign caregivers, a point we return to in Chapter 9.

The current system of dispatching caregivers and home helpers to individual homes is very labor intensive and, given the frailty of many of the family caregivers, there is a case to be made for transferring some elderly to modern, assisted living residential facilities. This could lower the nursing cost per patient, reduce the shortage of caregivers, and reduce stress on families. These facilities also promote a higher quality of life and independence than is the case in elderly homes with more comprehensive medical services and provide a much needed halfway option. However, due to underinvestment and a lack of incentives, Japan has a shortage of such facilities despite a growing market demand. The compelling logic of this option, nevertheless, is a basis for cautious optimism about expansion in this sector.

Pensions

Japan's pension system is in disarray, as in 2007 the government admitted it was "unable to match" some 250 million records with premium payers. As of 2010, nearly 50 million records remain "lost," and many pensioners believe they are being shortchanged as trust in the government has eroded considerably over this affair.

This saga of incompetence began a decade earlier when the pension records were being computerized. But the Social Insurance Agency (SIA) which was responsible for managing pensions has also been caught dipping into pension money for bureaucrats' housing and entertainment, losing money on ill-considered investments, and embezzling funds; and in 2005 several thousand workers were reprimanded when it emerged that they had been peeking at the personal records of politicians and celebrities. Then in 2008 SIA staff were caught advising companies on how to cut their premium payments by falsely reporting lower wages. Responding to voter anger, the DPJ disbanded the troubled SIA and from 2010 pensions are being administered by Japan Pension Services.

As of 2009 the government reports that about 40 percent of those obliged to contribute national pension premiums are not doing so, a marked rise from the 14 percent rate of premium evasion in 1992 when compliance peaked.[15] This problem has exploded in the early twenty-first century, fed no doubt by extensive media reports about what a bad deal pensions are for younger workers who are projected to receive less in total benefits than their cumulative contributions. There is resentment that today's retirees are relatively well-off and getting a good deal on their pension benefits relative to their contributions. For example, young people aged 24–34 today face an estimated JPY25 million deficit in their lifetime balance of tax and social security contributions to benefits, while people in their 70s are enjoying a JPY15 million surplus, making for a generation gap of some JPY40 million. There is also anger about inequality of pensions, with civil servants and politicians doing far better than ordinary citizens while premiums for low-income earners are relatively high. In addition, it is difficult to enroll non-regular workers because employers are under no obligation to do so and few can afford to pay their premiums even if they enroll themselves. By marginalizing these workers, society risks undermining social cohesion, and facilitating their enrollment in pensions could be a way of giving them a stake in a country that has treated them as a disposable underclass.

With the contribution rate sagging, the dependency ratio worsening from 3.6 workers per retiree in 2000 to 1.9 by 2025, and a vast increase in retirees claiming benefits over their longer lives, the situation is grim indeed. Clearly, the government needs to trim benefits while increasing contributions and is trying to do so. Under PM Junichiro Koizumi, unpopular reforms were enacted in 2004 that phase in increased premiums and lowered benefits. The stated goal is to ensure that pensions will equal 50.2 percent of after-tax working income, down from 62.3 percent in 2009, but experts are skeptical the government will be able to keep this promise.

The government is also stabilizing pension finances by raising the ratio of tax money used to cover the basic portion of the pensions from a little more than one-third to one-half, meaning this portion of pensions is less dependent on premium contributions. It is shifting towards funding the basic pension by taxes as a way of dealing with sagging premium contribution rates, but this means raising taxes in one form or another.

Figuring out how to sustain pensions and maintain living standards among the elderly is a key task not just in terms of their welfare, but also for the economy as a whole. Their spending and what they buy are becoming an ever more important mainstay of the economy.

Silver Business

As Japan's 7 million baby boomers retire, their savings are a target for silver businesses of all stripes. The boomers hold an estimated 10 percent of total personal financial assets in Japan, and overall 80 percent of Japan's financial assets are held by those 50+, suggesting attractive opportunities for businesses catering to the aging.

Drug companies are striking gold in Japan, the second biggest pharmaceuticals market in the world, with total sales of prescription medicine of $76 billion in 2008. Products already in use elsewhere are being rolled out in Japan as they pass lengthy clinical trials. From erectile dysfunction to mental depression, foreign drug companies are tapping a wealthy market with a growing appetite for drugs targeting geriatric ailments. Therapeutic treatment of age-related maladies such as arthritis, Alzheimer's, Parkinson's, eye ailments, etc. represent a major silver strategy for pharmaceutical companies. There is also a huge market for medicines that promote healthy aging as well as lifestyle-related and chronic diseases. Medical devices for the elderly and those who care for them are yet another market with exponential growth potential. However, Japan is an extremely competitive, closely regulated market with entrenched domestic players.

The government imposes price cuts for drugs that average some 5–6 percent a year, taking some of the glitter off the market. In the decade to 2004, spending on pharmaceuticals in the US tripled to nearly $240 billion, while in Japan during the same period, spending on prescription medicines rose less than 25 per cent from $53 billion to $65 billion. Governments in the EU also manage drug prices, but even there the spending on medicine nearly doubled from $70 billion to $135 billion.

The next big thing in Japanese medicine is the coming of generic drugs. The cost savings are too large for the government to continue to ignore. It is estimated that boosting generics market share and cutting prices to US levels could slash national drug outlays by one-third, cutting overall health spending by 7 percent. This explains the government's target of boosting the generic market share to 30 percent by 2012. Generics accounted for only 19 percent of Japan's pharmaceutical market in 2007 compared to a 59 percent share in the US. Teva, the world's largest producer of generic drugs, is forming strategic partnerships with Japanese pharmaceutical companies, and targets sales of $1 billion by 2015. Japanese firms are also on a buying spree, purchasing controlling stakes in overseas pharmaceutical firms to expand their offerings and cash in on the expected generic bonanza, for example acquiring Ranbaxy, the Indian generics giant.

Silver businesses are mushrooming in Japan, ranging from asset management firms and travel agencies to real estate, healthcare, and lifestyle services and products. Given that Japanese elderly enjoy the healthiest golden years in the world, there are promising long-term prospects for cashing in on affluent members of this generation. Health food sales are booming as older people try to maintain good health. There is also a booming market in talking dolls that help some elderly feel less lonely, and specialized toilets that provide medical feedback that can be linked with consultation centers, a boon for those living in isolated rural areas. Electronics companies are also producing and adapting all sorts of gadgets and gizmos targeting the elderly to make high-tech products more accessible while meeting specific needs.

Financial services companies are also aggressively marketing mutual funds and annuities to the elderly, but they are risk averse and suspicious. Developers are also seeking to lure retirees to live in planned communities, some even offering 3-month free trials. However, media reports about swindles are common, reinforcing cautious inclinations. After all, crime rates are rising in Japan, but old people are not only victims.

Crime and Punishment: Elderly Poverty and Isolation

The very first trial held under the new lay judge system introduced in 2009 involved a murder case.[16] Not just any murder case, but one involving two elderly who had a dispute over plastic bottles used to ward off peeing cats. A 66-year-old woman was stabbed to death by her 72-year-old male neighbor because of this spat over plastic bottles (and a history of similar confrontations), indicating that it is not only juvenile delinquents who resort to excessive violence for silly reasons. In this historic trial the perpetrator received a 15-year sentence – tough by Japanese standards, but jurors noted that he did not call an ambulance for the victim and instead went to the horse races and placed some bets, not exactly the behavior of one overcome by remorse. In 2008 alone, senior citizens committed some 123 murders, including some mercy killings of ailing relatives, so it's not as if they are only involved in shoplifting or other petty offenses.

One unexpected development in Japan is the increasing number of crimes committed by senior delinquents, mostly petty crimes such as shoplifting as it turns out. In Japan, the fastest-growing group of lawbreakers is over age 70. Around the world, it's teens and those in their young 20s who have the highest propensity to commit crime, but Japan seems to have a growing number of late bloomers. The Ministry of Justice's 2008 White Paper on Crime provides reassuring figures about declining levels of crime overall except for pilfering geriatrics. In 2007, 31,573 senior citizens were convicted of theft, triple the 1998 total. Between 2002 and 2007, arrests of people over 65 more than doubled even as the overall crime rate declined.

It is surprising that crimes committed by elderly people far exceed the increase in their population. While the elderly population doubled between 1988 and 2007 from 13.78 million to 27.46 million, the overall number of crimes committed by people aged 65 or over has risen fivefold. In 2007, police arrested 48,605 senior citizens (33,255 men and 15,350 women), accounting for 13 percent of the 366,002 suspects the police took action against that year.[17] Of this total, which does not include traffic violations, about 90 percent were petty offenses. In 1988, by comparison, elderly represented only 2 percent of all 398,208 criminal suspects, totaling 9,888 (6,675 men and 3,213 women).

Why are the elderly becoming more criminal? The economic crisis and inadequate pensions and welfare programs have driven many elderly into poverty, and shoplifting is one way for them to make ends meet on less. In terms of poverty rates, in 2007 the OECD ranked Japan fourth worst overall among its 30 member countries. Poverty affects 20 percent of elderly Japanese and there is growing inequality among them.[18] The critical role of economic distress in silver crime is evident in the northern island of Hokkaido, one of the poorest regions of Japan, where there were more elderly arrested for crimes than teenagers by a ratio of three to two.

Many elderly criminals are homeless and steal because they are hungry, while others are socially isolated and suffer from financial anxieties. Apparently, many fail to take advantage of existing welfare programs either because they are not aware or due to pride. Clearly, given the strong social stigma of arrest, the elderly are acting out of despair and desperation, but not all of it is about lack of money. The extended family provided various mutual support mechanisms and also conferred status on the elderly that reinforced a positive identity and a sense of belonging. With the breakdown of families and community, many elderly suffer from isolation, social exclusion, and loneliness. Many live apart from their children and grandchildren and don't have friends. Thus, aside from stealing food and other necessities because they are needy, some elderly commit crimes as a way of drawing attention.

The dilemma facing society is how to alleviate elderly poverty and their growing isolation, but there is no obvious panacea. Traditions of reverence for the aged and high status in the community are fading and now many elderly are feeling neglected because younger people are too busy and caught up in their own lives. In some cases, however, the problem is not just neglect.

Senior Abuse

The abuse of the elderly by their caregivers, often relatives, is a hidden scourge in Japan, one that does not get the same attention as domestic violence against spouses and child abuse. Caring for the elderly, especially those with senile dementia, is very difficult for professionals, let alone for relatives who are often over 60 years old and physically challenged, to provide the care needed by their "patients." Over time, even with nursing assistance, home care is fraught with tensions and, because it involves relatives, it can be an extremely volatile situation ready to explode. It is not surprising that abuse occurs because family caregivers are at their wits' end, don't get enough support or appreciation, are not trained to handle and defuse unpleasant situations, and, as relatives, have accumulated emotional baggage that makes it nearly impossible to retain a cool detachment.

Despite a tradition of filial piety, the government's emphasis on elderly care by relatives puts considerable pressure on families. A 2007 government survey reported 12,575 cases of elderly abuse by family members at home, with about 40 percent involving those with symptoms of Alzheimer's. The number of reports probably greatly understates the scope of the problem, but shows that the legal requirement for home nursing care workers to report abuses to authorities, introduced in 2006 as a provision of the senior abuse law, is having some impact. Popular images of daughters-in-law tormenting their mothers-in-law notwithstanding, sons are the most likely abusers (37 percent of cases), followed by husbands and daughters (14 percent each), while the oft-maligned daughters-in-law are implicated in only 10 percent of the abuse cases. Women constitute 75 percent of the victims and octogenarians are at greatest risk, with physical abuse involved in nearly two-thirds of the cases. Psychological abuse, negligence or denial of care, and economic abuse involving the selling-off of assets are legally considered abuse. Many of the abusers, however, are reportedly unaware of this and don't consider that what they are doing constitutes abuse.

The media also reports institutional abuse that is almost certainly more extensive than the number of reported cases. In many of these institutions, staff training is poor, the staff-to-patient ratio is poor, and there is little supervision by either managers or family. Such situations are a breeding ground for abuse. Some of the more horrific cases, such as caging of patients, involve unlicensed nursing facilities that do not meet government standards. They are relatively inexpensive, but offer poor-quality services. Safety problems are also rife, something the nation discovered when a fire swept through an unlicensed facility in Gunma in 2009, killing 10 of the 17 residents and leaving the survivors badly burned. There were no water sprinklers, doors were locked, and the few staff on duty were unable to help frail residents escape. These sorts of places are deathtraps and negligence is common, but eyes are averted as local authorities recommend them, and families entrust their relatives to unscrupulous operators, for want of reasonably priced alternatives.

Prospects

While Japan does face significant problems due to the aging of its population, it has a reasonably good track record in managing these challenges. It has already weathered a tremendous increase in the elderly population since the 1980s and has contained costs while delivering good medical services that help its old people enjoy the healthiest golden years in the world.[19] It is reassuring that the largest increases in the elderly population have already happened and that the government has managed to cope with the doubling of the elderly population over the first two decades of the Heisei era as well as it has, even while the economy was in the doldrums. Japan has survived this period of hyper-aging, and now faces a much more moderate and manageable 25 percent increase in the elderly population over the next two decades, reaching an estimated 34.8 million by 2030.

Dire projections and scaremongering about the future of a graying Japan underestimate the capacity to cope by pragmatically fine-tuning policies. No doubt there will be some zigzagging in policies and performance, and in some areas the chances for not getting things right are high, but it seems that the odds for an overall muddling-through scenario are reasonably good. Most Japanese agree that the nation's best days are behind it, and nobody is predicting a grand revival, but this does not mean that rapid aging puts Japan at risk of sinking into the abyss.

The Japanese record in controlling healthcare costs while maintaining a good and egalitarian medical care system is very impressive. The secret to cost-cutting lies in the biennial review of payment scales for medical services and products combined with relatively high co-payment rates (30 percent) and the political will to implement significant reforms in a timely manner. Underinvestment, however, is having a negative impact.

The downside of cost-cutting is richly examined in the Japanese media. Many patients are no longer eligible for the same benefits they have enjoyed, while co-payment fees are rising and are not negligible for those with significant medical problems. Many local hospitals have closed and regional alternatives are not as convenient, especially in rural areas. There is also a dire shortage of doctors in some regions and in certain specialties, meaning a denial of proper medical treatment in far more cases than one would imagine in an advanced country like Japan. There are also numerous cases of understaffed emergency rooms turning away ambulances carrying critically ill patients who end up dying for lack of care. Consultations with doctors also tend to be very brief, allowing for only straightforward diagnoses, while diagnosis and treatment of psychological problems remain inadequate.

Government policies have restricted the numbers of doctors and the medical system as a whole suffers from chronic underinvestment. Cutting-edge surgical techniques and medical procedures are not widely available, denying many patients modern medical advances that are less invasive and have shorter recovery periods that are life enhancing. According to the OECD, it takes two to three times longer in Japan than in other member countries to introduce newly developed drugs. This comparatively slow drug approval process also compromises the quality of medical care. Curiously, given the emphasis on cost-cutting, until now the use of cheaper generic drugs has remained very limited, but that is quickly changing.

The pressures to stay the course on cost-cutting are overwhelming, not only because medical expenditures have increased by 3 percent per annum since 1990 and the number of elderly needing more medical care is rising rapidly, but also due to ballooning budget deficits, constituting about 10 percent of GDP in 2010. In this context, the government has little leeway to make the sort of investments on the scale needed to have a significant impact, nor can it afford to cut co-payments or restore services without further mortgaging the future. The DPJ swept to power in 2009 promising to cut wasteful spending, but it will find slim pickings in the national health system.

Cost management has focused on controlling medical fees rather than restricting insurance coverage, an egalitarian solution based on the principle that access to medical services should be based on need rather than the ability to pay. The DPJ is inclined to maintain this principle, but in doing so will face soaring expenditures. To rein these in, experts call for a gatekeeping system in which general practitioners (GPs) exercise more effective control over referrals to specialists, but this is a long-term endeavor requiring a large increase in GPs and better training for them. In the meantime, the government will continue to squeeze fees and drug prices, but this approach raises concerns about maintaining the quality of care.[20]

The family-based caregiving model has limited shelf life because of changing employment, residential, and gender patterns and a declining familial support ratio. There are too few potential family caregivers relative to the soaring numbers of elderly needing care. As families shoulder less of the onerous burden of their honorable elders, more professional services and institutional options are necessary. Many older people don't want to become burdens to their children and favor such alternatives. To cope with surging demand for elderly care, the government will lower the age for mandatory contributions to LTC insurance and will also need to vastly increase the numbers of foreign caregivers. New technologies will provide some necessary support, but attracting and retaining foreign caregivers is necessary because the need is rising quickly and relentlessly. This means offering more incentives such as better wages and permanent residency to enhance Japan as a destination *vis-à-vis* other countries that are also recruiting care professionals. To manage costs and more effectively deploy caregivers, the government has to prioritize expanding assisted living residential facilities.

Where Japan has faltered most is in creating a family-friendly working and living environment. The drop in fertility in the post-WWII era is a result of many factors, but it is clear that companies and the government are not supporting families enough in helping them achieve a work–life balance. Women are voting with their wombs, refraining from having children because the opportunity costs are so high and rigid employment policies make many of them choose between raising a family or pursuing a career. Working couples have long work hours, but too few husbands do enough at home to help their spouses juggle work and household responsibilities. Changing such patriarchal attitudes is a significant impediment to achieving work–life balance.

The government's social welfare policies are also heavily weighted towards members of society heading for the exits and invest too little in supporting young couples and their children. In Japan, 70 percent of the social welfare budget goes to programs for the aged, such as pensions and medical services, while only 4 percent is earmarked for child benefits and childcare services. The government's education-related spending is also the lowest among industrialized countries in terms of its ratio to GDP. Modifying this balance is an urgent priority, but will not be easy.

The voting power of the old in Japan's graying democracy may make it difficult to shift priorities enough to make a difference, but the elderly do not necessarily constitute a monolithic bloc as there are considerable differences among them. Creating incentives for more flexible employment practices, small changes in daycare and spouse attitudes, and more support for elderly care are not a great stretch and could help women achieve a reasonable balance, fulfilling to them and beneficial to society.

As discussed above, the demographic time bomb presents Japan with a number of policy challenges and is serving as a catalyst for transformation. In general, during the Heisei era the government has implemented an impressive array of reforms aimed at dealing with the demographic crisis, ranging from elderly care to pensions. But nobody argues that this is enough, and the momentum behind ongoing reforms is sustained by the collective sense of urgency. These reforms will have significant consequences for the quality of life, the state of the economy, and the government's credibility, and as such serve as a barometer for Japan's future.

The socio-cultural consequences of Japan's rapidly aging population reverberate quietly throughout society, changing how people think about their world and act in it. Coping with such cultural upheaval and adapting to the repercussions is never easy, but seems to be causing less anxiety and tension in Japan than one would expect – testimony to collective resilience and fortitude in handling adversity. Thus, the prospects for managing the demographic crisis and adjusting to its consequences are reasonably good.

The major threats to a muddle-through scenario are deep fiscal vulnerabilities, the voting power of anti-reform elderly, and the marginalization of non-regular workers. Giving the latter a stake in the system and mitigating the widening gaps in society between rich and poor, old and young, urban and rural, and full-time and non-regular workers will be key to defusing the demographic time bomb. Managing these problems requires an understanding of the growing and interrelated risks facing the family and workers in the twenty-first century, issues we examine in the next two chapters.

Chapter 4

Families at Risk

The family in Japan conjures up images of stability that are increasingly out of step with emerging realities. Certainly, compared to most other advanced industrialized nations, Japan's families are not in crisis. For Japanese, however, the point of reference is not how much worse the situation is overseas, but how much better it seemed to have been in Japan until recent years when the media has reported extensively about various family-related problems. Stable and secure families and jobs have been the pillars of the post-WWII system, but both are less stable and secure, carrying significant ramifications for social policies.

Japan's social welfare system is heavily dependent on the family to provide critical support, assistance, and resources to family members in need. This outsourcing of basic livelihood security has worked reasonably well in Japan as long as the needs were limited and the family closely knit and able to provide. This has also been a convenient and cost effective strategy because the government has had little need to develop robust social welfare programs typical in many other advanced industrialized nations or budget for them. As a result, Japan's safety net is inadequate and increasingly so given the sustained economic crisis. The economic cross-currents in Heisei Japan, reinforced by changing norms and values, have undermined family ties while at the same time the burdens on them have been increasing. By invoking *jiko sekinin* (self-responsibility), a concept popularized under PM Koizumi, the government reduced support for families just as more of them are in greater need. The growing number of families at risk has exposed just how inadequate the social safety net is and constitutes a major challenge to the government because outsourcing social welfare to the family has been a central policy tenet. Problematically, government attitudes and policies towards the family have not adapted to the new realities of weakening family ties, more single-parent households, and rising divorce rates, creating a gap between policies based on the assumption of a conventional family model and atypical realities. These atypical families are especially prone to poverty, but government policies often reinforce their disadvantaged conditions. In this chapter we examine the rise of divorce, single-mother families, domestic violence, child abuse, and suicide in the Heisei era and how society is responding to the consequences. Pressures are building to overhaul social policies, and the DPJ promises to do so, because the existing social safety net assumes that vulnerable people can rely on their extended family for assistance. As we see below, however, this is no longer an option for increasing numbers of Japanese.

Divorce

Many families can no longer meet government expectations because of rising divorce rates. The spike in divorces since the early 1990s, featuring a 48 percent increase in the divorce rate between 1993 and 2003, constitutes a potentially devastating and expanding risk to affected Japanese families. More than 20 percent of marriages now end in divorce. Aside from the psychological and emotional impact on the divorcing couples and their children, and the lingering stigma attached to atypical households, many single parents swell the ranks of the working poor, those defined as earning less than JPY2 million a year. These families pose significant challenges to a society that is not prepared to cope with such uncertainties and the vulnerabilities they foster and expose. Rising levels of divorce not only challenge norms and values but also question patriarchal assumptions and inclinations embedded in social policies and laws while highlighting gender imbalances in employment and income.

Levels of divorce similar to prevailing rates in the EU (2.1 divorces per 1,000 people as of 2005; 3.6 in the US) are eroding the foundations of the prevailing ideology towards family in Japan based on the myth of a conventional household with a breadwinner husband, full-time housewife, and two children raised in a stable, nurturing environment who are afforded equal access to the range of opportunities expected in an affluent, middle-class society. While there has long been a yawning gap between this family ideal and reality – captivatingly conveyed in the classic films of Yasujiro Ozu depicting family travails in the 1950s – the surge of divorce has made this gap more visible and prominent in public discourse during the Heisei era.

Infidelity, spousal and child abuse, alcoholism, and Japan's workaholic culture have taken a toll on many marriages. Divorce is less stigmatized in contemporary Japan than in the past, but patriarchal attitudes towards women and their proper role linger. During the Heisei era, divorce has in many respects become less censured because it has become more prevalent and a fixture in public discourse. Certainly for many people divorce remains taboo, and even if it has become more common it does flout convention, leading in some cases to unpleasant consequences. For example, children suffer emotional trauma, landlords may be reluctant to rent, husbands may withhold child support, and employers may be less than supportive of single parents who face difficulties in balancing the needs of their families with the demands of their jobs. However, the media has played a key role in transforming popular images of divorcees, generating understanding and sympathy for the grim realities that undermine marriages everywhere and the tough consequences for single parents. There is now less social tolerance for abusive, philandering husbands and higher expectations for fathers and husbands to participate in family life. In contrast, adulterous women have always faced disapprobation and there has been a patriarchal assumption, now fading, that women tolerate their husbands' behavior while bearing responsibility for nurturing the family and other household responsibilities.

There is no simple explanation for why divorce has skyrocketed during the Heisei era.[1] Changing attitudes among women towards marriage is one factor. Conservative Japanese believe that as women become more educated and pursue careers they become more assertive and less willing to assume what are considered their proper roles and duties. It does appear that many women are more ready to challenge patriarchy than in the past. However, despite their doubts and reservations, and eagerness to have fun, work, and travel, most young women still express a desire to get married and have children even if it means sacrificing their careers. Given persistent gender inequalities in the workplace, it is not so surprising that women abandon careers for their families.[2] Women earn on average about 60 percent of men, and only 10 percent of managers are women. The wage gap reflects the higher concentration of women in non-regular work as contract, dispatched, or temporary workers. Their need for flexible work schedules to juggle work and family responsibilities is an important factor in this trend.

Women may be adjusting to marginal employment as non-regular workers, but they have high expectations of marriage and their attitudes towards the family are changing faster than men, for the very good reason they want to share the burdens more equitably. This widening gap in attitudes towards gender-ascribed roles is a serious risk factor for marriages. As divorce has become more prevalent and less stigmatized, people are less reluctant to end unfulfilling marriages. What was rare and an extreme measure of last resort that shamed the families involved has become a far more acceptable option subject to less social sanction.

Divorce has also risen because of the prolonged economic recession and is most pronounced among couples with lower educational backgrounds. They are the most vulnerable to job and salary cuts, accumulating debts and foreclosure. People get married for various reasons and one is economic security. To the extent that husbands are unable to fulfill this traditional expectation, and money problems become a source of contention, more women are hitting the reset button and trying to start their lives over.

Dekichatta kekkon, shotgun marriages, are also becoming more common in Japan, estimated at some 25 percent of all marriages, and another reason why the divorce rate is rising. It is estimated that 80 percent of such marriages involving teenage women, and 60 percent involving 20-year-olds, end in divorce, most within 5 years. According to the government, of the 569,000 first births recorded for 2000, 26 percent were to women who were pregnant before marrying, up from 13 percent in 1980. The rise among younger women, however, is even more marked. In 2000, 58 percent of first-born babies delivered to women ages 20 to 24 were conceived before marriage, compared with 20 percent in 1980. Among first births to teen mothers in 2000, 82 percent were conceived out of wedlock, up from 67 percent in 1990 and 47 percent in 1980.[3]

Until recently, many unhappy Japanese wives had two options: endure a miserable marriage or face financial ruin as a divorcee. Since 2007, however, Japanese wives who file for divorce are eligible to get up to one-half of their husband's pensions based on legislation passed in 2003. An estimated 11 million housewives, one-third of all adult women, have little or no full-time work experience, making it difficult for many to secure a job after divorcing, explaining their dilemma. The government, already weighed down with massive deficits, initiated the pension reform in order to trim welfare payments to indigent divorcees, not to empower women. Overall poverty alleviation spending ballooned 58 percent from JPY1.5 trillion in 1997 to 2.6 trillion ($22 billion) in 2005, explaining why the government is so eager to trim wherever it can.

The divorce rate among 45- to 64-year-old couples rose fifteenfold between 1960 and 2005. Since 1985, the number of divorces among those married at least 30 years has quadrupled. A popular book in Heisei Japan is, *Why Are Retired Husbands Such a Nuisance?*, and there was also a popular television drama "Jukunen Rikon" ("Middle Age Divorce") that focused on couples taking stock of their marriage. Retired husbands are often referred to as *sodai gomi* (large garbage) and *nure uchiba* (wet leaves) in reference to their clinging dependence on their wives once they no longer have work to absorb their attention. Men tend to lack social networks outside the workplace, leaving them isolated after retirement.

The media reports an epidemic of "retired husband syndrome," a condition that often appears in wives soon after their husbands retire. Symptoms range from skin rashes to ulcers, and an estimated 60 percent of older wives are affected. After decades of living their own lives, many couples have little in common and lack good communication. Suddenly thrust together, many couples find retirement a difficult transition. Some older wives, having raised their children and fulfilled their duty by them, decide to cut their losses and divorce; men take the initiative in only 25 percent of all divorces.

The number of divorces peaked in 2002 at 290,000, and then dropped to less than 260,000 in 2006, prompting speculation that many women held off divorcing until the pension revision came into effect in 2007. Given the frenzied media attention accorded this reform, there was widespread public awareness of what was in store. It turns out, however, that divorce rates did not soar as anticipated because women came to realize that it would not be easy to make ends meet on only half a pension. Women also still face significant hurdles in achieving financial independence because the courts have not awarded equitable divisions of household assets. Thus, the financial penalties of divorce remain high for women even after the pension reform.

Single Moms: Entrenched in Poverty

Rising levels of divorce mean there are more single-mother households and nearly half of them live in poverty. In 2009, for the first time, the number of single mothers receiving dependent allowances for their children topped 1 million. The total number of single-mother households is some 1.22 million, up 28 percent from 1998. Their rising numbers and high rate of employment challenge prevailing stereotypes of Japanese housewives staying at home while devoting their time and energy to raising their families.

Government subsidies for children of single-parent households are critical to these households because their average annual income of JPY2.13 million is only 38 percent of the national average and only just above the poverty line. Moreover, 41 percent of single mothers earn less than the poverty threshold.[4]

Unlike in the US and Europe, there are few teenage single mothers in Japan. Nearly 90 percent of Japan's single moms become single by divorce and most are middle-aged. Also, single mothers in Japan are much more likely to work than their counterparts elsewhere. However, as with women overall in Japan, many single mothers find it difficult to secure full-time jobs and thus most are engaged in non-regular jobs that offer lower wages, benefits, and job security. This explains why single-mother households earn only about one-third as much as two-parent households, in 55 percent of which both parents work. For some of these single moms, flexible part-time schedules are necessary to juggle child-rearing responsibilities, but for most it is the lack of regular, full-time employment opportunities that explains why they accept non-regular jobs and the attendant disadvantages.

For the vast majority of single mothers, their atypical status is a social and financial liability. The gap between single-mother households and married couples with children continues to widen. From 1975 to 1984, the income level of single-mother households stood at some 45–50 percent of married couples with children, dropping to 30 percent from 1991 to 2000.

The LDP-led government sought to save money by cutting subsidies and shifting from providing income security to supporting the financial independence of single-mother households. This initiative drew on inappropriate welfare-to-work models adopted in the US and UK where many recipients are unwed teenage mothers dependent on the dole. Single-mother households account for over 20 percent of all households in the US and UK, but only 7 percent in Japan. Another difference is that unwed mothers account for only 8 percent of single-mother households in Japan compared to 40 percent in the US, and most Japanese single mothers are divorced and in their 30s and 40s. Single mothers' work participation rate in Japan is the highest among major industrialized nations and is about 30 percent higher than that for married mothers in Japan.

Certainly, Japan does not have a problem of "welfare queens" as 83 percent of Japan's divorced middle-aged moms have at least one job and some 10 percent more than one. It is not the lack of a strong work ethic so much as limited opportunity and poor job prospects for single mothers, many of whom lack higher education. By legislating employment support measures and emphasizing vocational training, the government sought to help these women offset the cuts in public child support, but such measures did not anticipate how bleak the job market became for everyone, including recent university graduates. Chieko Akaishi, director of Single Mothers Forum, spoke at a Japan Federation of Bar Associations symposium in 2009, criticized the government for not alleviating poverty among single mothers, and drew attention to the poor job placement record for those who have gone through vocational training. The job placement situation is especially bleak for single mothers outside the major cities.

The problem facing many of these middle-aged divorcees is that they gave up their job to have children and when they reenter the job market they usually have to start over at the bottom. Unlike professional women with qualifications or civil servants who can interrupt their careers and resume them without penalty, many of Japan's divorcees tend to be less educated and less employable. As a result, they are relegated to the disadvantageous employment periphery where wages, job security, and benefits are lowest.

It was in 2003 that the LDP moved to trim payments to single-mother households, tightening eligibility criteria and placing limits on the duration and level of child support subsidies. The income ceiling for families eligible for the full allowance was lowered from JPY2.05 million to 1.3 million, well below the poverty line of 2 million, while 80 percent of whatever the former spouse pays in child support is counted towards this ceiling.

In order to support the new welfare-to-work model, the government stipulated that single parents be given preference in placing their children at subsidized public daycare centers that typically have long waiting lists. The government also moved to force deadbeat dads to provide alimony, introducing child support enforcement legislation in 2003 that enables women to collect back payments and garnish future wages. However, 90 percent of divorces are settled out of court and arrangements are typically informal. Only one-third of all divorcees negotiate alimony settlements and only about 18 percent regularly receive child support, helping to explain why most live in desperate circumstances.

Deregulation, outsourcing, and privatization have eliminated many of the stable low-paying jobs that single mothers previously depended on, forcing them into non-regular jobs. As of 2008, 59 percent of single mothers were so engaged, earning an average of only JPY1.35 million a year, 33 percent below the poverty line. As a result, 14.3 percent of Japanese children, the highest rate among OECD countries, are raised in poverty.

In its 2006 survey of Japan, the OECD reports:

> More than half of single working parents were in relative poverty in 2000, compared with an OECD average of around 20 percent ... Given the relatively high proportion of education costs borne by the private sector, it is essential to ensure that children in low-income households have adequate access to high-quality education to prevent poverty from being passed to future generations.[5]

There is legitimate concern that poverty is denying children in single-mother households access to the educational opportunities they need to improve their prospects. The OECD attributes increasing class stratification in Japan to educational differences, meaning that single-mother households are at risk of becoming entrenched in poverty. Given the grim conditions facing those living at or below the poverty line, the LDP-mandated cuts in government assistance created additional pressure on affected children to quit school and find a job to boost household income. In Japan, as elsewhere, lower educational attainment translates into lower lifetime earnings and greater job insecurity.

There is thus a class angle to the problems affecting single-mother households who represent a major subgroup of Japan's growing ranks of working poor.[6] The rising divorce rate in Japan is often attributed to women's increasing economic independence. Given this widespread perception, it is assumed that divorce is an individual choice and thus women should not ask the state to support their lifestyle decision to become a single parent. However, these assumptions are wrong; most divorcees are not well-educated, middle-class women with sparkling careers thumbing their noses at patriarchal social conventions. The divorce rate is higher among less educated women from lower-class backgrounds who often have low-paying jobs and are usually married to men from a similar background. Divorce trends track men's unemployment rates, and families with lower educational attainment are more vulnerable to economic crisis than those with higher levels of educational attainment.

Since coming to power in 2009, the DPJ has eliminated public school fees through high school, provided monthly child-rearing subsidies, and reinstated allowances for single-mother households. Consequently, the prospects for single-mother households and all impoverished Japanese families appear somewhat brighter even if they remain relatively dim.

Domestic Violence

In early 2007, the nation woke to lurid headlines about the dismemberment of a man by his wife in their upscale condo who later scattered the sawed-up body parts in a park and on the streets of Tokyo. At the murder trial, Kaori Mihashi, a slightly built 33-year-old looking more fashionable than murderous, testified that her husband beat her repeatedly since 2003, beginning only a week after their wedding. In 2005 she spent several weeks at a shelter recovering from serious injuries she said were inflicted by her husband, but like many abused women she returned home. However, unlike most abused women, she dealt with her problem by killing her husband and sought the court's understanding, and a shortened sentence, by invoking the battered wife defense. In recent years women's shelter advocates have testified in numerous similar trials to establish the legal basis for claiming that repeated abuse over a prolonged period is an extenuating circumstance. In Mihashi's case, however, the judge sentenced her to 15 years in prison, long by Japanese standards, saying that her hellish married life did not diminish her responsibility for what he termed a brutal crime. The defense lawyers argued that due to repeated beatings she was not mentally competent when she hit and dismembered her husband, but the judge dismissed two psychiatrists' diagnosis of insanity, saying she was capable of exercising judgment at the time the crime was committed.

During the Heisei era, the invisible scourge of domestic violence (DV) has surfaced with a vengeance, and what was long denied, condoned or otherwise tolerated has become a national concern prompting state intervention. Clearly, this tectonic and rapid shift in attitudes has been driven by greater awareness of global norms and the relentless work of Japanese activists and women's rights advocates to force the government to curtail domestic violence and support victims. In 2001, Japan enacted the Domestic Violence Prevention Law, signaling that no longer would this remain a private issue left to families. Crisis intervention by the police and criminal justice system based on this law demonstrates how changing social attitudes have translated into major government initiatives. The media previously portrayed domestic violence as a problem of Western societies while older generations of Japanese accepted husbands' resort to violence against their wives as normal.

The situation began to change following the 1993 Vienna Declaration and Programme of Action that explicitly recognized various forms of violence against women as a social problem warranting government intervention. More momentum, and pressure, was generated by the 1995 Beijing Women's Conference when women's rights activists began lobbying the government to act. In 1997 PM Ryutaro Hashimoto responded by asking the National Council for Gender Equality to study the issue, leading to a withering report issued in 2000 confirming the worst fears and urging immediate action. The previous year the government commissioned a national survey that also found appalling levels of domestic violence. One in seven women reported receiving medical treatment following spousal violence while 5 percent of women said they had experienced a life-threatening beating. Defying social expectations, the study found that domestic violence did not vary by class or educational attainment. At the same time, a study by the Osaka government found that two-thirds of women surveyed reported abuse by their partners.[7]

The Law on Prevention of Spouse Violence and Protection of Victims allows district courts to issue 6-month restraining orders against abusers and to evict them from the home for 2 weeks. Those who violate the court orders face up to a year in jail and a maximum fine of JPY1 million ($10,000). Anyone making a false report is subject to a maximum fine of JPY100,000 ($1,000). The law requires local governments to provide financial assistance to organizations that assist victims of domestic violence, and stipulates that the national government is responsible for establishing facilities to assist victims. The law is credited with expanding the number of shelters and counseling centers, but for many abused women these are remote from where they live and not of much help.

Critics of the law point out that it does not make domestic abuse a crime and requires women seeking a court injunction to provide affidavits from shelters, doctors, or police attesting to their claims of abuse, a requirement that increases the risk of dangerous delays. There is, however, a provision that allows courts to issue emergency restraining orders without a hearing if danger is deemed imminent. However, there is no injunction against marital rape and, in general, courts in Japan have not offered support to wives seeking protection from coerced sex.

Revisions of the law since 2004 broaden the definition of DV to include psychological abuse, verbal threats, or harassment by repeated phone calls.

Under the revised law, court-issued restraining orders are extended from a maximum of 2 weeks to 2 months and the courts can now order the abuser to stay away from the victim's children. The new law also calls on the government to develop a basic policy aimed at helping victims recover and orders each prefecture to develop an action plan to support this measure. As of 2010, the government has not issued specific policies to support victims and there are only 150 small, underfunded shelters mostly run by NPOs in a nation of 127 million.

The number of DV cases has surged since the government began compiling statistics in 2002, reaching 25,210 incidents involving the police in 2008. In 2,534 cases the courts issued restraining orders and there were 76 prosecutions of those violating such orders. Other laws were invoked in prosecuting 1,650 cases of domestic violence, including 77 murders. Almost all victims are women and most are in their 30s. Nationwide consultations for DV reached 58,528 in fiscal year (FY) 2006–7, up 63 percent from FY2001–2 when records were first kept. Part of this increase is because there are now 117 regional consultation centers compared to 87 in 2002, but it is also clear that what used to be considered normal is now increasingly seen as intolerable. In addition, there has been a dramatic transformation in attitudes as what used to be viewed as a private family matter is now seen to require state intervention. One suspects, nonetheless, that many women remain silent and endure abusive relationships behind closed doors, fearing retribution from abusive partners if they seek help.

Child Abuse Epidemic

As with domestic violence, the incidence of child abuse has exploded in Japan, with reported cases for FY2007–8 topping 40,000 for the first time, up from 1,101 in 1990 when the government began collecting data and marking a fourfold increase from the 10,000 abuse cases in 1999. This sudden sharp increase reflects the growing scale of the problem, changing attitudes towards what constitutes abuse, the prolonged economic malaise, and legally mandated reporting on the part of teachers, counselors, doctors, and police. Yet reported cases represent only the tip of the iceberg as many victims and their families remain reluctant to involve the authorities. This reflects not only the fear of social stigma, but also low levels of awareness and a lack of adequate counseling facilities.

Attitudes are changing and authorities have decided that something should be done to stop this hidden scourge. Global norms about proper parenting and what constitutes abuse have also driven policy changes. Social policy reforms affecting the family are happening against the back-drop of sweeping transformations in Japanese society.

Child abuse is an urgent matter as there are no signs that the epidemic is abating. Over the past decade there has been a horrifying cascade of media reports on beatings, burnings, deliberate starvation, suffocation, and drowning of children by their parents. Japanese have been forced to con-front the uncomfortable reality that what they had long regarded as excep-tional is in fact an everyday reality for many children and their abusers. What had long been a taboo topic is now a media staple. Heartrending tales of child abuse have raised public awareness and led the government to pass the Child Abuse Prevention Law (2000), since revised in 2004 and 2005. Significantly, the law introduces a legal definition of abuse so that it cannot be justified as discipline and requires police intervention under certain circumstances.

Mothers commit most cases of abuse, isolated as they sometimes are in anonymous urban communities living in many cases far from their rela-tives. Young Japanese mothers today face more stress in raising children because they more frequently shoulder the burden alone with little spousal or community support. This is especially true for single mothers. Moreover, three-generation households are increasingly rare and public care facilities are limited for infants and preschool children, and especially so for mothers who are not working. In addition, many parents may have been treated harshly as children and in turn subject their own children to the patterns of discipline and punishment that they grew up with. Social norms are changing in Japan, as elsewhere, and what once passed as acceptable is now considered abusive, but the legacies of past abuse linger.

The belief that "family problems are best dealt with in the family" is fading under the sustained pressure of activist groups and heightened media scrutiny. Japanese society is slowly and painfully emerging from a long period of denial. Bullying of students, corporal punishment, neglect, suspicious deaths, and spousal, child, and sexual abuse have all been invis-ible – taboo subjects that could not be openly discussed until recent years. Now people cannot avoid looking into the mirror held up by the media, and have been collectively horrified by a social problem that is far worse than most people had imagined. The consequent shift from denial of child abuse to mandatory state intervention has been astoundingly rapid.

The challenge now is to match the shift in policy and heightened public awareness with sufficient resources for overburdened child welfare offices; many victims are given too little information and there are too few staff to provide adequate counseling and assistance. The scale of additional resources needed to tackle the problem is enormous, but government has not responded adequately. As a result, many cases go undetected for too long, adding to the growing numbers of traumatized children whose suffering is compounded by a failure to give them the care they need. Tragically, some 60 children die of abuse every year.

Child support advocates argue that government authorities must go beyond identifying and punishing offenders by working with NGOs, support groups, and other activist organizations to improve systems to help both victims and their abusers to reestablish their lives. The scars of abuse often lead to developmental and behavioral problems that can affect victims throughout their lives. There is also considerable concern about a chain of abuse between generations.

Another key risk factor for child abuse is the growing incidence of poverty in Japan and a sharp rise in the working poor since the 1990s. This does not mean that wealthier families are immune from child abuse, but perhaps helps explain why the government's response has been inadequate. The persistence of poverty sits uneasily with the collective consciousness of a middle-class identity in a society where the appurtenances of prosperity are widely evident. Thus, there has been widespread denial of poverty and its consequences and therefore little in the way of policy initiatives or social programs targeting it.

The large percentage of children raised in poverty discussed above is one risk factor for abuse; another is the number of single-parent households. In an extended household there were more hands to help in raising children and also more eyes and ears to detect abuse. Single parents must shoulder the normally stressful task of child-rearing largely on their own. In addition, partners of single mothers commit many cases of abuse.

The fading of denial and social policy reforms represent a start, but the tasks of coping with and curtailing child abuse remain staggering. Fortunately, the media has kept national attention focused on the horrors experienced by far too many children and there appears to be growing awareness that the costs of inaction mean there is no turning back. Incrementally and fitfully, Japan is responding to many of its challenges in a quiet process of transformation. Sadly, for many Japanese children the promise of future action is an empty consolation.

Suicide

Perhaps the greatest trauma and risk facing Japanese families is suicide. Since 1998 more than 30,000 people have taken their lives every year in Japan and the national suicide rate has risen to one of the world's highest among large, industrialized societies. In general, for every suicide there are an estimated 10 attempts. What this means is that Japan's high suicide rate also signals that there are many more traumatized families and survivors in need of counseling and therapy. This national plague shows few signs of abating despite some government initiatives aimed at reining it in.

In the post-WWII era, Japan's suicide rate has been generally counter-cyclical, rising when the economy slackened and falling as it recovered. At the outset of the Heisei era Japan's suicide rate was not high compared to other developed countries, but it is now outpaced only in the former communist bloc countries, notably Russia, the Ukraine, and the small Baltic states. Japan's suicide rate is nearly twice that in the US and almost three times that in the UK.

Interestingly, reported suicides suddenly spiked in 1998, rising some 35 percent from 1997, a year when the government adopted deep budget cuts and closed the spigots of counter-cyclical spending. This policy blunder is credited with prolonging Japan's Lost Decade, forcing many small and medium-size firms into bankruptcy and putting many more at high risk of insolvency. The timing of Japan's 1998 suicide surge is circumstantial evidence that the government's abrupt cuts in stimulus spending in 1997, when the recovery remained fragile, may have been a contributing factor.

In 2008, a total of 32,249 people committed suicide, with the largest number among 50-year-olds.[8] More young people are committing suicide than in the past and 2008 marks the highest number of suicides among those in their 30s (4,850) since the government began compiling detailed statistics in 1978. Due to the stigma of suicide in Japan, experts believe that the number of deaths ascribed to suicide understates the true scope of the problem.

Officials determined the cause of suicide in only about two-thirds of the cases in 2008. The ranking of reasons for committing suicide in cases where this can be determined has been relatively stable during the Heisei era and is as follows for 2008: health problems (65 percent), financial problems (32 percent), family problems (17 percent), and work problems (10 percent). Depression is the most commonly cited health problem, accounting for

43 percent of the cases in which health problems were cited. The most depression-related suicides occurred among those in their 30s.

The international media has perpetuated the myth that Japan's high suicide rate is mostly a reflection of cultural influences and attitudes. The samurai practice of *seppuku*, involving ritual disembowelment to atone for serious transgressions of rigid ethical codes embodied in *bushido* (the way of the samurai), and allegedly neutral attitudes towards suicide in Buddhism and Shinto, are tired tropes frequently invoked in favor of the cultural explanation. Wartime images of *kamikaze* (pilots who flew their explosive-packed planes on one-way suicide missions, usually dive-bombing ships) and "*banzai* suicide charges" by infantry reinforce this perception of a people who seek honor in suicide and have scant compunction against it. If Japanese are culturally disposed to suicide, how can we understand the fluctuations in post-WWII suicide rates? Moreover, it is erroneous to suggest Buddhism is neutral about suicide; those who commit suicide are condemned to several rebirths. As for the *kamikaze* and *banzai* suicide charges, the soldiers involved were not in a position to make a free choice; there was considerable pressure and brainwashing compelling their actions. However, cultural factors do play a role in suicide, but more in terms of norms, values, and taboos that prevent people in distress, especially men, acknowledging they have a problem and seeking the assistance or therapy they need.

It is important to bear in mind that, as in other societies, suicide does carry a stigma in Japan and is a matter for concern at the personal and government level. The notion that suicide is not such a big deal in terms of Japanese culture is inaccurate and misleading. In the twenty-first century, it is not considered a respectable or honorable way to go. As elsewhere, suicides leave behind devastated families that struggle to cope with their loss.[9]

There are three powerful factors that explain the high rate of suicide in Japan and why it has stayed persistently high since the mid-1990s. The prolonged economic malaise, the rapidly aging society, and inadequate diagnosis and treatment of mental depression are the major causes of suicide in Japan. For middle-aged salarymen, a loss of job or other significant economic setback makes it difficult to provide for their families. Although insurance companies have extended the waiting period between when a life insurance policy is purchased and when it comes into effect, essentially aimed at addressing the costly problem of clients committing suicide shortly after enrolling, suicide does not invalidate the policy. Thus, in many cases it appears that breadwinners who are not able to meet their obligations make the ultimate sacrifice for their families, allowing them to collect on the life insurance policies to pay off accumulated debts and meet ongoing financial needs. There is a strong stigma to declaring personal bankruptcy and stiffer legal hurdles to doing so than in the US or UK, thus limiting this less radical option for those facing financial problems. Since Japan's post-1991 asset value implosion, many households are facing considerable distress because the value of the housing they purchased during the bubble years in the late 1980s is worth less than their mortgage.

It is a sad commentary on the state of Japan's public health system that many men who need treatment for depression or other psychological disorders find it difficult to get the therapy they need. General practitioners, the gatekeepers of the system, are not well trained to diagnose psychiatric disorders and miss many cases. In addition, due to the stigma attached to mental illness in Japan, there is a reluctance to diagnose; and drugs typically used to treat mental depression elsewhere were not often prescribed and not covered by national health insurance until 2003. In 2006, the government began introducing suicide hotlines and promoting counseling in schools and at work, a belated and limited response to a national crisis.

Counseling services remain in short supply, especially outside large cities, and people feeling suicidal have not had access to, or have been unaware of, emergency hotlines. Institutionalization is grim and excessive in many cases, but until recently doctors did not have many good intermediate options. The situation is improving, but there remain shortages of trained professionals and adequate facilities. Prefectures understand that more needs to be done at the local level, but are strapped for funds and thus mental healthcare programs remain underfunded and inadequate.[10]

In Japan, suicide has been viewed as an individual problem, but there is growing recognition that suicide is a social problem requiring a collective response.[11] The prefectural government in Akita, a traditional rural farming area with one of the nation's highest suicide rates, drew inspiration from a successful suicide prevention program in Finland where suicides dropped by one-third between 1990 and 2007. Akita has emulated Finland's multi-pronged suicide prevention strategies by establishing a community-based program relying on hotlines and local volunteers who make people aware they are there for those in need, inform them about what services are available, and respond when required. This program launched in 2004 has been a success and is credited with lowering Akita's suicide rate, demonstrating that prevention measures can be effective. It is indicative of what is possible that every prefecture in Japan has an extensive traffic accident prevention program running to billions of yen annually that has cut road fatalities by almost 50 percent from peak levels; a similar commitment of government resources could reduce the national suicide tally.

Japan's rapidly aging society is another reason why the suicide rate has remained obstinately high. Elderly people over age 75 have the highest rate of suicide in Japan due to anxieties over failing health and poverty. In addition, elderly couples have added stress when the healthier partner takes care of the other. Even with public health assistance the burden is heavy on the elderly, and *roro kaigo* (elderly nursing elderly) is the sapping reality that many face. Not surprisingly, in the absence of adequate assistance, the burden can become too heavy for a 70-something taking care of an 80-something, and the caregiver in some cases accedes to the wishes of their partner to assist them in committing suicide or even commits suicide themselves to escape their nursing hell. In twenty-first-century Japan the elderly are increasingly isolated as community- and family-based support structures are overwhelmed and/or unraveling. Many elderly live in isolation and are stoically self-reliant until this is no longer possible.

Conclusion

This review of the risks to Japanese families highlights just how much worse the situation has become during the Heisei era even if the situation is not nearly as bleak as elsewhere. Clearly, there has been a major shift from collective denial to widespread recognition of social ills that have been ignored and allowed to fester. The media has played a critical role in transforming taboo subjects into news features while civil society organizations have lobbied for necessary legal reforms. While the government has responded to some degree, and there has been a rapid and largely welcome shift from treating these problems as private family matters to recognizing them as issues of national concern requiring public intervention, the challenges to Japanese society remain immense. Changing public attitudes, norms, and values towards the risks facing families have driven reform, but this groundswell remains unmatched by adequate resources to alleviate the risks. Civil society organizations have helped fill the gap, but activists maintain the scale of the problems requires national solutions. Policies towards divorce and single-parent families have been more punitive than supportive, and those targeting domestic violence, child abuse, and suicide tend to address symptoms rather than causes while offering little support to victims and those close to them. Given how far Japan has come in a relatively short time, there is a basis for cautious optimism that such lapses will gradually fade, especially given the DPJ government's inclinations, but probably not as fast as most would wish. Perhaps the greatest fundamental risk to the family in twenty-first-century Japan is the decline of job security and incomes for growing numbers of Japanese who are joining the ranks of the unemployed and working poor, the subject of our next chapter.

Chapter 5

Jobs at Risk

The fading of stable and secure employment patterns and the proliferation of less stable and riskier non-regular employment practices is one of the dramatic upheavals reverberating through contemporary Japan.[1] This significant structural change in the labor market began in the 1980s and has gained momentum since the 1990s. Some aspects of the paternalistic employment model that characterized post-WWII Japan remain evident, but the transition continues apace. From nearly one-fifth of the workforce in the early 1990s, by 2009 more than one-third of workers were employed on the disadvantageous terms common to non-regular employment, featuring low wages and limited job security. This new precariat (precarious proletariat) numbers some 20 million workers. The plight of these workers and their vulnerability to labor force adjustments during downturns has highlighted the limitations of Japan's social safety net and ignited debate about a society of "haves" and "have-nots," winners and losers, and widening income disparities.

The problems of the *kakusa shakai* (society of disparities) constitute a major challenge to policy-makers and national identity. Japan's working poor, those earning less than JPY2 million a year, and their families are a growing underclass that pushed Japan's relative poverty rate up to 15.7 percent in 2007, meaning 19 million Japanese live in poverty. For a proudly middle-class society that values the absence of differences and poverty, this expanding precariat of working poor has been an unexpected, unwelcome, and wrenching development. Aside from undermining social cohesion, there are also grim implications for Japan's low birthrate and troubled pension and medical care insurance systems.

Given prevailing norms valuing corporate paternalism and lifetime employment, rapid deregulation in the job market has had unanticipated consequences that are undermining the implicit social contract. The situation facing job-seekers is grim as the unemployment rate in 2009 peaked at 5.7 percent with the jobless figure totaling some 3.76 million, including an estimated total of 1.14 million who lost their jobs due to corporate restructuring. According to the government, GDP in 2008 alone declined by over 4 percent, while in FY2008–9 the surge in unemployment for the year at 710,000 was the highest on record and 75 percent (530,000) of this total lost their jobs due to corporate restructuring.[2] This is not the way Japan wants to see itself – a heartless capitalist economy that treats workers as disposable items. Japanese have taken a measure of pride, for good reason, in their more paternalistic employment system and the values it embodies. Thus, the undeniably stark realities of a deregulated and risk-oriented labor market have rumbled uncomfortably throughout the archipelago as Japanese digest the stark statistics and the ebbing of job security, one of the pillars of post-WWII Japan's strong sense of solidarity and social capital. As the inclinations and practices on the insecure labor market periphery become ever more mainstreamed, the government has also had to reassess its social welfare model that is based on the assumption of stable families, secure jobs, and low unemployment.

Past as Prologue

It is a sign of the times that in 2008 Karl Marx's *Das Kapital* was published in manga form, and the 1929 classic of Japanese proletarian literature *Kanikosen* (*Crab Cannery Ship*) was reissued in 2008 and became an unlikely hit, selling some 600,000 copies. *Kanikosen*'s sudden popularity also spawned four manga versions and a film.[3] In a country where light entertainment dominates the fiction market, the sudden appeal of the haunting and angry tone of *Kanikosen* focusing on the brutality of employers and the battered dignity of oppressed workers resonated with the shifting national mood. A book highlighting the heartless exploitation of workers tapped into Japan's zeitgeist as confidence in Japan, Inc. evaporated. For young Japanese, the grim job market and the difficulty in finding regular, full-time jobs are devastating because they understand quite well that once you enter the periphery the chances of escaping and landing a good job are remote.

Running Amok

In June 2008 a young man, Tomohiro Kato, rammed a truck into crowds of Sunday shoppers in Akihabara, Tokyo's mecca for Japan's cool culture of anime, manga, and video games that is equally famous for its electronics and high-tech gadget shops. After running over several people and crashing the truck, the disgruntled temp staffer then went on a stabbing spree, in the end killing seven and injuring 10 others. Somewhat surprisingly the Internet community, at least partially, rallied in his defense; and the national media, while condemning his actions, also tried to explain with some degree of sympathy why he lashed out so dramatically.[4] He is one of the young and disenfranchised, deeply frustrated in his dead-end job, anxious about his job security and future. Believing, incorrectly it turns out, that he was about to be fired, he rented a truck and drove it through his fellow "netizens" who throng the streets of Akihabara, although warning them on the Internet beforehand about his intentions. It is striking, given this random and violent rampage in a nation where violent crime is relatively rare, that some Internet blogs took his side while the media delved into why he ran amok; seldom does such a callous crime meet with such compassionate understanding. The deranged man's absence of hope and the shared reality of unrealized dreams struck a chord with the nation's youth and sent a shiver up the collective spine. His thwarted aspirations, as for so many young people, are emblematic of what the media dubs as the *rosu gene* (the "lost generation," youth who suffer from diminished career opportunities *vis-à-vis* older generations of Japanese). For a society that puts a high premium on social cohesion and order, this anti-hero represents much to be feared as Japan tries to come to terms with what he did and what his actions may portend for others in similar situations. Haphazardly, this rampage became a horrifying symbol of what has gone wrong in contemporary Japan, compelling some national soul searching about collective complicity.

Economic Crisis

In the wake of the subprime loan crisis in September 2008, the Japanese economy imploded. What started out as a US problem rapidly spread around the world, depressing global markets, and suddenly the export-addicted Japanese economy hit the wall. Exports dropped 30 percent in 2009 and GDP for FY2008–9 fell 9.4 percent, the worst in the OECD and double the EU average decline.[5] At no time during the Heisei era were the signs of economic upheaval ever so obvious. There was a spike in suicide-related train delays, bankruptcies and homelessness increased, once-thronged stores and restaurants were quiet, and the nation collectively lost confidence, battening down the hatches, knowing from the days of the Lost Decade that worse may come. The powers that be seemed overwhelmed by the typhoon that was sweeping through the nation's factories, leaving despair piled up in its wake. Errant, fumbling leaders at the top found themselves upstaged by a grassroots response to this national calamity.

Haken Mura: Village of the Damned

With some 3.5 million unemployed Japanese greeting the dawn of 2009, the public was treated to an unusual New Year's media spectacle, a sea of tents and tarps in central Tokyo dubbed *toshi koshi haken mura* (New Year's village for contract workers). Makoto Yuasa, head of a homeless NPO, was the driving force behind creating a tent village and soup kitchen at the end of December in Hibiya Park – a brilliantly conceived made-for-media event. This facility was for contract workers who had suddenly lost their jobs and company-provided housing. They were the new face of the homeless, disposable workers who found themselves out on the streets with no recourse. Some of them were ineligible for government assistance while others faced a long wait before getting the help they urgently needed. By staking out a section of Hibiya Park that faced the Ministry of Health, Labor, and Welfare (MHLW), as dawn broke on January 1, *haken mura* drew the nation's attention to those who needed help and to those who weren't responding. The newly displaced descended on the park, lining up for blankets, food, and legal advice, basking in the limelight of saturation media coverage. This was the media event of New Year's 2009 as the public looked on at a rare display of social activism on prime time.[6]

More than 20 organizations involving NPOs and an umbrella group of unions (Zenkoku Yunion), and the closely affiliated Anti-Poverty Network (Han Hinkon Nettowaaku), joined forces to create this village of the damned, victims of the new riskier employment model ushered in by deregulation.[7] The organizers and the displaced gave countless interviews.

The media informed the public that up to 10 million workers in Japan would not qualify for unemployment benefits under existing regulations, highlighting the degree of risk and the gaps in the safety net. Timing the event at the New Year, when the more fortunate are counting their blessings, and news is slow and the media is desperate for human-interest stories, was a shrewd move that maximized publicity and put pressure on the government to do something.

Respond it did by opening up unused public housing, on a temporary basis, for the suddenly fired and by fast-forwarding government assistance. The eligibility criterion for receiving unemployment benefits was slashed from one year of contributions to six months, and those still ineligible were given welfare assistance, an unusual situation because very few applicants are usually able to qualify for welfare and must have a handicap or demonstrate inability to work. Yuasa and other representatives of NPOs gained a seat at the table where the government cobbled together stopgap policies aimed at addressing the problems and consequences of non-regular and indirect employment under which nobody takes responsibility for the workers' welfare and the risks are shifted entirely to the worker.[8]

A tiny underfunded NPO representing people who don't exist, blessed with a media-savvy, intelligent leader, had irrevocably changed the terms of debate, shamed the government into action, and on television lifted up the national *tatami* mat, where the inconvenient and unwanted are usually swept into oblivion. By doing so, nobody could ignore the dispossessed or deny them their due. *Haken mura* represented a subversive attack on the powers that be, shining a harsh light on the callous disregard of business leaders, bureaucrats, and politicians towards those who were feeling the sharp edge of the risks unleashed by deregulation. They had created a riskier Japan that the Japanese were not prepared to accept or ignore. This turnabout is all the more stunning given how the mantra of deregulation, privatization, and *jiko sekinin* (self-responsibility) invoked regularly by the popular PM Junichiro Koizumi resonated powerfully in Japan, with media support, and appeared to enjoy widespread acceptance. The naysayers who at the time warned of dire consequences were marginalized in public discourse until *haken mura* held up a mirror for society, making it look at what people had not wanted to see. Confronted with the desperation of the underdogs, and sensing that they too faced unanticipated risks, public sentiments shifted in their favor. By mainstreaming the consequences of riskier employment in this manner, *haken mura* shifted the terms of debate and raised expectations for government intervention.

Haken mura encapsulates the problems of riskier employment regulations, oversold faith in the benefits of deregulation, and the potential for civil society to promote reform and instigate government action. The bold stroke embodied in *haken mura* demonstrates that civil society is more influential than is generally conceded. As in the aftermath of the 1995 Kobe earthquake, when bureaucrats were caught unprepared and responded sluggishly to an urgent crisis, NPOs again intervened to make a difference and play a helpful crisis role that the government had been unable or unwilling to fulfill. Unlike in Kobe where the yakuza shamed the government by opening up the first soup kitchens for displaced survivors, in *haken mura* it was citizen volunteers and NPO activists taking the lead just across the road from the very bureaucrats charged with labor and welfare issues.[9] In Hibiya Park they made a stand, and in doing so challenged the stereotype of overly deferential Japanese ever bowing to government authority. Activism may not be common in Japan, but this case shows how powerful it can be and, in demonstrating what can be achieved against the odds, *haken mura* serves as an inspiration to others.

Anatomy of a Crisis

Japan has long been famous for its paternalistic employment system based on the so-called three jewels of lifetime employment, seniority-based wages, and enterprise-based unions. The system is based on reciprocal obligations and has been widely admired for valuing employees, promoting teamwork, and instilling loyalty. There was also a compelling economic logic to this system. Lifetime employment made sense because after WWII there were shortages of skilled workers and companies had to invest heavily in on-the-job training. By promising secure jobs and providing seniority-based pay, firms offered golden handcuffs that addressed workers' lifecycle income needs while ensuring that firms reaped the fruits of investing in their employees' human capital. In addition, lifetime employment helped ease anxieties about the introduction of labor-saving technologies on the factory floor because workers knew it would not mean losing their jobs. Enterprise unions created good channels of communication within the company, nurturing a team-oriented atmosphere between management and workers, thereby minimizing antagonistic labor relations and the costly strikes and work actions that had erupted extensively in the early post-WWII era. Extensive training and rapid innovation facilitated by the three jewels were key to boosting productivity and propelling the emergence of world-beating export manufacturers.

The three jewels don't glitter quite like they used to. It has long been known that lifetime employment only applied to about 30 percent of the full-time workforce, mostly employees of large enterprises. For employees of small and medium companies, and for women who often worked as part-timers after leaving their previous job to get married and raise children, jobs were never that secure. Women workers, and the subcontractors of larger companies where workforce adjustments were concentrated, served as the shock absorbers for larger companies and their mostly male core workers. Since the onset of the Heisei era, companies have scaled back the hiring of full-time workers and relied increasingly on non-regular workers, those who are beyond the remit of the three jewels.

The logic of the three jewels also unraveled because the workforce has become top-heavy with older workers collecting on their seniority. When most of the workers were young in the 1950s, wages were low and workers were content to have a job and dream of eventually pulling down good salaries. However, as the baby boom generation (1947–9) moved up the rungs, and productivity did not keep pace, especially among white-collar workers, companies suddenly confronted the Heisei recession and intensified global competition in the 1990s. In this stagnant but highly competitive environment, escalating wage outlays posed a significant challenge. Throughout the 1990s companies met this challenge by expanding reliance on contingent workers, those who had no claims to lifetime employment or seniority pay.[10] These workers also largely remained outside the sphere of unions that organized a shrinking percentage of the workforce, less than 19 percent by 2006, down from 50 percent in 1950. Companies further met this challenge by cutting overtime pay, but in many cases not overtime work, and introducing merit pay schemes that emphasized results over seniority.

Thus, the foundations of the Japanese employment system embodied in the three jewels eroded rapidly in the 1990s. The economic logic that made these practices appealing to management changed and thus they have been progressively abandoned in favor of a more flexible employment system featuring less security and more risk for workers. Conditions that used to be associated with the labor periphery of non-regular employment have now become mainstream.

Big Bang?

In the early years of the twenty-first century the Japanese economy seemed to be on the rebound. Some observers credited PM Koizumi's resolute policies that forced banks to write down their dud loans and, more importantly, the revitalizing impact of his emphasis on deregulation, privatization, and *jiko sekinin*. Koizumi was seen as Japan's answer to Thatcher and Reagan, embracing market-oriented reforms, slashing red tape, and unleashing private sector entrepreneurial initiative and individual self-reliance. He campaigned for deregulation with the slogan "no pain, no gain." However, the Heisei Big Bang has fizzled, failing to deliver the promised benefits while undermining the norms and verities of Japan's employment system. What went wrong?

Deregulation generated greater risk while the government did not make necessary adjustments in the social safety net to deal with the possible consequences. Deregulation was articulated as a job-generating measure, reducing employer obligations and thus making them more inclined to offer jobs. The government saw it as a risk worth taking in order to reinvigorate the economy. With productivity lagging, and unemployment rising along with the costs of social services for the unemployed and indigent, deregulation offered the possibility of some improvement. As elsewhere, deregulation was oversold as a remedy. There were more jobs created, but often on unattractive terms with little security. *Jiko sekinin* was promoted as a way of shifting responsibility for and costs of workers' welfare from firms and government social programs to individuals and their families, putting the most vulnerable at greatest risk. As we noted in the previous chapter, increasing numbers of families were in no position to assume greater financial burdens or higher risk given their dire circumstances and cuts in social welfare.

The media initially romanticized the rise of freeters (free arbeiters, referring to job-hopping youth mostly in part-time or contract jobs), but as the grim and ineluctable realities of life on the labor market periphery sunk in, there has been greater concern that these young people have been given a one-way ticket into poverty. These youth were once depicted as conscientious objectors to the life of corporate drones, but in reality most were unwilling "rebels" who could not find a regular job and they face bleak prospects. The proliferation of such workers carries implications for the solvency of pension and medical care systems since most do not pay social insurance at a time when demands on these systems are rapidly escalating.

Recognition of the new risks associated with emerging employment trends is reinforcing concerns about growing income disparities. The notion of a ubiquitously middle-class society remains appealing to many Japanese, but in the early twenty-first century it has been more difficult to sustain this myth. Studies on mobility and income disparities indicate that Japan has long had a self-perpetuating elite and disparities, but now, as with so many other taboo subjects, it has become acceptable to draw attention to what society has hitherto averted its eyes from. Income disparities are not only due to differences between regular and non-regular workers, but the growth of non-regular employment has contributed to a widening of the gap and drawn more attention to it.

During the 1990s, despite severe economic problems, corporate Japan largely avoided firing workers. There were fewer new hires, and retiring full-time regular workers were replaced with non-regular workers or positions were left unfilled, but by and large companies kept faith with their regular, full-time workers. This was possible with the help of public subsidies. In some respects, jobs are maintained as a form of welfare. This is in preference to a restructuring that would entail large numbers of unemployed workers receiving government assistance. This job subsidy system was first introduced in the 1970s to soften the fallout from the oil shocks and recession. In 2009, 2.4 million jobs were maintained at 88,000 companies by government subsidies, up sharply from only 1,343 jobs at 63 firms in 2008; the subsidies cover two-thirds of wages at large firms and 80 percent at small and medium firms. Adding these 2.4 million jobs to the 3.76 million officially unemployed means that in the absence of these subsidies Japan's unemployment rate would have been 9.3 percent rather than 5.7 percent as of mid-2009.[11]

From the late 1990s beginning with the Obuchi administration (1998–2000), employment laws were gradually deregulated to enable wider use of temporary, contract, and dispatched workers hired by firms through intermediary agencies. The 1999 Dispatched Manpower Business Act set in motion a fairly rapid spread of contract work arrangements in many sectors of the economy. In 2004, on Koizumi's watch, contract workers were also allowed in manufacturing, sparking a skyrocketing of their numbers in this critical sector where increased global competition led to fierce cost-cutting measures and a need for more flexibility.

The consequences of shifting risk to employees became apparent after the global economic crisis that began in 2008 slammed Japan's major export markets. Japanese manufacturers saw their orders drop dramatically, creating a domino effect throughout the economy. Employers cut their losses by sacking contract workers. Since many of these workers were on short-term contracts or indirectly employed through an intermediary, Japanese firms felt no moral obligation to keep them on the payroll and legally were not obliged to do so. Tens of thousands of contracts were not renewed, while in some cases firms exercised opt-out clauses that permitted them to sever contracts. The costs of risk hit the headlines as suddenly unemployed workers protested outside factories and jammed Hello Work offices.[12] Again, the media gave these jobless workers prominent and sympathetic coverage, raising the stakes for the companies that dismissed them while also pressuring the government to take action. Television crews took viewers into the cramped factory dorms of workers who had been given notice, giving them an opportunity to voice their sense of betrayal and draw attention to the miserable pay and terms of employment. Their stories of woe and impending eviction from company-supplied housing gave a human face to risk that sent shockwaves through the nation. Responding to the backlash and public outcry, some companies backed down and rescinded job terminations or extended contracts, but such cases were rare. It was this cold corporate calculus, unwelcome and unfamiliar to Japan, combined with the government's floundering response that propelled civil society groups to take action and prepare for the consequences. And, they made sure that there would be as many witnesses as possible by staging the *haken mura* spectacle.

Desperate Youth

Young workers are increasingly locked out of the regular job market, meaning their prospects for job training, skill development, and promotions up the career ladder are remote. As of 2007, according to the OECD, 31 percent of Japanese age 15–24 (excluding students) are non-regular employees.[13] Youth unemployment ranged from 4 to 5 percent in the 1990s but then doubled in the final years of the 1990s, reaching 9.2 percent in 2000 before peaking at 10 percent in 2003 and then declining to 7.7 percent in 2007.[14] Although Japan's youth unemployment rate is well below some of the more extreme cases in Europe, the OECD also notes that the incidence of long-term unemployment in Japan is above the OECD average.

Young Japanese are facing unprecedented upheaval in a job market marked by adverse structural changes that dim their prospects. Until the 1990s, in general, young people made a smooth and swift transition from education into stable jobs and experienced low unemployment and job turnover. However, this system disappeared under the wave of restructuring and deregulation prompted by prolonged recession during the Lost Decade. The Ice Age for young job-seekers during the 1990s thawed somewhat during the modest economic recovery from 2003 to 2007, but returned with a vengeance in 2009. The consequences for young workers are bleak indeed, as mobility from non-regular jobs to regular jobs is negligible. Whereas the transition from school to work used to be a ticket to a stable career and middle-class life, for many young Japanese this transition has turned into a one-way ticket to the employment periphery of precarious jobs and the working poor. These freeters face high job turnover in dead-end jobs with little access to vocational training that could improve their prospects.

While young people overall are increasingly finding it hard to grasp a rung on the career ladder and are trapped in low-level jobs, those with lower levels of educational attainment are most at risk. They have a harder time making the transition from school to work, change jobs more often, and also experience higher and longer periods of unemployment. Less educated youth have always fared more poorly in the job market than better educated counterparts, but one of the dire legacies of the Lost Decade is the much higher propensity of such outcomes; far more end up as non-regular workers. This tendency highlights the problems generated by slackening demand for regular workers by companies eager to save money and maximize flexibility and the consequent decline of lifetime employment and attendant training programs. To reiterate, non-regular workers are much less likely to receive skill training than their regular counterparts, reinforcing their marginalization and lowering the possibilities of shifting into better jobs.

There are significant weaknesses in the education and training system in Japan that have become all the more apparent due to these structural changes in employment, especially the poor linkages between what students study and what firms are looking for in terms of graduates' skills. In the context of fewer opportunities for on-the-job training, wherein the company invests heavily in nurturing firm-specific human capital, the general skills learned as students are all the more critical in determining employment prospects and career trajectories. Secondary and tertiary education curricula, however, have not adapted to the new prevailing market realities and thus graduates are often not the "off-the-rack" workers companies are seeking. The government has unveiled a raft of measures aimed at addressing these critical problems affecting the transition from school to work, but they don't seem to be working.[15] Meanwhile, young Japanese face bleak futures where their dreams and aspirations seem impossibly remote.

Women Workers

Women have long been shunted to the labor market periphery and borne the brunt of labor force adjustments. They have served as the shock absorbers for Japan, Inc., earning lower wages and lacking the job security that is commonly accorded to their male colleagues in the core, regular workforce. Part-time women workers have provided human resource managers a degree of flexibility, in terms of layoffs and shortened hours, that has underwritten the costly and rigid lifetime employment and seniority wages enjoyed mostly by male workers. The changes in Japan's employment system during the Heisei era discussed above have also affected women workers, who are now disproportionately represented among contract workers, those who are the most vulnerable to corporate downsizing.

For women, the Lost Decade has been a time of declining opportunities and lost gains. It is telling that Japan ranks number 8 on the 2008 UNDP human development index, but only 54 on the gender empowerment index, down from 42 in 2006. Average wages for women workers have been about 60 percent of the male average overall, and 70 percent for full-time workers. Since the early 1990s, overall job growth has been concentrated in non-regular work where women are most likely to be employed, explaining why the wage gap in Japan remains persistently large despite the Equal Employment Opportunity Law (EEOL-1985, amended 1999) and other measures aimed at combating gender discrimination in the workforce. The courts have been increasingly supportive of women's efforts to seek judicial redress, and they have won landmark cases. It is now against the law, for example, to arbitrarily assign workers part-time status if they are working similar hours and have similar responsibilities as regular workers, once a widespread practice that mostly affected women.

Women remain underrepresented, however, among managers and corporate board members. As of 2005 only 10.1 percent of managers were women, up from 6.6 percent in 1986. Since this figure includes women who own their own businesses, it doesn't fully reflect just how limited their presence is in corporate Japan's fusty management circles. The *sogo shoku* (career track) system involving lifetime employment and seniority wages represents a barrier to managerial positions for women because it is oriented towards male workers who can rely on their wives to bear and raise children and take care of household tasks and responsibilities. Women find it very difficult to juggle managerial responsibilities and long working days with child-rearing, so in many cases it is an either/or choice: career or children. As noted in the previous chapter, the Japanese employment system is geared towards continuous work and heavily penalizes a few-year hiatus, meaning women are not normally able to resume their careers and assume the same position on the corporate ladder as when they left. With inadequate public support and family-friendly corporate policies, many women drop off the career track, withdraw from employment to raise children, and then return usually on a part-time basis. These policy failures have put women's careers at risk while squandering their talents and human capital.

Childcare leave policies are aimed at addressing this problem, but typically jobs are held for leave takers only one year while social norms dictate that mothers spend at least the first three years with their infants. Even for modern mothers who return by the end of their allowed maternity leave, companies do not make sufficient allowance for their special needs or give the sort of family-friendly support that working mothers need to balance the demands of work and home. The "samurai" work culture expects lots of overtime and total devotion to the workplace that is only possible for male workers who can "outsource" household duties to their wives. One of the risks corporate Japan faces in not retaining women workers is evident in the finding that companies with more women employees and family-friendly policies tend to be more profitable.[16]

The employment rate for women aged 25–29 in Japan rose continuously during the first two decades of the Heisei era, reaching 71 percent by 2007, a level that exceeds the OECD average of 69 percent. However, the employment rate of young mothers with a child under the age of 2 remains very low at 29 percent, compared with the OECD average of 52 percent. Furthermore, most returning mothers work in precarious jobs, many needing a flexible schedule because of the relative scarcity of public childcare facilities and little help from husbands around the house; as of 2008, only 1.23 percent of men eligible for childcare leave take it. One reason may be that in times of economic uncertainty and corporate downsizing, men don't believe taking childcare leave is a good career move and don't want to somehow jeopardize their job security by putting family first.

Conclusion

The sudden proliferation of risky jobs and insecure employment carries stark implications for Japan. What has happened because firms sought individually to save money on wages and benefits and gain flexibility in terms of shedding workers at will has collectively turned into an expensive national crisis that dims the outlook for business, government, and society. Spreading insecurity and declining income are undermining household consumption and contributing to deflation because more workers have less money in their wallets and are reluctant to spend when they are not certain of keeping their job. Already about 40 percent of Japanese who should be contributing to the national pension system are not doing so while the rising number of non-regular workers means a larger number of people are not obliged to pay in. Greater job insecurity, however, means that more people will rely on the safety net and the government will need to expand this net to cope with the consequences of risky jobs and growing numbers of working poor. The increased reliance on non-regular workers is also depressing productivity because training for non-regular workers is not common and they are relatively cheap, meaning that firms have little incentive to boost their productivity and instead use them as low-value-added workers. The persistence of a large wage gap in Japan between male and female workers is emblematic of Japan's failure to tap the human capital of women workers and discourages the most highly educated from pursuing careers.

The main problem is that there are very important incentives for employers to hire non-regular workers; wages and benefits are low, there is no need for the employer to contribute to medical care insurance or national pension schemes, and such workers can be fired virtually at will. While regulations and protections for non-regular workers are lax by OECD standards, those for regular workers are very strict and backed up by social norms and court decisions. Japan's dual labor market, based on the gap between regular and non-regular workers, is a consequence of policy choices and has encouraged a structural shift in labor market demand. These policy choices have facilitated the emergence of a precariat and put pressure on the social safety net, leaving bureaucrats racing to narrow the gap between existing regulations and policies and these new realities. For many young workers who have already been shoved off the career ladder, the gap in job status, incomes, and prospects is likely to persist.

The growing gap embodied in the dual labor market poses serious challenges to policy-makers on a number of fronts. First, the solvency of the medical care and pensions schemes, certainly a government priority, is at greater risk the more that workers are at risk. Second, the precariat is much less likely to marry and procreate, exacerbating Japan's fertility woes. Lower fertility means fewer consumers and taxpayers in the future and a rising dependency ratio, with fewer workers supporting retirees, suggesting the eventual need for higher taxes and lower benefits. Third, there is also a relatively high correlation between unemployment and suicide, another major social ill that the government is trying to reduce.[17] By presiding over the proliferation of less secure employment and neglecting job protection or exit strategies to full-time work for non-regular workers, however, the government appears to be undermining its campaign against suicide. Thus, current deregulation policies encouraging firms to hire more non-regular workers because of the savings and flexibility they confer come at a high cost to society. Greater job insecurity and lower incomes dim economic prospects overall, have a deflationary impact, burden the safety net, boost suicide rates, and also lower fertility because poor economic prospects are incompatible with assuming the responsibilities of raising a family. The DPJ is trying to address this dysfunctional situation by revising labor regulations, but whether it will succeed is an open question.

The economic implications of risky jobs are indeed grim, but the consequences of risk also affect national psychology, identity, and social cohesion. Widening income disparities and the emergence of a dual labor market are dividing people and relegating some to less appealing careers and a depressed standard of living. One of the "miracles" of Japan's rapid recovery from WWII was how evenly the fruits of economic growth were distributed compared to other industrialized societies. Since the 1990s, however, the *kakusa shakai* has emerged along with rising rates of poverty.[18] In 2007, the number of working poor earning JPY2 million or less rose to 10.23 million workers out of a workforce of some 65 million, while the average salary for regular full-time workers was about JPY5.3 million.

The binding myth of the middle class generated cohesion in Japan, but it no longer enjoys the credibility that it once had, raising questions about how to manage the inevitable social tensions of a society in which divisions between "haves" and "have-nots" have become more apparent, larger, and more entrenched. Breaking the self-perpetuating cycle of poverty remains difficult. Until the recent explosion in non-regular employment, Japanese took a measure of pride in their employment system and the reciprocal obligations it embodied and the relatively equal outcomes it created. People largely bought into the system because it seemed reasonably fair and inclusive. Now that many Japanese are on the outside looking in, what is the new Big Idea that can bolster a strong sense of shared interests? Certainly it seems that Japan still has a large reservoir of social capital and a strong collective identity, but for many of the "lost generation," the young people who can't realize their ambitions and cannot find employment security, the shared sense of purpose that motivated successive generations of post-WWII Japanese is waning.

Work has been a critical element of individual identity in Japan and long careers with a firm fostered a reassuring sense of group attachment and institutional affiliation. Aside from securing a desirable social identity, work created a structured and predictable life course. One's job also facilitated a degree of social intimacy and connectedness. In a society where work has been so integral to identity and a critical sense of belonging and shared values, norms, and aspirations, the fraying of the employment model during the Heisei era, and the sudden emergence of risk among a people more accustomed to certainty, has been wrenching. In the wake of the bursting of the bubble in the 1990s, a society habituated to muted disparities and secure life trajectories has suddenly confronted the onslaught of economic stagnation, globalization, job cuts, and non-regular employment. Job risk has led to dramatic disparities and uncertainties that are altering Japan's social landscape and remapping assumptions and expectations in unsettling ways. As Japan sheds the ways and means of the discredited Japan, Inc. model, it is cobbling together a new social paradigm. This transformation, however, is a gradual and incremental process, and as is common amidst such upheavals, not always onward and upward.

Whither Japan depends on policies affecting transition from school to employment and nurturing skills that endow workers with lifetime employability rather than lifetime employment. It depends on regulations bolstering employment protection for non-regular workers, promoting equal pay for equal work, and addressing the problems specific to contract employment that leave workers in the lurch. The DPJ government is restricting indirect and non-regular employment, at least to some degree, while also improving the safety net and vocational training programs to cope with the consequences of riskier employment and dislocation. There is a consensus, reinforced by the economic malaise and bleak projections, that Japan needs to innovate and that greater risk taking is part of this process; the agenda of ongoing reforms focuses on sharing, managing, and coping with these risks.

The DPJ won a historic landslide victory in 2009 because it promised to address widespread anxieties by improving job protection, expanding the safety net, and helping the most vulnerable; but as discussed above, these are immense problems that defy easy solutions. Targeting disparities and risk is high on the political agenda, and it is encouraging in many ways that the DPJ is shifting government priorities away from public works to social welfare programs, but it will be difficult to translate the glimmer of hope it offers into sustainable reforms. In the next chapter we examine Japan's political system and how it is evolving to better understand the prospects for managing twenty-first-century Japan's enormous challenges.

Part III
Politics and Consequences

Chapter 6

Contemporary Politics

The Japanese political system is in crisis because the public has lost faith in its politicians and trust in government. Endemic corruption and economic policy failures have made voters less forgiving of a ruling class they hold in low regard. A more vibrant civil society, greater transparency, and a somewhat more feisty press have raised public expectations of politicians that have not been met. Since the beginning of the Heisei era people have been reeling from what seems like an endless recession and are increasingly frustrated with politicians' inability to improve the situation. The public wants the government to reinvigorate the economy, but without trampling on egalitarian ideals.

In the 2009 elections the Liberal Democratic Party (LDP) that has dominated Japanese politics since being established in 1955 discovered to its regret that widespread anxieties about growing disparities and social cohesion carry political consequences. Certainly voters have many reasons for being disheartened by Japanese politics, but despite these misgivings many were hoping that the Democratic Party of Japan's (DPJ's) historic victory in 2009 would usher in sweeping transformation. The severe fiscal problems it has inherited from the LDP, however, are growing apace due to the economic downturn and the rapid aging of society, limiting options while highlighting the urgency of reform. Voters are feeling disappointed that for all the DPJ promises of change, there are many shady continuities in mainstream politics. PM Yukio Hatoyama has been a big disappointment, failing the test of leadership on a number of issues.

The change of government and advent of party competition are not the only encouraging signs of reform in Japanese politics. Japan is also on the brink of a generational shift in political leadership that carries the potential for significant political change. Some of Japan's emerging younger leaders may surprise by demonstrating expertise and skills that may help revive Japan or at least lessen some of its more pressing problems. Many are more cosmopolitan than their elders, having traveled, lived, and studied overseas and observed the strengths and weaknesses of other political systems. Many will place more emphasis on policy initiatives and addressing critical socio-economic issues rather than porkbarrel projects and influence peddling. This new generation of politicians will no longer be so preoccupied with the scars of defeat and occupation by the US, or with battling neighbors over war responsibility, an issue we further examine in Chapter 10. Some of these Young Turks also will be helping to promote Japan's transformation, responding to and invigorating a more robust civil society while also addressing the multi-faceted challenges of a rapidly aging society.

Political Revolution

In 2009, the LDP lost an epic landslide victory in the lower house Diet elections to the DPJ, chiefly because the economy has been stagnant for nearly two decades and the LDP implemented neo-liberal economic reforms that the media and voters blame for widening income disparities. This is a tectonic political event because the LDP has ruled Japan since 1955 except for a brief hiatus spanning 1993–4. Voters gave their verdict on deregulation and the LDP's failure to revive the economy and provide either hope or a safety net for the growing ranks of marginalized workers. As the economy spiraled downward in the runup to the elections, momentum grew in support of *seiken kotai* (political change), a phrase that became emblematic of a national mood dooming the LDP. The DPJ victory was mostly due to the failings of the LDP rather than its own platform, but its pledge to curb the excessive powers and perquisites of bureaucrats, and assert political control over policy-making, resonated powerfully with voters. The DPJ also emphasized *yuai* (fraternity), vowing to restore a sense of mutual support that implicitly rejects *jiko sekinin*, an LDP signature policy that came to mean, "if you are in trouble you are all on your own."

The LDP was blamed for neo-liberal structural reforms promoting deregulation and privatization that have increased risk and disparities dramatically in a society that has long tried to minimize and mitigate risk and inequality. As noted in the previous chapter, labor market reforms that began incrementally under PM Keizo Obuchi in 1998 and gathered sweeping momentum under PM Junichiro Koizumi (2001–6) have produced "winners" and "losers" in a society that highly values its egalitarian ideals.[1]

Rapid economic growth between 1955 and 1973 did not lead to the wide disparities evident in other advanced industrialized societies. The Gini coefficient, a measure of income equality, showed a high level of equality until the 1980s. From the mid-1980s, however, disparities began to widen and became more pronounced in the 1990s. Disparities thus did not start with PM Koizumi, but they did become more prominent in the media and in twenty-first-century political discourse, and are indelibly associated with the LDP. Now, in a society no longer overlooking widening gaps between "winners" and "losers," the plight of the latter attracts considerable attention. The Hibiya Park tent village spectacle discussed in Chapter 5 was a game-changing event that powerfully influenced the 2009 campaign and was a key factor in determining the outcome. Amidst the subsequent media scrutiny, one clueless LDP politician suggested that the fired workers lacked a proper work ethic, provoking acerbic criticism in the media while making his party look out of touch and unsympathetic.

Through structural reforms and cuts in welfare spending the LDP increased risk in society, but failed to manage it well by not preparing for the foreseeable consequences. The LDP now knows the cost of not keeping faith with the people. The lower house election landslides of 2005 and 2009, swinging from the LDP to the DPJ, show that increasingly fickle and feisty voters are desperate for change they can believe in and ready to punish a party that does not deliver.

Revitalizing Japanese Democracy

It has become popular for politicians to score points by railing against the bureaucracy, and many observers dismiss parliamentary politics as mere theater because the bureaucrats are really in charge. In the Iron Triangle of big business, the LDP, and the bureaucracy, the bureaucracy has held sway and drew up the budgets and policies that propelled Japan, Inc. during its glory days.[2] Under this system, bureaucrats defined national interests and prepared legislation accordingly. Cabinet ministers essentially rubber-stamped the bureaucrats' decisions while the LDP enacted the bills drawn up by them. Bureaucrats dictated policy-making while politicians did their bidding.

The DPJ is working to tame the bureaucrats and assert political control over policy-making. It has resolutely moved forward on this agenda, initiating a series of changes that are subjecting the civil service to greater political guidance exerted by the Cabinet. This is an extraordinary change and is occurring with no apparent resistance. The DPJ came into power targeting wasteful spending for budget cuts and the bureaucrats have complied by sacrificing numerous projects they had put into the budget. The public hearings on the budget held at the end of 2009 under the auspices of the Government Revitalization Unit proved riveting and immensely popular political theater. Bureaucrats asked to defend their budget requests suddenly became tongue-tied and unable in many cases to make a compelling case for their projects, demonstrating how unaccustomed they are to being questioned and how tone deaf they can be to public sentiments. The public enjoyed the hearings as much for the cuts in wasteful spending as for the embarrassment of the bureaucrats, a well-deserved comeuppance in the media limelight.

The DPJ is also targeting the practice of *amakudari* (descent from heaven) whereby senior bureaucrats retire into well-paid sinecures at companies they previously supervised in their official duties or take up top positions at state-subsidized "public interest" corporations related to the ministry from which they retire. The conflict of interest, inflated contracts, bid-rigging, and sense of unfair advantages bestowed on bureaucrats fuel public support for ending *amakudari* and help explain why successive governments have tried to curb this practice. Greater transparency and tighter regulations have had some impact, but *amakudari* has survived because of lax supervision and enforcement. The DPJ is showing it means business and has banned bureaucratic practices such as compulsory early retirement that have created a need for *amakudari* posts. It remains to be seen, however, if it can succeed in its quest, even if it has the political will to do so because bureaucrats are seasoned infighters.

The DPJ's strategy to impose political control over the bureaucrats is to provide general guidelines laying out its priorities for the bureaucrats to implement. The DPJ government issues directives and supervises, but still relies extensively on the technocrats. The difficulty for the DPJ remains the bureaucratic monopoly on policy expertise; there are no independent thinktanks like the Brookings or American Enterprise Institutes in the US that play a crucial role in shaping policies, and Diet members have relatively few staff or resources compared to the US Congress to work on developing policies.

More aggressive policy guidance by Cabinet ministers, however, marks a significant shift from the LDP that often deferred to the bureaucrats. Another major difference with the LDP is the shift of spending away from public works projects to social welfare spending. In addition, whereas the LDP presided over a system that systematically favored producers over consumers, and business over workers, the DPJ favors consumer and worker interests. It is also rolling back LDP deregulation and privatization initiatives involving the labor market and postal system and is reconstituting government advisory panels, including more voices from civil society organizations.

The DPJ represents a wide spectrum of political interests and is led by mainstream politicians with populist inclinations. It understands that the Japanese seek a new social contract because structural reforms have generated job insecurity, amplified disparities, and created a Japan most Japanese don't want. Many of Japan's youth have been marginalized as contingent workers and the DPJ believes that giving them a stake in the new Japan is crucial to maintaining social cohesion. Revitalizing Japan's democracy is vital to this project. Booting the LDP out of government and putting the unelected bureaucracy under political control represents an encouraging start, but the DPJ understands that regaining the trust of people and addressing their concerns about risk remain imperative. Having done their part by voting for change, the people are waiting impatiently for positive results. The corruption scandals engulfing leaders of the DPJ seem more like politics as usual and as such reinforce the public's low opinion of politicians.

Japan's Enigma

Why did Japanese voters support prolonged one-party rule under the LDP despite its glaring shortcomings? The short answer is that the 1955 system sustained that one-party rule (1955–93, and in coalition 1994–2009), creating an ossified democracy that curbed voters' expectations and options. In addition, the LDP delivered on economic growth and improved living standards, at least until the Lost Decade. The apparent inevitability of LDP rule fostered inclinations (loyalty to local champions) and incentives (porkbarrel projects) inimical to robust democratic practices and perpetuated conservative hegemony and top-down rule. Systemic corruption favoring those in power also limited the prospects for meaningful change at the polls.[3]

As elsewhere, the odds are stacked in favor of incumbents. The percentage of hereditary politicians, 25 percent in the LDP after the 2005 elections, was quite high compared to other democracies, creating strongholds for family dynasties where challengers have had little chance. In addition, campaign laws and regulations also created barriers to entry and favored incumbents. In the 2009 elections, however, hereditary politicians fared poorly, mostly because the LDP, in which they have been most prominent, suffered such a resounding rout.

Overrepresented rural constituencies have been yet another brake on reform, long favoring the LDP because voters in the countryside have been wooed with large public works programs and various agricultural subsidies and protectionist measures. The DPJ, by promising to shift spending away from public works to social welfare programs, challenged this system, but won anyway because even conservative strongholds in the countryside gave up on LDP-style politics.

In the twenty-first century the two dominant parties have been the LDP and the DPJ. The LDP has been somewhat more conservative while the DPJ is more of a rainbow coalition ranging from LDP renegades on the right to unionists and former Socialist Party members on the left. In general, the DPJ appeals to the urban, younger, more educated, and more progressive voters while the LDP's strength has been among the more conservative business community, rural voters, the self-employed, and the elderly. In order to better understand contemporary politics, however, it is important to examine the system that perpetuated one-party rule since 1955.

The 1955 System

The 1955 system is a reference to the conservative, one-party hegemony that prevailed in Japan until 2009.[4] This system mainstreamed conservative politics and involved close cooperation between politicians, big business, and bureaucrats, the so-called Iron Triangle also known as Japan, Inc. This triumvirate of interests has not always agreed on policy issues, but has found enough common ground to maintain a level of cooperation that ensured extended political hegemony. Political scientists attribute Japan's persistent structural corruption (*kozo oshoku*) to this triangle of interests and the means they have adopted to sustain their power.[5]

In November 1955 two conservative parties merged – the Liberals and the Democrats – creating a grand coalition of the right. Samuels refers to this as one of the most overdetermined events in Japanese political history, a culmination of lobbying by the Japanese business community, US meddling, and Nobusuke Kishi's resolute maneuvering combined with the reunification of the Japan Socialist Party in October 1955.[6]

The CIA was involved with the creation of the LDP through direct funding and vigorous public diplomacy aimed at highlighting the dangers of, and neutralizing, left-wing political influences in Japan.[7] Chalmers Johnson concludes that the US was the architect of Japan's one-party democracy and the ascendancy of conservative political and cultural forces.[8] The US, he argues, was eager to ensure that Japan did not opt out of the Cold War and choose neutralism, and thus pressured the bureaucracy, and helped orchestrate the rise of the LDP, to enlist support. US officials have acknowledged making payoffs to the LDP between 1955 and 1972, a meddling that underscores just how flawed and inconsistent US efforts were in promoting democracy in Japan.

The 1955 system was shaped by the tension between conservative and progressive political forces. Progressive in this context meant the left-wing political culture that prevailed in trade unions and the Japan Socialist Party (JSP), the largest opposition party in Japan until its demise in the mid-1990s. From its inception in 1955, the LDP opposed and sought to defuse efforts to pursue a "class struggle" supported by the union movement.

The 1950s and 1960s featured divisive ideological battles between supporters of the JSP and the LDP. The LDP championed conservative causes including overturning many of the US Occupation-era reforms even though, paradoxically, it also stood for close ties with the US. On many of these issues, especially constitutional revision and the US alliance, progressive forces vigorously opposed the LDP, resulting in strikes, street protests, and occasional JSP boycotts of the Diet.

The LDP enjoyed the support of the middle classes represented by farmers, merchants, and the owners and employees of family businesses and small manufacturing concerns. The JSP represented the modern sectors of a rapidly developing Japan, attracting unionized blue-collar workers, white-collar "salarymen," and younger, well-educated urban voters. Back in the late 1950s the LDP seemed to represent a shrinking, backward-looking, tradition-bound constituency, but one of the interesting stories of Japanese politics is how the LDP managed to reinvent itself to become a party with broader appeal. The JSP, meanwhile, pursued an ideological agenda that became increasingly irrelevant and unappealing to Japanese voters. Perhaps the highpoint of the socialists' political fortunes came with the mass street protests in 1960 opposing the renewal of the Security Treaty orchestrated by Prime Minister Kishi (1957–60).

Kishi is the founding father of the 1955 system, a wartime Minister of Commerce and Industry who was an influential official in Manchuria where he reportedly learned the dark arts of money raising and laundering. He was arrested, but never prosecuted, by the International Military Tribunal for the Far East as a suspected Class-A war criminal. Following the US Occupation of Japan (1945–52), Kishi stood for revising the US-drafted Constitution. He lobbied against Article 9 and the constraints it places on Japan's rearmament so that Japan could become a more equal ally of the US and carve out an autonomous foreign policy.

Kishi became prime minister in 1957 and remains notorious for his role in securing Diet approval of the US–Japan Security Treaty (known as AMPO in Japan) in 1960. The Japanese left led mass demonstrations against ratification of the revised treaty, tapping into popular anger against the continued *de facto* occupation of Japan by the US and the dangers this might incur should the superpowers have a showdown. Hundreds of thousands thronged the streets of Tokyo and surrounded the national Diet building, forcing the government to cancel a planned visit by US President Dwight Eisenhower. Kishi managed to ram the legislation through the Diet in June 1960 without the opposition present, but then resigned under duress a week later, making way for Hayato Ikeda and his Income Doubling Plan.

After Kishi resigned, the party steered away from ideologically divisive issues such as security and constitutional revision and focused instead on bread-and-butter economic issues. The LDP staked its future on raising living standards and policies aimed at stimulating high-speed growth, presiding over the so-called economic miracle of double-digit growth in GDP.

By the end of the 1960s, however, the LDP's popularity was waning because of its support for the US during the Vietnam War and growing concerns about the environmental impact of rapid growth. Demonstrating a flexibility that has sustained the LDP over the decades, the party co-opted the opposition platform and promoted relatively progressive environmental legislation in the 1970 Diet session that broadened its constituency, and undermined its critics, by addressing issues that mattered to voters.[9]

There are many factors that explain prolonged one-party dominance, but perhaps the most important was the LDP's success in making this seem inevitable and beneficial. The LDP cultivated the image of being the sole political party ready for prime time, portraying itself as the only safe hands in times of crisis whether economic or security. Oddly, despite the prolonged Heisei recession, one often attributed to poor policy decisions and inept leadership, the LDP managed to convince enough voters that only it had the expertise to manage the economy. Voters sent the LDP a chastening message from time to time, most notably in 1993 when it ceded power for 11 months, but these outbursts were limited rebellions until the bloodbath of 2009.

In 2009, the 1955 system came to an end. Prime Minister Koizumi began dismantling this system in 2001, cutting the LDP off from its rural base by slashing public works spending and privatizing the postal system.[10] He tried to reinvent the LDP, the party of the status quo, as the party of reform and managed to convince the public in the 2005 elections, but his successors reverted to form. Finally, voters ended LDP dominance because they were certain that the LDP had run out of fresh ideas. For more than a half-century they had placed their faith in the LDP and the 1955 system, but turned against it with a vengeance because it was no longer delivering on the economy and implemented policies that increased risk while shrinking the safety net.

LDP Factions and Structural Corruption

The faction (*habatsu*) system in the LDP is another legacy of Kishi that facilitated the institutionalization of corruption. Factions are subgroups within the LDP that coalesce around leaders, less for ideological or policy reasons than for practical benefits – financial support for election campaigns and allocation of influential posts inside the party and in the Diet. Thus while business groups like Keidanren and Nikkeiren provided regular political contributions to the LDP, they were also vigorously lobbied by faction leaders or aspirants for additional funds needed to wage internal campaigns to determine the party's all-important presidency. This faction infighting was expensive and generated strong pressures for increased contributions. The institutionalization of factions, and their role in funding candidates, securing seats in the Diet, electing party presidents, and ensuring that members got named to cabinet positions, have been critical factors sustaining money politics and a cash for favors system. Faction competition intensified and, in response, party leaders played a critical balancing role, ensuring that plum posts were widely distributed to ensure party unity. Cabinet reshuffles became routine and frequent, involving a division of the spoils, as politicians with their faction's support sought the influence, prestige, and lucrative opportunities of ministerial portfolios. Thus, a critical function of a faction leader has been the ability to deliver and that has depended on fundraising. The LDP's statesmen are the party's preferred face, but its bagmen have played a critical role behind the scenes to bolster the party's fortunes and sustain its hegemony.

Bureaucrats also played a role in this system through *amakudari*. The enormous regulatory and discretionary powers of the bureaucracy over industry made it imperative for the latter to call on the services of these retired officials to maintain good relations and channels of communication with the government over critical matters. Given politicians' influence over regulations, these former bureaucrats also worked to promote their new employer's interests by tapping into political networks developed during their careers. This Iron Triangle collusion between the bureaucracy, politicians, and big business proved a hotbed of corruption, and nobody knew better how to work the system than Kakuei Tanaka.[11]

Tanaka was the most notorious politician in post-WWII Japan and also one of the most popular. From the early 1960s he rose in the party ranks because he had no peer in raising money and figuring out how to use it to gain power. He systematized and developed the existing money-raising schemes and built the most powerful faction in the LDP. He served as prime minister (1972–4) despite humble origins, limited social graces, and a lack of university education. Under Tanaka, the golden rule was, "he who holds the gold, rules." His success in campaigns was based on the Etsuzankai (Niigata Mountain Association), a local support group based in his prefecture with some 100,000 members at its peak that helped orchestrate the porkbarrel projects and patronage for which he became infamous. He advocated large-scale construction projects not merely because of the opportunities for graft and kickbacks; Tanaka also wanted to raise living standards in one of Japan's most backward regions. By developing transportation links, including a highway and *shinkansen* (high-speed railway line) between Tokyo and Niigata, his home prefecture, Tanaka was one of the architects of the *doken kokka* (construction state). While the rest of Japan may remember him most for sleazy politics, in Niigata he is still revered as a local hero. He also had a deft touch with bureaucrats, cultivating them in order to use them, while he was admired in the business world for cutting through red tape and getting things done. He was a gifted populist, giving a voice to the many Japanese leery of the privileged governing elite while responding to their needs in colorful dialect and in a practical, gruff manner they could relate to.

In 1974, however, the Japanese media broke a story about Tanaka's shady land deals that spurred his resignation as prime minister. Then in

1976, investigations in the US Congress into the corrupt business practices of US companies overseas led to revelations about $1.8 million in payoffs by Lockheed Corporation to Tanaka aimed at securing a large order for aircraft by ANA, Japan's second largest carrier. Marubeni, one of Japan's largest trading houses with a stake in the order as the representative of Lockheed, was also implicated. The subsequent scandal led to his prosecution and finally conviction in 1983, but his appeal dragged on and throughout this period he continued to effectively rule the LDP through his huge faction and acted as the "shadow shogun" (kingmaker) through the mid-1980s. Soon after Tanaka's conviction, the LDP was in disarray over how to deal with their *de facto* leader's disgrace, leading PM Nakasone to dissolve the Diet and hold new elections in which Tanaka won more votes than any other politician, a stunning vote of confidence from his constituents. The resulting "Tanakasone" cabinet, as the media dubbed it, was packed with Tanaka faction members, including Noboru Takeshita, the man who eventually took over the faction. Soon after Takeshita's revolt in 1985, Tanaka suffered a debilitating stroke and in 1989 resigned from the Diet due to failing health. This came just as the LDP was reeling from the Recruit scandal, one that shocked even jaded Japanese voters, regarding the incredible extent of influence buying in Japanese politics. Tanaka's death in 1993 came just as the LDP was suffering yet another major scandal, this time involving large under-the-table payments from a trucking company, Sagawa Kyubin, and embarrassing yakuza connections. Despite an unending cascade of scandals implicating the LDP, however, the Socialist Party was unable to take advantage.

Demise of the Left

The LDP regained power in an unlikely coalition government in 1994 including the Japan Socialist Party (JSP), its long-time opponent.[12] The coalition elected JSP leader Tomiichi Murayama as prime minister in what turned out to be the party's last hurrah. Soon thereafter the JSP committed a surprising act of institutional suicide, repudiating its core policies on security and the Constitution. Accepting the US–Japan Security Treaty and the constitutionality of the Self-Defense Forces alienated its political base and also signaled the party's growing irrelevance in the post-Cold War era. Declining union membership, prolonged opposition status, and the ideological "defeat" heralded by the Soviet Union's collapse had sapped the party's strength. Joining the LDP in coalition government and deciding to bury the two parties' major differences over the key ideological issues that had animated their battles over the decades was the equivalent of surrender and marked the end of the JSP as a political force. One of the most prominent developments since the mid-1990s is the retreat of left-wing political influence and the ongoing hegemony of center/right parties.

Voice of the Dispossessed?

The Japan Communist Party (JCP) is the main representative of the left, but remains a small fringe party that has suffered from the reform of the electoral system discussed below. In the post-Cold War era it faced extinction, but because it had always maintained a distance from Moscow the impact of the Soviet Union's collapse was limited. The party faced a reckoning, however, given that it appeared to have lost its *raison d'être* and, more importantly, had a dwindling membership.

The JCP managed to reinvent itself during the Heisei era, downplaying ideology and class warfare and cultivating a less stodgy image under an astute new leader, Kazuo Shii. Circulation of the *Akahata*, the party newspaper that generates significant revenues for the JCP, peaked at 3.5 million in 1980. In the subsequent three decades the party's fortunes went into a tailspin, despite the prolonged Heisei recession when the growing income gap and "contradictions of capitalism" became more apparent. Sales, membership, and funds sank relentlessly until 2008 when the party began to experience a slight rebound. *Akahata* sales rose to 1.6 million and membership exceeded 410,000 with the media reporting growing interest among young voters. At a time when the phenomenon of floating voters, those with no party affiliation, was becoming more widespread, the JCP was bucking the trend, gaining a reported thousand new members a month since 2007, mostly under age 30. The LDP's membership, in contrast, plummeted from 5 million at its peak to an estimated 1 million in 2009 and it is becoming more geriatric.

The JCP maintains unwavering support for Article 9 of the Constitution banning Japan from maintaining armed forces and waging war and opposes the US–Japan Security Treaty. It supports a foreign policy that strictly adheres to the UN Charter and seeks to distance Tokyo from Washington. It also believes that Japan needs to more forthrightly accept war responsibility and do more to atone for past excesses committed in Asia between 1931 and 1945. While opposing mandatory singing of the Kimigayo (national anthem) and veneration of the Hinomaru (national flag), it acknowledges the emperor as the symbolic head of state.

Alone among the political parties the JCP does not accept government campaign funds, instead relying solely on its own formidable fundraising capacity. Given voter anger about endemic political corruption, the JCP stands out as a clean party. It is also the most women friendly with more elected at the local, prefectural, and national levels combined than any other party.

The JCP has adopted a more pragmatic approach, shrugging off dialectical materialism and dense manifestos in favor of attractive websites and graphically appealing poster messages such as one featuring a young woman criticizing employment deregulation by saying, "We are human beings, not things." This makeover with a web-savvy campaign and a message targeting the young and disaffected repositioned the party and broadened its constituency. Amidst prolonged economic stagnation, the JCP's message struck a chord with the growing ranks of working poor and newly unemployed while also attracting students.

The JCP is the voice of some of the "lost generation" of Japanese who have experienced just how tough the job market is in Heisei Japan. The old norms of lifetime employment and employer paternalism have given way to rising levels of temporary work contracts and abrupt dismissals, generating widespread discontent among the working poor. Between 2002 and 2006, the ranks of working poor grew by 40 percent, accounting for more than 10 million out of a total labor force of some 66 million.

Growing anxiety about jobs, the inadequate social safety net, and a vibrant public discourse about the growing income gap should be making more people more receptive to the JCP's message, but this has not translated into electoral success. Its share of the vote has steadily declined from 11.3 percent in 2000 to 8.2 percent in 2003, 7.3 percent in 2007, and 7 percent in 2009. Although it polls nearly 5 million votes in national elections, making it one of the world's largest communist parties among countries with a multi-party democracy, the JCP remains a small party with only nine members in the 480-seat lower house, all proportional representation seats.

Electoral Reform

The overhaul of the electoral system in 1994 was the most important political reform in the first two decades of the Heisei era. Ironically, a coalition of small parties that briefly ousted the LDP ushered in a mixed system of single seats and proportional representation that favors large parties. The idea was that the old system, in which constituencies were represented by three to five politicians, relied too much on personalities, local networks, and lavish campaign spending that awarded seats to the candidates winning the most votes, often meaning multiple LDP members from a single district. Since multiple LDP candidates would vie for seats in each multi-seat district, they could not compete over policy or party affiliation, thereby personalizing campaigns and structuring incentives towards swaying voters with money and porkbarrel projects.

Under the new system, there are 300 first-past-the-post, single-member districts (SMDs), and 180 seats from 11 regional blocs allocated on a proportional basis. Citizens aged 20 or older cast two ballots, one for a candidate in their constituency and one for a party to determine proportional representation. Each party submits a list of candidates for the proportional system and seats are allocated according to the party's proportional vote and the candidates' ranking on the list. Candidates can run both in an SMD and on the proportional list provided their party has five or more Diet members or gained more than 2 percent of the votes in the previous election. This system produces so-called zombie candidates, those who get voted out of office in their SMD, but come back to political life, and remain in office, courtesy of proportional representation.

Advocates hoped that this electoral reform would encourage candidates and voters to focus more on parties, issues, and policies. One of the major consequences of this reform is that smaller parties have become more marginalized. In more than half of the 300 SMDs in 2009, voters had a choice between only two candidates, reflecting the high cost of entry that discourages smaller parties from fielding candidates. To run in an SMD the candidate must pay a deposit of JPY3 million, about $30,000, but this is not returned to candidates who garner less than 10 percent of the vote. To do well under this electoral system there are incentives to field candidates in as many districts as possible, putting a premium on well-organized and well-funded campaigns that favors larger parties. Because candidates risk losing their substantial deposits, the highest of any democracy, smaller parties without deep pockets are sidelined.

Advocates of electoral reform assert that as campaigns become less personal and more party centered, shifts in party and party leader popularity may create more volatile swings in elections that facilitate changes in government along the lines of what happened in the UK in the 1997 elections when Tony Blair's resurrected Labour Party swept to power, ousting the long-entrenched Conservatives. The last two lower house elections in 2005 and 2009 were landslides for the LDP and DPJ respectively, suggesting that in some respects electoral reforms are having this anticipated impact of making politics more party-centric and nurturing a stable two-party system of alternating governments. However, given that in 2009 most voters did not support many key provisions in the DPJ's manifesto, voting the party into power *despite* its policy pledges, it is not clear that campaigns are necessarily becoming more policy oriented.

The 1994 electoral reform did not address the more fundamental problem of political corruption that disillusions so many voters. Campaign financing laws have not sufficiently closed loopholes or promoted transparency to regain public trust and enforcement has been lax. So electoral reform is a significant reform, but not one that has restored the legitimacy of a tarnished political system. In addition, electoral reform has not yet addressed the overrepresentation of rural voters that has favored the LDP. Politicians elected in crowded urban districts represent vastly more voters than those elected in sparsely populated districts; this bias reached a high of 4.86:1 *vis-à-vis* urban voters in the 2007 upper house elections. The Osaka High Court ruled in 2009 that disproportionate representation, defined as exceeding a 2:1 ratio of per capita voter representation, is unconstitutional and urged a speedy remedy while allowing the results to stand. Based on this ratio, results in 45 out of the 300 SMDs in the 2009 lower house elections were unconstitutional.

Koizumi

Junichiro Koizumi was the most gifted politician of his generation, a brilliant campaigner oozing charismatic appeal, an outsider often dismissed as strange until he outmaneuvered party leaders in winning the LDP leadership battle in 2001. He previously had served three times as a cabinet minister, but he was a rank underdog in the battle to head the LDP because faction leaders had already anointed former Prime Minister Ryutaro Hashimoto, making it a done deal. Or so they thought. Undeterred, Koizumi staged a stunning grassroots rebellion in the party's prefectural chapters that carried the day and swept him to power. He vowed to take on the factions and destroy the LDP, a message that resonated powerfully among the party rank and file, eager to project a different image. Outgoing

LDP president Yoshiro Mori left with single-digit approval ratings as prime minister and the LDP was desperate for a leader who could dramatically change voter perceptions of the party. Paradoxically, it was his high-risk, flamboyant style and trampling of taboos that made him so popular in a society where safety, conformity, and compromise are so highly valued.

While he was premier, Koizumi was a controversial leader due to his Thatcher-like economic reforms at home, growing security cooperation with the US, and ardent support for President George W. Bush's "war on terror" in the wake of 9/11. These reforms and expanded security cooperation with the US were unpopular, but Koizumi was never a weathervane politician. Part of his appeal was his willingness to be bold and decisive, demonstrating leadership qualities that people admired more than his policies and agenda. Under Koizumi, Japan adopted structural reforms, including deregulation of the labor market and privatization of the Post Office and the nation's highways, while he supported initiatives that helped resolve the problem of banks' vast portfolios of non-performing loans. His economic czar, Heizo Takenaka, forced banks to come clean on their dud loans and write down massive losses in exchange for government support. Takenaka's hard line on non-performing loans made bankers wince, but he is credited with reviving bank fortunes and leaving the financial system in good shape when the global banking system was poised at the edge of the abyss in 2008–9.

Koizumi presided over a shift towards greater accommodation of market forces as a means of promoting greater productivity and competitiveness. His policies won considerable praise from business circles, neo-classical economists, and foreign observers because they attributed Japan's economic problems to the long-standing muting of market forces by successive LDP governments. Many Japanese, however, blame him for embracing market fundamentalism, widening disparities, and creating an inadequate safety net that left many people vulnerable to the riskier model he promoted. In the 2009 elections, voters gave a verdict against his reforms principally because they are blamed for growing disparities and the government had not prepared for the increased risks of deregulation and its likely consequences.

While he was in office, Koizumi's self-indulgent gestures at Yasukuni Shrine in Tokyo, including six visits, were an unmitigated disaster, dividing Japanese while alienating China and Korea. He didn't convince very many observers that those annual pilgrimages reflected his commitment to peace and desire for harmonious neighborly relations, for the very obvious reason that this particular shrine is not about peace and harmony. Drawing a line in the gravel at Yasukuni accomplished nothing except to remind people how costly and self-defeating nationalistic impulses can be.

At a time when one of the most critical issues facing Japan was the rapid emergence of China as an economic superpower and regional hegemon, Prime Minister Junichiro Koizumi derailed bilateral relations and thus postponed a critical top-level dialogue between Asia's main powers. As Japan's bid for a seat on the United Nations Security Council imploded, territorial disputes festered, and China proved conspicuously unhelpful on North Korean missile launches, the costs of alienating Beijing were clear. Climbing out of this deep hole and mending fences with Beijing was left to his successors.

Many pundits dismiss Koizumi's impact, insisting that the DPJ will roll back his reforms and that his legacy will be ephemeral. This may, however, underestimate both the constraints on those who follow and the reforms that have been set in motion. In fact, Koizumi departs having presided over a sweeping transformation of Japan. Not all of it was his doing, as some changes were ongoing when he took office, but he made lots of things happen.

Certainly he leaves a mixed legacy, but there has been a tectonic shift in Japan's security posture, and significant changes in its political economy. Moreover, new information disclosure legislation implemented on his watch has improved transparency and government accountability, and a series of judicial reforms is creating a more activist and accessible legal system. He has, for better and worse, exerted leadership – an uncommon quality in Japanese politics.

In Japan's staid political world, style and showmanship now matter. "Cool-biz" Koizumi, the leader who popularized light clothing in summer heat, gave his sclerotic party a heart transplant. Keizo Obuchi, prime minister from 1998 to 2000, was known as "cold pizza." By comparison, Koizumi was nouvelle-fusion cuisine, trendy to the max. He was the leading *choiwaru oyaji* (cool older guy), with a coiffed mane of hair and snazzy duds. He was a master of political gestures and barking out snappy sound-bites. His masterful campaign in 2005, ostensibly about postal reform, was a brilliantly orchestrated, media-friendly three-ring circus featuring "madonna assassins" (outspoken female celebrity-candidates), superb PR, and a battle between good (reformers like me) and evil (all who opposed). Japanese voters had never seen anything like it and, even if they did not understand the finer points of postal reform, they knew they wanted to stand with the lionhearted leader who was putting everything on the line for his cause.

Koizumi gambled his political life on postal reform by calling a snap election when the Diet rejected his postal privatization bill. He then put some of the party's geriatric rebels out to pasture for opposing him, and brought in some celebrities as lawmakers to add sparkle to his party's image. This crowd-pleasing gesture reinforced his reputation as an eccentric maverick with guts and verve. There are not many politicians who fearlessly risk getting booted from power because they won't take no for an answer.

If one reform stands for Koizumi-nomics, it is the privatization of the postal system. This quixotic initiative is also directly linked to the downsizing of Japan's construction state, since postal savings have long been the ready source of cheap funds for public works. Privatization aimed to make it increasingly difficult for bureaucrats and politicians to siphon off these funds for their pet projects. Given the enormity of Japan's fiscal crisis, Koizumi's moves towards reducing profligate spending constituted a major step towards reducing budget deficits. The privatization of the highways was another milestone on the road to fiscal discipline.

One of the profound changes under Koizumi that affected powerful LDP politicians and their supporters was the huge cut in public works spending from some 8 to 4 percent of GDP. This translated into fewer roads and bridges to nowhere, and much less "uglification."[13] The tightening of the spigot on such porkbarrel projects, important sources of employment in the countryside, accentuated urban–rural income disparities, but also undermined the nexus of corruption linking construction firms, politicians, bureaucrats, and mobsters. Local chapters of the LDP had much less largesse to spread around among voters. The impact of this squeeze was fully evident in the upper house elections in 2007 when the LDP lost its majority. It is telling that when the DPJ came into office in 2009 one of the new administration's first moves was to immediately cancel two major dam projects and it followed this move with much more of the same, slashing the public works budget by 18 percent in its first budget. The downsizing of the construction state thus continues apace, one of Koizumi's positive and lasting legacies.

Koizumi carried through on his threat to destroy the LDP in other ways too. He marginalized the factions, purged dissenters, and alienated significant constituencies like the postmasters who opposed his privatization initiative and have considerable influence in rural Japan. The LDP's once-vaunted voting machine was rusty when he came to power, and thus became even more decrepit.

Finally, in 2009 Koizumi's vow to destroy his party was nearly fulfilled as the LDP shrank to a mere 119 seats, down from 296 in the 2005 landslide. Only 10 of Koizumi's 83 "children," those he handpicked and were first elected in 2005, retained their seats in 2009.

Politically it makes sense to find a scapegoat for widening income disparities, but it is not accurate to place all the blame on Koizumi-nomics. The gap between rich and poor had already opened up before the Koizumi era, due to a rapidly aging workforce and employers' shift toward hiring more part-timers beginning in the 1980s. Nonetheless, Koizumi's deregulation initiatives amplified existing disparities and his mandated cuts on social welfare spending had a devastating impact by reducing the safety net just as more people were at risk.

In foreign policy, Koizumi embraced an assertive policy toward East Asia while cultivating closer ties with the US. Sidestepping the constitutional constraints of Article 9, he sent troops to Iraq and increased security cooperation with the US. As discussed in the next chapter, his breakout gambit of visiting Pyongyang to normalize relations with North Korea backfired, raising bilateral tensions and distrust. Under Koizumi, Tokyo developed a lopsided relationship with Washington that rested uncomfortably on expanded security cooperation – while relations with East Asia were left in tatters.

For all his foibles, no other prime minister in Japan left office with such a high level of popularity. Koizumi offered vision, hope, and leadership and the Japanese people responded enthusiastically. His successors have all paled in comparison to this once-in-a-generation politician. Although Koizumi retired from politics in 2009 with his legacy of economic reforms under attack, he changed Japan by giving the dated and tawdry ways and means of Japan, Inc. a big shove towards the exit and invigorated Japanese democracy by promoting transparency and contributing to the LDP's fall from power.

Prospects

Electoral reform was supposed to foster a stable two-party system, but as of 2010 this remains a distant prospect. Unlike in 1993–4 when an unstable coalition of small parties took over, the DPJ is a major party with staying power, but its popularity has plummeted, while the establishment of new small parties suggests further realignment is on the cards. The LDP faces a difficult task in rebounding from its devastating defeats in 2007 and 2009 that saw it lose a majority in both houses of the Diet. Reinventing the LDP and broadening its constituency are essential, but not easy given the top-heavy presence of senior lawmakers who are most responsible for the party's demise. Significant defections from the party in the run-up to the 2010 elections carry bleak implications about the LDP's future prospects.

Japanese voters want more and better reforms than either party has been offering. In the last two lower house elections (2005 and 2009), the landslide victories went to the party that convinced voters that it was the party of reform. This is not surprising given how unappealing the status quo is. There is no sense that returning to the old ways and means of Japan, Inc. is viable, but there is also little confidence in the half-baked structural reforms Koizumi launched and his successors neglected. Koizumi campaigned on the slogan of "No Pain, No Gain," but he and the LDP delivered considerable pain without tangible gains. Since the beginning of this century, voters have voiced desperation for reform, but also want the government to provide a better safety net to prepare for the predictable consequences. Public skepticism towards the DPJ's promises of subsidies and handouts suggests that voters are discerning and seek more compelling and sustainable change they can believe in. Their growing impatience for tangible economic improvement and sustainable reforms that address crucial issues like widening disparities and the aging society is creating a new dynamic in Japanese politics. Citizens expect more from politicians, and having thrown the bums out of office are ready to do so again. Japanese democracy stands to benefit from this decline in loyalty and deference among feistier voters.

The DPJ is moving resolutely against the bloated *doken kokka* and practice of *amakudari*. There are numerous "public interest" corporations established and subsidized by supervising ministries that have been expected, as quid pro quo, to provide lucrative sinecures for retiring officials. They accounted for more than half of *amakudari* posts in 2008. These public interest corporations depend on subsidies and government contracts. Cutting these subsidies and reorganizing most of these public interest corporations as private entities while instituting competitive, open bidding on the services and projects they have been providing will be a major hurdle, but could save money and reduce the scope for corrupt practices.

Canceling and postponing numerous ongoing dam and road projects and shelving other planned public works is freeing up funds to spend on social welfare programs. Certainly there is plenty of fat to trim from public works, a sector long notorious for corrupt practices such as bid-rigging that inflates project costs and has involved under-the-table payments to politicians and bureaucrats. Rural regions, however, have become dependent on public works spending and the jobs this generates. Certainly many projects are proceeding and the construction spigot remains open, but the reduced flow of funds for the *doken kokka* is having a negative impact on regions that are already hurting and there is an urgent need to facilitate a transition towards sustainable rural economies. The emphasis on expanding jobs in forestry management, conservation efforts, and agriculture, however, is not a panacea for what ails the Japanese countryside.

The DPJ favors decentralization and devolution of powers to regional governments, based on the assumption that local knowledge can reshape regulations, practices, and budget priorities that are better suited to local conditions. Giving local governments greater leeway and abolishing central government local offices might tap regional dynamism and save money. Regional sovereignty will remain a laudable slogan, however, until the Diet passes enabling legislation and, more importantly, transfers authority and sources of revenue to cover operational and personnel expenses. Bolstering local finances by allocating specified tax revenues is an urgent matter in facilitating the devolution of power.

So too is expanded partnering with civil society organizations. Japan has over 80,000 non-profit organizations and non-government organizations, but most are small, underfunded, and lacking in significant capacity as a result of government policies. Many DPJ Diet members favor changing the tax code to liberalize charitable deductions that would bolster their fundraising and see great prospects in partnering. In order to rapidly expand social services that meet local needs at a reasonable cost there are strong incentives to rely more extensively on citizen groups. In this and other ways the DPJ agenda is shifting government closer to the people and their needs than was the practice under the LDP.

Seiken kotai (political change) has finally happened, raising public expectations of government and the hope that the DPJ can tackle Japan's numerous problems more effectively than the LDP. The relatively smooth transition of power testifies to the strength of Japan's democracy, but voters remain skeptical that politicians can deliver. The policy implications of political change are significant. National security and the alliance with the US remain divisive political issues in contemporary Japan. The Hatoyama–Obama relationship got off to a rocky start because the DPJ battled for changes in an agreement negotiated by the LDP regarding US military bases in Japan and seeks a less subordinate association. In the next chapter we explore the evolving security debate in Japan and battles over relaxing some long-standing constraints.

Chapter 7

Security and the Peace Constitution

With the end of the Cold War in 1989, there were high expectations around the world that security concerns would diminish and that governments could cut defense budgets. It has not worked out that way as new threats to security proliferated, defense spending increased, and the predictability of the Cold War era suddenly looked more attractive in some respects than the messier and more ambiguous post-Cold War environment. During the 1990s, governments and international organizations faced unprecedented challenges ranging from nuclear proliferation to genocide in Rwanda, devastating war in the Congo, soaring numbers of refugees, ethnic cleansing in the Balkans, and extensive human rights violations by governments stretching from Burma to Haiti and Sierra Leone to North Korea. And then 9/11 etched its place in history.

For Japan, the Heisei era has been a time of growing anxieties concerning China's massive increases in defense spending and modernization of its armed forces, and North Korea's missile tests and nuclear weapons program. Relations with both countries are troubled due to unresolved historical issues and legacies of animosity. In addition, the bedrock of Japanese security, its alliance with the US, has faced considerable challenges and adjustments in this era. Growing cooperation between the two nations on security under PM Koizumi has not masked frustrations and unease on both sides about how the alliance is evolving. Pressures from Washington to take on a greater security role are increasingly hard to deflect, but Japan remains a reluctant partner, doing the minimum necessary to placate the US. In Japan there are also growing uncertainties about the US commitment and the value of its security umbrella that confront the very real threat poised by Pyongyang and worries stemming from China's rapid economic rise and military modernization. The Japanese public remains leery of cozier security ties with the US and where this may lead, and the presence of US bases and military personnel on Japanese soil generates significant tensions in local communities while underscoring Japan's continued dependence and subservience. It is striking that during the Heisei era Japan emerged as an official development assistance (ODA) superpower focusing on promoting human security through development and technical assistance programs that enjoy an enthusiastic public support that eludes the government's security cooperation with the US.

The security discourse in Japan is powerfully shaped by history.[1] Japan's military rampage through Asia in 1931–45 still resonates loudly in the twenty-first century, combining with Article 9 in the Constitution to constrain Japanese security initiatives. However, there are signs that some Japanese want to shrug off the burdens of the past and constitutional constraints to assert a bolder security posture they believe is normal and in the national interest.

Normal Nation?

For Japan, armed with Article 9 of its Constitution, one that bans war and maintaining armed forces, security issues have become more nettlesome in the Heisei era. The post-WWII US security alliance meant an outsourcing of defense and reliance on the US nuclear umbrella. However, following the first Gulf War (1990–1), Ichiro Ozawa, a prominent conservative politician who rose to become Secretary General of the DPJ in 2009, sparked national debate about Japan's security posture, arguing that by only providing money, Japan had not played a sufficient role in supporting the international community's response to Iraq's invasion of Kuwait.[2] Japan contributed some $13 billion of the total $60 billion used to push Iraq out of Kuwait, but garnered little kudos for its large contribution. Ozawa asserted that Japan was widely criticized in the international community for shirking its responsibilities by not committing troops and other essential personnel. While Japan did not get much public gratitude there was very little criticism, as coalition forces needed its financial contributions more than its troops or logistical support. But Ozawa struck a chord in a nation that keenly cultivates its international stature and is very sensitive to criticism, real or contrived.

Ozawa advocates Japan becoming a normal nation, one that can only dispatch troops overseas under United Nations' auspices. He criticizes Japan for free riding on the sacrifices of other nations and emphasizes that if Japan aspires to join the UN Security Council, it cannot evade deploying troops overseas in support of UNSC resolutions and actions. In a nation accustomed to hiding behind Article 9 to fend off US demands for expanding its security posture and responsibilities, Ozawa's stance in the early 1990s provoked heated debate both domestically and regionally. At home and in the region, the ghosts of war remain persistent reminders of the risks of Japanese militarism. Japan may not be as repentant and contrite about its shared past with Asia as many of its own citizens and those in neighboring countries would like, but the horrors of war have been a powerful constraint on the security debate among Japanese and nurture support for the war-renouncing Article 9 we discuss below. Hiroshima is one of the most popular destinations for school trips from all over Japan, an experience that etches the reality of war on the minds of these students. In addition, every August, the month of the two atomic bombings and Japan's surrender, the media extensively covers various aspects of the war that remind everyone of what is at stake. General Toshio Tamogami, the former head of the Air Self-Defense Force forced to resign at the end of 2008 for his apologist views on Japanese imperial expansion 1931–45, chose Hiroshima to deliver a speech on August 6, 2009. In Hiroshima, this anniversary of the first use of the atomic bomb is usually a day devoted to commemorating the sufferings of the atomic bomb victims and renewing pledges to promote nuclear disarmament, but Tamogami chose it, with obvious political purpose, to challenge the unilateral pacifism enunciated in Article 9. He argued that Japan must develop nuclear weapons to protect itself, a decidedly minority view, demonstrating how desperate the right wing is for attention by making his remarks at a time and place where they would be most unwelcome.

The war-related taboos, and apparent constitutional restraints, that shackle Japanese defense policy debate have not been uniformly effective in shaping actual policies. Article 9 states:

> Aspiring sincerely to an international peace based on justice and order, the Japanese people forever renounce war as a sovereign right of the nation and the threat or use of force as means of settling international disputes. (2) In order to accomplish the aim of the preceding paragraph, land, sea, and air forces, as well as other war potential, will never be maintained. The right of belligerency of the state will not be recognized.

Thus, it would seem there is little ambiguity and no scope for Japan to maintain large modern armed forces as it currently does. However, Japanese courts have upheld the government's position that defensive military forces are not banned by Article 9, a huge loophole that the government has fully exploited.[3]

The US actually insisted on insertion of Article 9 in the Japanese Constitution, but has regretted it ever since. Even during the US Occupation (1945–52) the US pressured Japan to remilitarize, but was rebuffed by Prime Minister Shigeru Yoshida who countered by insisting that Japan was too poor and needed to concentrate on economic recovery from the devastation of war. Even so, since then the Japanese government has revived its military forces and has incrementally beefed them up under sustained pressure from the US to do so. In the context of the Cold War, Japan was above all a showcase of the virtues of US-style democracy and capitalism, a shining example that contrasted with miserable conditions in the Soviet Union's orbit of influence. But Japan was never only an ornament and served as an "unsinkable aircraft carrier" enabling the US to project its military influence in Asia. The San Francisco Peace Treaty enacted in 1952 allowed the US to retain its military bases in Japan and gave it control over Okinawa where most US bases and forces are still located. The agreement on reversion of Okinawan sovereignty to Japan in 1972 also provided for the US to retain its base rights there. So even if Article 9 seems to limit the Japanese government's security options, it never affected its willingness to accommodate US demands for base privileges, nor it appears did it constrain repeated US violations of Japan's Three Non-Nuclear Principles.

Japan's nuclear weapons allergy is understandable and Prime Minister Eisaku Sato (1964–72) first enunciated Japan's Three Non-Nuclear Principles in 1967 that prohibit the production, possession, or introduction of nuclear weapons on Japanese territory. In 1974 he won the Nobel Peace Prize for doing so, but subsequently it is clear that he was aware of, and tolerated, repeated US violations of these principles, generating a storm of controversy. In 2009, this controversy was reignited when retired high-level officials from the Foreign Ministry confirmed a persistent rumor, and declassified US documents, that there was a secret bilateral agreement that allowed US nuclear weapons into Japanese territory. This agreement was concluded when the US–Japan Mutual Security Treaty was revised in 1960 and allowed US ships carrying nuclear weapons to transit Japanese waters and call at Japanese ports. There also was a similar secret agreement allowing the US to bring nuclear weapons into its bases in Okinawa in a crisis; nuclear weapons were actually stored in Okinawa prior to reversion in 1972.

Reflecting the logic of greater transparency in contemporary Japan, in 2009 the *Asahi* newspaper called on the government to stop lying about the no longer secret agreements and come clean. With the Cold War over and the secrets now declassified in the US and thus in the public domain, the *Asahi* fumed:

> There is absolutely no reason why the Japanese government has to keep those secrets under wraps. The government must acknowledge the existence of those agreements and admit to the people that it has lied time and again. Without such an admission, the government will not be able to win the public's ready understanding on the future of US security cooperation. Continuing to bury its head in the sand is unacceptable if the government hopes to regain the public's trust in diplomacy.[4]

Well, wherever its head is buried, the Japanese government does operate in abnormal circumstances. It has to consider its security options in light of a past invoked by its neighbors, nurture a close relationship with the US as an insurance policy, and pretend to observe Article 9 while clearly violating it.

Finally, two decades after the Cold War ended, the government led by the DPJ reversed the long-standing LDP policy of denial and tacitly acknowledged the secret agreement on nuclear weapons, one already confirmed by retired Japanese diplomats and US disclosures. Perhaps the most surprising revelation is that since the 1960 accord, bureaucrats briefed politicians and prime ministers at their discretion; some leaders were not privy to this agreement. Thus, this key area of Japan's diplomacy was not subject to oversight by elected politicians except to the extent that bureaucrats opted to let them in on the secret. It is this type of bureaucrat-led governance that the DPJ is seeking to end.

Steering the DPJ into power in 2009 with adroit campaign tactics, Ozawa may have the opportunity to push his normal nation agenda, although there are many in his party, and in the ruling coalition, who embrace dovish inclinations at odds with his more robust security stance. For advocates, the normal nation debate is about how Japan's uses its military power and under what conditions so that it can assume a more influential role in shaping global affairs to promote its national interests. For critics, this debate tramples constitutional constraints, ignores public sentiments, and puts the nation at risk.

Unarmed?

Japan's Self-Defense Forces (SDF) were first established towards the end of the US Occupation, modestly beginning as a National Police Reserve of 75,000 lightly armed infantry in 1950 during the Korean War, and have since grown into a formidable force. In this all-volunteer military, there is a total of nearly 240,000 personnel with 148,000 in the Ground Self-Defense Force (GSDF), 45,000 in the Maritime Self-Defense Force (MSDF), and 46,000 in the Air Self-Defense Force (ASDF). There are an additional 58,000 reserves. Recruiting and retention are difficult given better paying options, poor benefits, tough working conditions, and low public esteem.

There is a widespread misperception that Japan lacks a military or has only a token defense force. In fact, Japan has a larger army than the UK or France, the fifth largest navy in the world, and the most advanced naval and air force capabilities in Asia. It lacks long-distance missile and aerial refueling capabilities, and amphibious units, but it has advanced Aegis destroyers, sophisticated anti-submarine helicopters, helicopter carriers, and spy satellites, and is participating in a US-led ballistic missile defense system.

The defense budget is nearly $50 billion, or approximately 1 percent of GDP, putting it in the top seven worldwide. The government also provides support for US forces stationed in Japan amounting to more than $2 billion a year. Limiting the defense budget to no more than 1 percent of GDP is symbolically important, signifying that Japan is not aspiring to be a military power, but there is a sleight of hand involved to maintain spending below this magic threshold. If Japanese defense spending is tallied according to NATO accounting standards, it has long exceeded the 1 percent barrier. To get a sense of the delicacy of the military's standing in Japan, it was not until 2007 that the Defense Agency became a full-fledged ministry. Political controversy and deep-rooted pacifist sentiments confront attempts at enhancing the SDF's capabilities or budget. It has an exclusively defense-oriented policy and only defensive weapons capabilities, although in 2009 a government advisory panel recommended scrapping such constraints. Civilian control is strictly observed and it was not until 1992 when the Diet approved the Peace Keeping Operations (PKO) legislation that the SDF was permitted to operate overseas under extremely strict rules of engagement. It remains on a tight leash as enabling legislation is subject to periodic review and renewal.

Certainly Japan is a significant regional military power and, since its first overseas dispatch of troops in Cambodia in 1992–3 under UN auspices, it has taken on further PKO missions in Africa, the Middle East, and Asia. The first overseas deployment not under UN authorization was to Iraq in 2004 as Japan joined the "coalition of the willing" under pressure from the US. This deployment was extremely unpopular with the Japanese public, but was regarded as an unavoidable quid pro quo for US protection from North Korea in the context of its repeated missile tests and nuclear weapons development program. However, Japan's engineering units engaged in reconstruction efforts in Iraq proved embarrassing not only because they actually provided little clean water, ostensibly their main mission. The main problem from the coalition forces' perspective was that other troops had to be dispatched to protect the Japanese troops given their strict rules of engagement. This meant that Japan's deployment to Iraq was more of a burden on the coalition than a welcome contribution, pinning down troops for guard duty when they were desperately needed elsewhere. The limits placed on the SDF to ease domestic political concerns made them little more than a token force that earned the nation little international kudos. This is not what Ozawa had in mind when he promoted the idea of a normal nation. In contrast, Japanese airlift logistical contributions based in Kuwait involving the ASDF, and naval refueling operations for coalition forces in the Indian Ocean by the MSDF, were significant and appreciated. However, the fact that some of the fuel was diverted to Iraq operations rather than for exclusive use by NATO forces in Afghanistan, as specified by the legislation, became yet another political controversy in the minefield of Japanese security debate. This is a debate shaped by Article 9, one exposing deep rifts rooted in history and the US alliance.

Contesting Article 9

There is strong support for retaining Article 9 among the Japanese people. The government's concerted and ongoing efforts to enhance security ties with the US during the Heisei era are not widely supported. Especially after 9/11, the government has emphasized developing security cooperation with the US, offering troops for reconstruction in Iraq, opting for participation in ballistic missile defense, expanding guidelines for defense cooperation, participating in an anti-piracy mission off the Horn of Africa, and agreeing to a refueling mission in the Indian Ocean in support of US-led forces in Afghanistan. In each of these cases, the government was redefining and expanding Japan's security profile well beyond what would have been politically possible at the beginning of the Heisei era. Collectively, these security initiatives suggest that Article 9 has diminished sway over government security policy.

During the Clinton administration (1992–2000) security ties were enhanced through a series of defense guidelines that stretched incrementally the envelope of what Japan was prepared to do, but the emergence of North Korea as a serious military threat with missile capabilities and a nuclear weapons program in the late 1990s created a heightened sense of urgency. Against the backdrop of double-digit annual increases in China's defense budget over the past two decades, and anxieties about the tectonic shift in regional power to Beijing, Japan's security policies became less restrained and tread on various taboos. For example, the government has long ruled that collective self-defense was prohibited by the Constitution. However, participation in US-sponsored theater missile defense, clearly covering not only Japan, appears in violation of this long-standing stricture. Similarly, the 1 percent limit on defense spending, not specified in the Constitution but informally adopted by the government as a ceiling, has also been broached. And, the line between offensive and defensive weapons has become ever more blurry as Japan has upgraded its arsenal. Moreover, overseas deployments of the SDF, once politically impossible, have become normal during the Heisei era.

Living in a dangerous neighborhood with unpredictable neighbors has created opportunities in Japan for advocates of enhanced security capabilities to achieve their long-standing agendas. These influential revisionist officials, pundits, wonks, and politicians have long chafed under the limits imposed by Article 9 and have worked hard to sidestep them. However, during the Showa era the shadow of war and a vibrant left-wing opposition created significant obstacles. Ironically, the end of the Cold War ushered in an era of opportunity, one helped no doubt by the death of the Showa Emperor the same year as the fall of the Berlin Wall. Long-suppressed war memories and tragedies actually came to the fore in public discourse following his death, but in some respects the constraints that war devastation had sustained since surrender in 1945 were buried with Emperor Showa. Since then, constitutional revisionists and normal nation advocates of various stripes have seized the opportunities of circumstance provided by North Korea, China, and 9/11.

PM Shinzo Abe (2006–7), a pro-revisionist, took the gloves off, taking up where his grandfather Nobusuke Kishi had failed in leading a fight for constitutional revision back in the late 1950s. Abe will mostly be remembered as a hapless politician out of his depth who had one of the most ignominious exits from politics of any Japanese premier, but during his brief tenure he pushed through legislation promoting patriotic education and also established legal guidelines for holding a constitutional referendum. Mandating patriotic education was aimed at instilling greater pride in nation, and willingness to fight for it. The referendum legislation was aimed at facilitating revision of the Constitution targeting Article 9. Under the Japanese Constitution, the bar for revisions is set high, requiring two-thirds support in both houses of the Diet and the approval of more than 50 percent of voters in a referendum. However, until 2007 there were no legal guidelines for holding such a referendum. After passing the legislation, PM Abe signaled that he would target Article 9.

The public backlash was unexpectedly strong, resonating throughout Japan. The Article 9 Association was founded in 2004 by a number of intellectuals and pundits who favor retaining the Peace Constitution. Since then, like-minded citizen groups aimed at mobilizing public support for retaining Article 9 mushroomed all over Japan in communities, workplaces, and schools, totaling nearly 7,500 as of 2009. Most of these were established in response to Abe's declaration of war on the war-renouncing Constitution.

For many Japanese it is a point of pride that Japan's Constitution embraces pacifism, a powerful symbolic break with the wartime past and an ongoing guarantee. It is the foundation for an attractive Japanese national identity shorn of militarism and supporting peace and non-proliferation. Many see it as a source of soft power and view any attempts to alter it with grave suspicion. There is also concern that altering or expunging Article 9 would provoke regional neighbors and become an excuse for mischief or worse. Some mainstream conservatives pragmatically favor retaining Article 9 because it prevents Japan from becoming entangled in American wars by ensuring that the US–Japan Mutual Security Treaty is a one-way street: having the national hands tied by the Constitution has its conveniences. These pragmatists, with the support of pacifists, have been instrumental in protecting Article 9.

Advocates of revision are a heterogeneous group, with some seeking national autonomy and muscularity, reminding Japanese that it was imposed by the US to keep Japan weak and subservient.[5] Others suggest that it is a matter of honesty, asserting that the SDF's very existence means that Japan is living a lie that deceives nobody and nurtures dangerous illusions. Then there are those who wish to revise Article 9 to reinforce the constraints that are now routinely evaded.

Momentum for revision gained impetus following the 1991 Gulf War. Ozawa and others portrayed Article 9 as an obstacle to international cooperation, an embarrassing constraint that made Japan look selfish and unwilling to assume its international responsibilities. The image of Japan paying large sums of money to have others do their fighting, so-called checkbook diplomacy, helped shift the terms of debate, but revision of Article 9 remains hotly contested. PM Abe badly misjudged public sentiments in making revision a priority. When PM Koizumi agreed to expand security cooperation with the US by sending troops to Iraq, the majority of Japanese were opposed. They have also opposed the refueling mission in the Indian Ocean and US-led NATO operations in Afghanistan. The Japanese people are wary that enhanced security cooperation with the US will drag it into conflicts and look to Article 9 as a useful hedge against such a scenario. The resounding repudiation of Abe in the 2007 upper house elections was due to a variety of factors, and constitutional revision was not the most important of them, but his initiatives reinforced perceptions that Abe was KY (*kuuki yomenai*, a sobriquet commonly used for someone who is clueless), out of touch, and unable to gauge the public mood.

The revisionists have suffered a serious setback, galvanizing opposition to their agenda, but they now have a referendum law in place and can bide their time until a new opportunity arises. The revisionists, pragmatists, and pacifists have contested Article 9 under almost continuous LDP rule since 1955. The emergence of a DPJ-led government carries uncertain implications because it is as internally divided as the LDP has been over revision. As in the past, external developments and the windows of opportunity they create for domestic actors will play a decisive role. Clearly, the abnormal context of security policy shaped by contests over Article 9 complicate aspirations to normal nation status. To the extent that normal is defined by US security policy, Japan will not measure up. However, Japan believes it can make a significant contribution by emphasizing human security.

Human Security

Human security is an approach to promoting political stability based on focusing on improving living standards and addressing humanitarian problems that is well within Japan's comfort zone. Japan's Ministry of Foreign Affairs states, "Human security aims to protect people from critical and pervasive threats to human lives, livelihoods and dignity, and thus to enhance human fulfillment."[6] In practical terms this involves Japanese aid and development programs focusing on community development initiatives, education and healthcare, reconciliation and reconstruction in wartorn areas, and other projects that emphasize improving individual lives and prospects.[7] In addition, Japan is a leading contributor to the UN Trust Fund for Human Security.

While the US targets militants in its war on terror, Japan focuses on mitigating the underlying conditions that propel people to extremism and emphasizes the wellbeing of people, especially those left behind in their societies. Some critics insist that Japan's human security policies are a coy and misleading mask for its fundamental support for US traditional security measures.[8] Tokyo, however, sees human security as a practical means for it to assume a greater role in international affairs than its military constraints allow.

When Ozawa invoked the 1991 Gulf War to admonish the nation about its free riding on US security, the litmus test shifted to "boots on the ground." Normal nation advocates reasoned that Japan would only enjoy the respect of other nations if it would commit its soldiers to UN-sanctioned operations and put them in harm's way. Thus in 1992 Japan hastily passed PKO legislation permitting the first overseas deployment of Japanese troops since 1945, safely monitoring elections in Cambodia as it turned out. Since then, Japan has put boots on the ground all over the world in support of UN missions, showing that it no longer shirks its responsibilities, while demonstrating to its neighbors and its own citizens that it can be trusted. In connection with the conflicts in Iraq and Afghanistan, operating without UN sanction, Japan also put boots on the ground, planes in the air, and boats in the ocean to support its ally. With the escalation of the war in Afghanistan under the Obama administration, encompassing Pakistan, Japan under the DPJ faces renewed pressure to put more boots on the ground. Following the dictates of human security, these boots will belong to medical professionals, engineers, agronomists, educators, economists, and development specialists. The adverse conditions prevailing in these two countries will test the resourcefulness of Japan's human security policy and the depth of its commitment.

North Korea, Abductees, and Impasse

Despite an image of reticence and low-profile diplomacy, Tokyo does want to assert autonomy from Washington. In September 2002, PM Junichiro

Koizumi held a dramatic summit with Kim Jong-il in Pyongyang to discuss normalization of relations, this at a time when Washington was isolating North Korea, a member of what President Bush had memorably termed the "axis of evil." The two nations do not have diplomatic relations and North Korea regards Japan as a belligerent in the Korean War because US bases in Japan were used in the war. North Korea also remains incensed by the depredations of Japanese colonialism (1910–45) and Tokyo's unrepentant attitude while envying the reparations paid South Korea in 1965 in connection with normalization.

At the summit, the two leaders signed the Pyongyang Declaration and exchanged apologies, Japan for the colonial past and North Korea for the abduction of Japanese nationals during the 1970s and 1980s. It was also a chance for Koizumi to express Japanese concerns about nuclear issues and to request a moratorium on further missile tests. But the showstopper was the admission by Kim-Jong-il that North Korean agents had abducted 13 Japanese nationals and that eight of them had died. Three weeks after the summit, five surviving abductees returned to Japan.

Normalization talks between the two countries began way back in 1991 and proceeded slowly and fitfully until fizzling out in 2000, reportedly over the abduction issue.[9] Koizumi hoped that a meeting of leaders could remove this massive stumbling block to normalization. The Bush administration made it clear that it had not been consulted about the mission and was unhappy that Koizumi was not following Washington's lead. Soon after Koizumi's less than triumphal return, the US divulged that North Korea had acknowledged it was pursuing uranium enrichment for its nuclear weapons program in violation of its past commitments. The timing of the US revelation, and questions about its veracity, generated suspicions that it was primarily aimed at derailing Japan's normalization initiative, but Washington need not have bothered.

The domestic backlash regarding Kim Jong-il's revelations about the abductions capsized normalization, sparking a furor among the Japanese public. Rumors about the abductions, possibly involving several dozen Japanese nationals, had been swirling around for years, but Kim's admission generated demands for a full accounting about the fate of all abductees and demands for the return of any still alive. The Japanese media, which had heretofore done little reporting about what had been unsubstantiated rumors, suddenly shifted into high gear and embraced the hardline position on North Korea that had been confined to the far-right margins of public discourse. Koizumi may have wanted to focus on the big picture of normalization, hoping that improved relations might facilitate progress on curtailing Pyongyang's nuclear weapons program, but the abductee issue launched a sustained media frenzy about what is known in Japan as the *rachi mondai* (kidnapping problem) and catapulted the Kazokukai (Families of Abductees Association) into the national limelight. These parents and siblings tour the country giving speeches and receive sustained saturation media attention. Indeed, in 2006 the government actually ordered the national broadcaster NHK to devote coverage to the abductee issue, ensuring that it remains in the public spotlight. The Kazokukai, the sympathy-generating public face of the abductee movement, also enjoys influential organized support from the Sukuukai (The Abductee Rescue Association) and the Rachi Giin Renmei (Diet Members Association for Abductees). These organizations have played critical roles in shaping policy and public attitudes towards North Korea that brook no dissent.[10]

It is difficult to overstate the impact of the abductee issue on Japan's foreign policy, or the political meddling and opportunism that ensure this impact has continued unabated. North Korea has been the biggest foreign policy dilemma for Japan since it tested Taepodong missiles in 1998 by shooting them over Japan's main island of Honshu. In some respects, it appears that the public shaped Japan's foreign policy, especially when Koizumi arranged the return of five of the abductees and the government indicated that there was an agreement to return them to North Korea after a brief visit so they could make decisions about their futures and that of their families in North Korea. Given outrage over the deaths of some abductees, returning the returnees to Pyonyang after 2 weeks was a bizarre plan that quickly became politically impossible for the Japanese government. Apparently the public reaction came as a surprise to the officials who had brokered the agreement, revealing them to be inexplicably tone deaf in anticipating how their diplomatic handiwork would play in the arena of public opinion. Japan thus reneged on its end of the bargain, resettling the five returnees while demanding Pyongyang allow their families and remaining abductees to also return and provide credible explanation about the fate of those not accounted for.

To credit the public with orchestrating this shift in foreign policy and prioritizing the fate of the abductees over the normalization process and the Six-Party Talks, however, is to overlook the key role of the media in whipping up the frenzy and the behind-the-scenes role of right-wing groups in manipulating this issue to promote their own agenda.[11] Anyone suspected of favoring dialogue over diatribe was subject to unrelenting and unrestrained attacks carried in the media impugning their characters and motives; the voices of reason were vilified as the voices of treason. In essence, right-wing groups opposing normalization with North Korea hijacked the abductee issue. They, and a number of influential conservative politicians, sought regime change, and could not abide cutting a deal with a ruthless despot who, in their opinion, could not be trusted. North Korea drew their ire for, *inter alia*, the mistreatment of ethnic Korean repatriates from Japan. Some of these right-wing activists had been involved in that repatriation effort involving some 90,000 repatriates between 1959 and 1984, and nurtured a grudge on behalf of those they had unwittingly put in harm's way. These people exploited the very real suffering of the abductee families to arouse public opinion against normalization and stifle any media criticism or questioning about how such extremists hijacked Japan's foreign policy. There are strong parallels with government efforts in the mid-1950s to normalize relations with the Soviet Union by cutting a deal on the disputed northern territories. At that time right-wing groups campaigned aggressively to capsize the deal and sustain the stalemate because they found the regime in Moscow objectionable and did not want improvement in ties that might benefit left-wing forces in Japan.

Prime Minister Shinzo Abe (2006–7) was Deputy Chief Cabinet Secretary under PM Koizumi at the time of the Pyongyang summit and a hardliner on North Korea. Subsequently, as LDP Secretary General, he pledged in 2003 that normalization would not happen, and no reparations for the colonial era would be paid, until there was a full accounting and all the abductees had returned to Japan. He propelled and rode the wave of public hysteria about the abductions into the premiership, leapfrogging several more senior politicians in the ruling LDP. More than any other high-ranking politician, Abe is associated with benefiting from the abductee issue and keeping it in the limelight. He cultivated a high-profile involvement with the Kazokukai and as a result gained considerable popularity despite mediocre political skills. He also sabotaged PM Koizumi's normalization initiative. When Abe became premier in 2006 he created a cabinet portfolio dedicated to the abductee issue and was instrumental in mandating NHK coverage.

Privately, journalists and officials acknowledge the right-wing's kidnapping of the abductee issue to hijack Japan's foreign policy, but nobody wishes to go public for fear of reprisal. The house of a senior diplomat involved in brokering the initial Koizumi summit in Pyongyang was bombed; for promoting dialogue he had been castigated as pro-North Korea. Arch-conservative Tokyo Governor Shintaro Ishihara, rather than condemning this act of terrorism, even suggested that the diplomat had it coming to him. In this chilling context, it is no wonder that nobody is eager to draw back the curtain and expose what is going on behind the scenes. At a Tokyo symposium in 2009, in off-the-record remarks, a Japanese journalist detailed the pressures she felt in reporting on North Korea and the abduction issue and the impossibility of raising questions or voicing doubts in a nation where journalists have been targets of violent reprisal by right-wing groups in the recent past.

Given this climate of hostility directed against North Korea, it is amazing that PM Koizumi attended a second summit in 2004. On this occasion he persuaded North Korea to allow the families of returned abductees remaining there to leave and reunite with those who had resettled in Japan. Pyongyang also agreed to further investigate the fate of the eight dead abductees given lingering doubts about the circumstances of their deaths.

This saga took a macabre turn when North Korea returned the remains of one of the most celebrated abductees, Megumi Yokota, whose parents had prominent roles in the Kazokukai. Megumi reportedly was one of the dead abductees. Some of her cremated remains were returned to Tokyo in 2004 to corroborate her death, but the government announced that DNA tests showed that the remains were not those of Megumi and contained the DNA of two other unknown people. This provoked further vilification of the North Korean regime and lent credence to those who said it could not be trusted. For trying to deceive the Japanese about Megumi, the media and their puppet masters renewed calls for sanctions and a tougher line.

Having whipped up public outrage over the DNA tests, the government was embarrassed by an article in *Nature*, an international scientific journal with considerable prestige and impeccable credentials. In February 2005 *Nature* carried an interview with the Japanese scientist who had conducted the DNA tests and he admitted the tests were inconclusive, contradicting the government line. He elaborated that the samples could easily have been contaminated with the DNA of anyone who came into contact with them and also admitted he had no previous experience analyzing the DNA of cremated specimens. Given the extremely high temperatures in cremation, it is not surprising that Megumi's DNA was not detectable. Suddenly, the government's assertions of North Korean duplicity boomeranged. However, the Japanese media buried this evidence that the Japanese government misled the public, taking months to report this scandalous political meddling, but with none of the headlines and fanfare that had accompanied the government's original announcement. Oddly, the forensic scientist who conducted the tests and exposed the government's duplicity suddenly became unavailable for interviews.

While controversy raged over the abductee issue, Japan's security concerns were put on the backburner. Prioritizing the abductee issue over negotiations addressing North Korea's nuclear weapons program, and linking full resolution of the former with starting the latter, highlights just how powerful the "hijackers" had become in controlling Japanese foreign policy. The Six-Party Talks involving both Koreas, the US, China, Russia, and Japan were launched in 2003 following North Korea's withdrawal from the Nuclear Non-Proliferation Treaty earlier in the year. Japan was a reluctant participant from the outset and all the more so when the other participants refused to include the abduction issue on the agenda. Even the US, Japan's closest ally, regarded the Japanese desire to link the abduction issue with denuclearization negotiations as an unwelcome distraction. Essentially, Japan was trying to hold the nuclear weapons negotiations hostage to the abductee issue, a recalcitrant stand that may have made sense given the domestic political climate, but one that undermined national security interests and marginalized Japan in the Six-Party process. From Tokyo's perspective, however, the Six-Party Talks were an appropriate forum for the abduction issue that would give it more leverage over North Korea.

This oft-suspended process failed to rein in North Korea's nuclear weapons program and ended in bitter recrimination. Japanese perceptions of US betrayal during the talks underscore fears that the US is not a reliable ally. The US failed to keep Japan informed about its bilateral talks on the sidelines with North Korea and stunned Tokyo when it announced towards the end of the Bush administration that it was removing Pyongyang from the list of state sponsors of terror, and lifting related sanctions, in exchange for verbal assurances that North Korea would decommission sites related to its nuclear weapons program. Giving away this valuable leverage undermined Japan's policy of sanctions and isolation to pressure North Korea to come clean on the abductees.

The morphing of President Bush's hardline position and public support for Japan's concerns about abductees into "let's make a deal" accommodation was an object lesson for Japanese in Washington politics and how quickly and decisively US foreign policy can shift when interests dictate. The US had always had difficulty in walking the tightrope of loyalty to its ally on abductions and the press of larger security issues, but in the end the Japanese knew where they stood. By refusing to decouple the Six-Party

Talks from the abductee issue, Japan undermined the process while alienating its ally. Watching Pyongyang renege on its end of the bargain by enjoying the lifting of sanctions, but not ending its nuclear weapons program, was small comfort for Japan. In the end, Washington and Tokyo failed to imagine the impact of their choices on each other, while losing their gambles and a degree of mutual trust and respect.

Normalization with North Korea seems a far more distant prospect now than during the Koizumi era, while mutual recriminations over the abductee issue remain shrill following various failures to break the impasse. Thus, Japan's security interests have been undermined by North Korea's obdurate resumption of its nuclear weapons development program while most of the abductees' families remain in the dark about the fate of their missing relatives. This is a story of missed opportunities that will haunt Japan for some time.

Prospects

Japan's anxieties about the rise of China and fears that Washington will prioritize that relationship to the detriment of its alliance with Tokyo are widespread and introduce new challenges to Japanese security policy. This zero-sum thinking about this strategic triangle is a dead-end. The Bush administration quietly chastised PM Koizumi for his repeated provocations of Beijing over history and annual pilgrimages to Yasukuni Shrine because this ran counter to Washington's strategy of cultivating China as a stakeholder in the international system. Alienating China, thus, created a rift in bilateral relations with Washington that had generally been very good because of Koizumi's strong support for closer security ties. After PM Shinzo Abe took office in 2006, keenly aware that the road to warmer relations with Washington led through Beijing, he made it his first overseas visit on a fence-mending mission that thawed relations with China and earned kudos in the US. Broadening and deepening ties with China have become the new mantra in Japan under the DPJ despite some lingering misgivings.

President Barack Obama and Secretary of State Hillary Clinton have worked hard to allay Japanese concerns, making Tokyo their first stop on initial tours of Asia, but all the symbolism doesn't mask emerging realities. Indeed, at a watershed strategic summit of US–China policy-makers in mid-2009, President Obama stated the obvious in noting that US–China relations will shape the twenty-first century, and calling this bilateral relationship the most important in the world. It is exactly this troubling reality that spurs Tokyo to ponder where it fits in and what its options are. It remains unconvinced that better relations between Beijing and Washington are really to its benefit even as it seeks ways to downplay disputes with China and improve relations. Having long been America's leading strategic partner in Asia it is naturally wary about losing this status even if such concerns are overblown.

Leaders in China and Japan recognize that the bilateral relationship should not be held hostage to history because way too much is at stake. Japan under the DPJ is actively cultivating closer relations with Beijing, not to distance itself from Washington as some pundits suggest, but rather to enhance ties and address a number of divisive issues, including conflicts over resources, overlapping territorial claims, product safety, intellectual property rights, transparency in military spending, and environmental issues. The DPJ understands that improved bilateral relations with China are indispensable for enhancing the trilateral relationship involving the US.

Since 2006, China has become Japan's leading trading partner and both nations know how much they benefit from booming economic ties and understand how much is at risk by politicizing history or territorial disputes. During the Koizumi years, Sino–Japanese relations were shoved into the deep freeze by venomous disputes over history and war responsibility that spilled over into domestic politics and poisoned mutual perceptions. Attacks on Japanese spectators at the 2004 Asia Cup, anti-Japanese demonstrations in Shanghai the following year, and an Internet petition gathering more than 22 million signatures in 2005 opposing Japan's bid for a permanent seat on the UN Security Council were some of the lowlights as mutual perceptions reached a nadir since normalization of relations in 1978. This came at an inopportune time amidst a tremendous power shift towards Beijing, generating anxieties in Japan that would have been difficult to manage even under the best of circumstances let alone during a bilateral pout. Since then leaders in both nations have been working to manage disputes over territory and resources in the East China Sea and dialing down the rhetoric about the past. While Japan remains wary about China's rise and its intentions, and popular sentiments are somewhat chilly, a continuing strong alliance with the US provides reassurance.

In contrast to these pragmatic inclinations, Japan has painted itself into the corner over the abductions issue. The government now is hostage to an aroused public and will have a hard time decoupling resolution of the abductions from its larger strategic interests. It is very likely that the fate of all the abductees will never be known, and suspicions that North Korea is withholding information or harboring some will persist given the deep distrust among Japanese towards its estranged neighbor. However, ongoing missile tests, the testing of nuclear devices in 2006 and 2009, and uncertainty about what the departure of Kim Jong-il portends, suggest the need for more engagement rather than isolation. Hardliners in Japan, and the US, imagined that if Pyongyang was squeezed enough through sanctions it would collapse, but these hopes remain unfulfilled. In fact they backfired in 2009 by provoking North Korean withdrawal from the Six-Party Talks, resumption of its nuclear weapons program, and repudiation of the cease-fire on the Korean Peninsula, all alarming developments. Certainly, North Korea has a history of dramatic diplomacy to enhance its leverage, but given Japan's proximity there seem to be few benefits of isolation or regime collapse. Resuming dialogue at some level to manage tensions, never easy, is now complicated by the domestic politics of the abductions. Pyongyang has also deftly exposed and amplified differences between Tokyo and Washington that have introduced tensions in the bilateral relationship.[12] Japan, by maintaining a hardline, risks isolating itself diplomatically.

Despite rising threat perceptions and expanding security cooperation and overseas deployments, it is striking that the Japanese defense budget has remained modest and relatively stable. Certainly Japan has fiscal woes that militate against sharp increases, but the absence of growth in defense spending contrasts with China's annual double-digit increases. This reassuring non-development reflects the value of the US security alliance. Getting back on the same page on China and North Korea, and taking the initiative in Afghanistan and Pakistan via human security and nation-building initiatives, are vital to nurturing and modifying this alliance. But with Japan ramping up its contributions, it will want a greater say, putting the spotlight on President Obama's avowed commitment to a multi-polar global order.

There are anxieties that the DPJ has undermined bilateral relations with the US, but these concerns are overblown. Tensions between allies are normal and the landslide victory of the DPJ carries political consequences that affect security ties. The DPJ seeks a more equal relationship with the US, but this also means that the Obama administration expects more from Japan. The Yoshida consensus, however, remains resilient in Japan, meaning economic problems trump security. Thus, Japan will not deliver as much on security cooperation as the US wants. Growing fiscal constraints and economic stagnation also cast a shadow over future defense cooperation as Japan will have relatively fewer resources to devote to its own defense and the alliance. Improving relations with Beijing is a hedging strategy playing to such concerns.

Reworking bilateral ties, especially security cooperation, is complicated and will have rancorous moments. The US–Japan 2006 agreement on base realignment and reduction of US forces in Japan resulted from long and often testy negotiations during the Bush administration that left ill will on both sides. One area of contention involves environmental compliance on the bases. As we see in the next chapter, the environment is a DPJ signature policy issue. More importantly, the Japanese public remains ambivalent about and sometimes hostile towards the US military presence, especially in Okinawa where most of the 47,000 US troops are stationed. Reducing the US military footprint in Japan without compromising security, however, remains a shared goal. The evolving framework of cooperation between the US and Japan will test alliance management skills, especially over base realignment, but is key to sustaining healthy bilateral relations.

The Japanese government signals that it wants to assert more autonomy and go beyond its reactive diplomacy, defined as essentially doing as little as possible to meet or assuage US demands. During the first 20 years of Heisei what was once anathema has become normal, and once sacrosanct verities have tumbled aside as Japan has modified its security posture and taken on more overseas missions while enhancing cooperation with the US. Overseas deployments, constitutional revision, human security, and an independent course on North Korea are signs of change and incipient autonomy.

Advocates of a more muscular Japan, however, have suffered a string of surprising setbacks in the twenty-first century. The revisionist/normal-nation camp had political momentum under Koizumi and Abe, and after the referendum for constitutional revision was passed in early 2007 it seemed that Article 9 was doomed because the LDP controlled both houses of the Diet. However, the voters threw the LDP out of power in successive elections in 2007 (upper house) and 2009 (lower house) and what seemed certain is unlikely as long as the DPJ remains in power. The revisionists' ideological agenda remains on the margins of the mainstream and public opposition is robust. Thus, in assessing prospects for changes in Japan's foreign policy, it is crucial to understand the constellation of political forces that are contesting this agenda and the continuing resilience of norms and values that have defined Japan's security policy in the post-WWII era.

Policy planners and security experts have become more vociferous, however, in suggesting the government modify its defense-only policy and reconsider the official ban on collective self-defense – proposals that would have been unthinkable at the outset of the Heisei era. Taking it even further, Toshio Tamogami, the former Air Self-Defense Force Chief ousted over his apologist views concerning Japan's militarist past, sparked a furor and reopened wounds in his speech "Casting Doubt on the Peace of Hiroshima," delivered in that city on August 6, 2009. He said, "As the only country to have experienced nuclear bombs, we should go nuclear to make sure we don't suffer a third time." His views are not representative – indeed 80 percent of the Japanese continue to support the Three Non-Nuclear Principles – but they demonstrate that the right wing is less reticent on security issues and provoking debate over taboo topics. Indeed, earlier in 2009 former Prime Minister Yasuhiro Nakasone, a hawkish LDP heavyweight who did much to expand Japan's security role in the 1980s, also suggested that Japan might have to exercise the nuclear option. This is highly unlikely, but again, what was unthinkable at the end of the Showa era in 1989 is now an issue that even voices from the political mainstream are openly putting on the table. As we see in the following chapter, nuclear controversies are also at the heart of environmental battles in contemporary Japan.

Chapter 8

Environmental Issues

In 2009 at the United Nations General Assembly, in his debut on the world stage, Prime Minister Yukio Hatoyama made a bold offer of cutting CO_2 emissions by 25 percent by 2020 from 1990 levels in an effort to regain a leadership role on the environment that Japan has relinquished since launching the 1997 Kyoto Protocol. By drawing a line in the carbon, Hatoyama tried to galvanize global efforts to tackle climate warming. In doing so, he signaled a major shift away from the failed environmental policies of the LDP.

A nation that brought us the Kyoto Protocol and the Prius hybrid car, and produces only 4 percent of global CO_2 emissions compared to 20 percent each for the US and China, must be doing something right. Its factories are energy efficient and conservation efforts have worked. In the three decades since 1979, Japan's GDP has doubled while its industrial sector energy consumption has remained flat. Certainly, Japan is miles ahead of the US when it comes to mass transit. Japan has also invested in developing various green technologies and it has provided green aid to China to help reduce emissions from its power plants and factories that end up as acid rain in Japan. Indeed, its cutting-edge environmental technologies are in high demand and offer considerable potential for reducing emissions and global warming. Government and industry sources often tout Japan's green credentials and reel off impressive statistics, but a lot depends on what you look at.

Greenwashing

Japan's record on the environment is not as stellar as commonly thought. Is it a global leader in energy efficiency, reducing use of oil and promoting renewable energy? Not really.[1] Japan has not met its Kyoto Protocol target of a 6 percent reduction in CO_2 emissions from 1990 levels, instead chalking up a 9 percent rise since then. In terms of carbon emissions per capita, Japan is about one-half US levels but is roughly the same as the UK, Germany, and South Korea and exceeds Spain, Italy, France, and Sweden. Surprisingly, household emissions of CO_2 have increased a dramatic 40 percent in Japan since 1990 despite the nation embracing what is perceived as a relatively green lifestyle with extensive recycling and widespread residential use of solar energy panels.[2]

Japan relies on oil for 48 percent of its energy needs, exceeded only by Italy in the OECD; oil accounts for 40 percent in the US, 35 percent in the UK, and 37 percent in Germany. In Japan, coal-fired plants account for nearly 30 percent of total power supply, up from only 10 percent 30 years ago. Coal releases more CO_2 when burned than oil or natural gas, so increases in its use are not consistent with achieving the goal of a low-carbon society even if the new clean-burning technologies make coal-fired plants more environmentally friendly. Surprisingly, primary energy consumption was increasing in Japan by 2.3 percent between 1997 and 2007 while declining in Germany by 8.7 percent.

In terms of CO_2 emissions relative to GDP, based on purchasing power parity, Japan in 2004 had a ratio of 0.35, far better than the US (0.54), but lagging the UK (0.32), France (0.23), and Italy (0.31) and only just ahead of Germany (0.39). In 2008, German Watch's Climate Change Performance Index ranked Japan only 42nd among the top 56 CO_2 emitting nations based on a weighted average of emission trends, levels, and climate policy.

Renewable Energy

To cut emissions, under the LDP Japan relied on market forces and voluntary reductions. This approach contrasts with the EU approach of mandatory emissions cuts and "feed-in tariffs" which promote use of renewable energy by obligating utilities to purchase target amounts at above market rates set by the government. Such incentives promote use of renewable energy sources and achieve economies of scale.

In the 2000s Japan not only surrendered its lead in solar power, but also made very little progress on other renewable energy sources such as wind, waves, and biofuels. In general, Japan's reliance on market mechanisms to achieve emission reductions means the government did not adopt aggressive public sector measures involving compulsory emission targets, carbon taxation, feed-in tariffs, and other subsidies promoting renewable energy options. In 2009 the government adopted a feed-in tariff limited to solar energy, but it is sensible for the DPJ-led government to extend this to promote the full gamut of renewables and put its ambitious carbon emissions reductions target within reach.

The LDP target for renewable energy by 2014 was less than 2 percent of Japan's total energy supply, well behind Denmark where 20 percent of all its power needs are generated by wind alone, based on generous subsidies and tax incentives. In Germany, wind produces about 7 percent of total power while in Japan wind produces less than 0.3 percent of total electricity output as of 2007. The share of electricity generated by all renewable sources of energy in Japan as of 2007, excluding large-scale hydropower, stood at 0.7 percent; in Germany this was 14 percent, up from 6.3 percent in 2000, with a target of 27 percent by 2020. The DPJ is looking for renewable energy generating 10 percent of total energy supply by 2020, an ambitious goal given the existing situation.

In 2005, the Japanese government eliminated a small subsidy targeting household adoption of solar energy, but in 2009 it reinstated this subsidy in order to reduce greenhouse gases, promote eco-products and stimulate economic recovery. This was in conjunction with government incentives for consumers to purchase energy-efficient cars and appliances, again a resounding success that suggests how much more the government could be doing. Clearly, incentives work and much more can be done to promote renewable energy. There are also ambitious plans to create green-collar jobs, some 3 million by 2020, but this will depend on the government structuring incentives and projects that spur private sector investments in such jobs. The DPJ is pursuing this agenda, over the objections of big business, because it is popular with voters, plays to Japan's strengths in environmental technologies, and is an area where Japan can play a global leadership role.

Resuming subsidies for household solar panels will help rejuvenate the solar power industry, but much depends on modernizing and integrating the national power grid network to handle the fluctuating energy input from various renewable energy sources. Failing to create a "smart" power grid capable of handling and storing a range of renewable energy supplies will ensure that renewable energy remains a bit player, and thus it is encouraging that the government is at least putting this hugely expensive and technologically challenging undertaking on the table. Getting industry on board will require significant incentives and subsidies, but such investments are critical in the transition to a sustainable, low-carbon economy.

Japan's Green Revolution

Japan boasts some green technological marvels such as a train station near Tokyo that produces all its energy needs through solar panels and photovoltaic windows that lower heating and cooling needs. The government is also subsidizing household adoption of eco-friendly hydrogen fuel cells that generate electricity and heat water. They are becoming more affordable through innovation and economies of scale. Solar power generation is expanding again after the government reinstated a subsidy providing up to JPY500,000 ($5,000) to defray installation costs for households. Homebuilders are now much more conscious about energy efficiency and new electrical appliances feature large energy savings. The cool biz campaign urging workers to ditch their ties and wear lighter clothing in the summer and tackling the heat island effect by topping roofs with greenery may have only a small impact, but prod people to rethink lifestyle and design issues affecting the environment.

Under the LDP, Japan's environmental strengths were largely lost in translation. The DPJ, however, is serious about creating green-collar jobs and tapping Japan's green technology prowess. The government understands that exports of green technology and conservation know-how to China and India are potentially very lucrative. It is indicative that in his first substantive policy speech after the 2009 elections, PM Hatoyama focused on the need to cut CO_2 emissions. This means abandoning campaign promises to eliminate highway tolls and reduce gasoline tax surcharges, moves that would encourage greater use of automobiles.

The DPJ has made its pledge for CO_2 emission cuts contingent on other nations also getting on board, giving it some wiggle room that might also facilitate backsliding. PM Hatoyama gave momentum to global efforts, but clearly Japan is not going to press ahead unless other major polluters make similar commitments. The Copenhagen Summit in 2009 demonstrated that the global community remains distant from a viable action plan to reduce carbon emissions. It is unclear what Japan is prepared to do if other major polluters are not willing to cut emissions and to what extent it will rely on carbon offset schemes in lieu of actual reductions. There is also uncertainty regarding plans for carbon taxes, a domestic emissions trading scheme, and how Japan will count its assistance aimed at helping developing countries reduce their emissions towards its own reduction target.

Nippon Keidanren, Japan's leading business lobby, has criticized the targets for being overly ambitious and advocates a 4 percent decrease in emissions by 2020 from 2005 levels, meaning a 4 percent increase from 1990 levels. It describes the DPJ target as mission impossible, one that would do substantial harm to the economy, because Japan's factories are already some of the cleanest and most efficient in the world. True, but this doesn't mean that Japan cannot reduce its dependence on carbon fuels and expand reliance on renewable energy as other industrialized nations have done while promoting greater household conservation as the current eco-products subsidies are doing. Some businesses will suffer, but most will figure out how to innovate while others look to thrive by tapping the possibilities of a global green revolution. Consumer interests are often invoked to justify inaction as businesses assert that customers are unwilling to pay a premium for more eco-friendly products and do not want to shoulder the financial burden of carbon reduction despite evidence to the contrary. For example, customers purchased large numbers of Prius cars, even before eco-incentives, although they cost more than comparable non-hybrid models. There is considerable environmental awareness among Japanese and, given the sense of urgency about global warming, they are not the main obstacle to CO_2 reductions.

Nuclear Follies

The Japanese government puts a great deal of faith in, and spends massive amounts of money on, nuclear energy. This reflects policy-makers' dream of securing energy self-sufficiency and explains why two-thirds of the national energy research and development budget is devoted to nuclear power.[3] In terms of reducing carbon emissions and reducing dependence on oil imported from the Middle East, it is a sensible policy. However, there are good reasons why the majority of Japanese remain skeptical about nuclear power.

Japan has witnessed a series of nuclear accidents over the past two decades that raise serious concerns in an earthquake-prone nation with ambitious nuclear power plans. Japan is totally dependent on imported energy and has thus invested billions of dollars since the 1950s in developing its nuclear energy program. Public concerns about the safety of nuclear power contrast sharply with official insistence that the nation's facilities are both safe and necessary. Polls consistently reveal that 70–75 percent of Japanese have misgivings about nuclear power and fear that serious accidents might happen.

With dwindling reserves of fossil fuels, high prices, and growing concern about greenhouse gases related to consumption of these fuels, the prospects for the nuclear power industry have brightened considerably. Advocates assert that nuclear power is the trump card in the battle to reduce emissions and curb global warming while critics suggest it is more of a wild card given the risks, high costs, and long-term waste disposal issues involved.

Japan currently operates 55 nuclear power plants, up from 32 in 1987, that supply nearly 35 percent of its electricity needs. The government plans to raise the share of energy generated by nuclear power to 41 percent by 2014. Since 1998 two nuclear power reactors have started up with six more currently slated for installation or expansion. In the following sections we examine some notorious incidents and aspects of Japan's nuclear power program that help explain why so many Japanese have considerable qualms about the potential environmental consequences.

Tokaimura

The world's most serious nuclear accident since the Chernobyl meltdown in 1986 occurred in Tokaimura in September 1999. This small village, about 70 miles from Tokyo, is known as "Nuclear Alley" because it is home to 15 nuclear-processing facilities. In 1999 workers at a uranium-processing plant accidentally triggered a runaway chain reaction that lasted for 20 hours in a facility that had no containment barriers. Mistakes in preparing nuclear fuel caused an accident that was not supposed to happen.

A stunned nation learned that the accident occurred while the workers were transferring enriched uranium in stainless steel buckets and mixing the uranium by hand and then pouring it into an open holding tank. The failsafe high-tech safety procedures lauded by nuclear industry proponents were ignored in favor of manual mixing of highly dangerous and unstable radioactive materials. The workers erred in the quantities of the solution they mixed, instead of using processing equipment at hand that had automatic controls to prevent such an accident from occurring. Investigators discovered that the workers were actually following company instructions in violating safety protocols. Since there would be no risk of an accident if workers abided by these protocols, there was no contingency plan for such an accident and no form of containment to protect area residents from the radiation.

Despite three previous nuclear mishaps at Tokaimura, public authorities were slow to react. The town authorities had no contingency plans and firefighters arrived without protective clothing because they were not informed about the nature of the accident. It took 2 days to arrange proper medical care for the three workers directly exposed to the nuclear fission and two of them died from their injuries because the hospital designated for treatment of radiation victims was not prepared to handle such cases. In 2002 the Mito District Court fined JCO, the company operating the nuclear fuel facility, JPY1 million (about $10,000) and its president an additional JPY500,000 ($5,000) while issuing suspended prison terms of two to three years for the six managers prosecuted. The cost of nuclear negligence, thus, proved rather modest.

This exposure of official bungling and the consequences of a business more concerned about profits than safety left the public even more skeptical about a nuclear program that has been plagued by safety flaws, radiation leaks, shutdowns, fires, falsification of inspections, and cover-ups.

Whistleblowing

In the summer of 2002, revelations about extensive falsification of safety records over the previous decade involving potentially dangerous problems in a number of the nation's aging nuclear power plants indicated the low priority accorded public safety. In the aftermath, 17 reactors were shut down for a year to recheck safety systems and perform necessary maintenance and repairs. Amazingly, dozens of high-level industry executives knew of the problems and participated in a well-orchestrated cover-up to falsify inspection and repair records and certify the safety of power plants where engineers had found fissures that could prove dangerous if left unattended. More stunning was the initial handling by the Ministry of Economy, Trade, and Industry (METI) of the whistleblower's report about the falsified safety records. A foreign subcontractor who participated in the inspections and found the problems later discovered that the results of his inspections were ignored and subsequently falsified. Later he reported these criminal acts to METI, the government ministry with oversight responsibilities for the nuclear power agency, and was again ignored. Moreover, ministry officials apparently alerted the power companies of the whistleblower's identity and efforts to expose their negligence. The problem was identified as how to handle the whistleblower as opposed to responding to the allegations by investigating wrongdoing, making repairs, and ensuring public safety. The media eventually blew the lid on this case, forcing the government and power industry to do what they should have done in the first place: put safety first. Ironically, the cover-up was motivated by a desire to avoid raising public concerns about nuclear power and avoid the costs of plant shutdowns that have been the financial bane of the industry. Those concerns and costs rose substantially due to this failure to comply with existing regulations. Yet again, the public learned about the need for better oversight and the low level of corporate and government ethics that lay at the heart of this scandal. In considering how Japan is changing, it is significant that this story ever came to light. As in so many other areas of life in Japan, there is a great deal more openness about topics that were once taboo or suppressed.

Alas, inadequate maintenance and inspections carries real consequences, claiming the lives of five workers in 2004 at the Mihama nuclear plant. They were scalded to death when exposed to steam leaking from a corroded pipe that had not been inspected since it was installed in 1976. Tests on the pipe after the incident showed it had lost 85 percent of its thickness, something that could have been discovered in an inspection. Nine months before the accident, a subcontractor had informed the operators about the urgent need for such inspections, but his warning was ignored. Regulations did not require regular inspections of secondary cooling cycle steam pipes so they weren't inspected. This in a country where every car more than 3 years old is required to undergo extensive and expensive safety checks every other year. The culture of safety that should be intrinsic to nuclear power operations appears lax in far too many instances in Japan – an institutionalized complacency in industry and government that raises legitimate environmental concerns.

Kashiwazaki

In Japan, Kashiwazaki has come to mean "close call." On July 16, 2007 a 6.8 magnitude trembler jolted beneath the world's largest nuclear power complex located in Niigata Prefecture in a place that was not supposed to have a tectonic fault. This earthquake serves as a vivid reminder of the risks generated by nuclear power, especially in zones of seismic risk.

The good news is that a mega-disaster did not occur and, thanks to design safety margins, the seven reactors with a capacity of 8,000 MW were not damaged by an earthquake that exceeded all assumptions in the design specifications. The three reactors in operation and a fourth in start-up mode did shut down automatically as designed. Kashiwazaki had been shut down previously in 2002 because of falsifying safety data.

Tokyo Electric Power Company (TEPCO) reassurances about the negligible risk associated with this incident rang hollow in a nation accustomed to the nuclear utility industry's lack of transparency, tardy notifications, cover-ups, and mishaps. TEPCO informed local government authorities about the radioactive leakage nearly 9 hours after the earthquake. Industry advocates emphasize the effective functioning of nuclear-related safety equipment and the absence of damage to the reactor buildings. Critics have called on the government to shut down some one-third of the nation's 55 nuclear reactors for more robust inspections to investigate and reassess seismic risks in light of the lessons drawn from Kashiwazaki; the tremors were more than double the design benchmark. Nobody knows how many reactors may have been built on similarly flawed assumptions. The discovery of a fault beneath Kashiwazaki's nuclear reactors has also raised concerns about relying on power companies to select and assess site suitability.

NHK aired an investigation featuring interviews with the staff that were at the plant when the quake hit. The supervisor explained that the crisis control room door jammed because of the earthquake, meaning that he and his staff were unable to enter and monitor the situation. Instead they set up a whiteboard in the parking lot and used their private mobile phones to maintain communications and monitor the seven reactors spread over the complex. The supervisor admitted that the absence of effective centralized crisis control and poor communications with local authorities could have turned a dangerous event into a more serious disaster. Sometimes it is good to be lucky.

There are grave concerns about seismic science and the government's credibility on safety. In 2005 a judge ruled in favor of TEPCO in a case filed by local residents of Kashiwazaki to revoke the license to build a nuclear reactor at the site. The judge ruled that the scientific evidence overwhelmingly proved that the plaintiffs' assertion – that the plant was vulnerable to an earthquake due to a hitherto undetected fault – was baseless. Proof is in the eye of the beholder, but clearly this faulty judicial ruling has been a black eye for seismic evaluations conducted by the nuclear power industry.

Deregulation

Deregulation of the utility industry is putting pressures on operators to boost profits at the expense of safety. So just as Japan's aging nuclear power plants, many entering their fourth decade of operation, are in more need of inspections, maintenance, and repairs, bottom-line concerns are forcing cutbacks in safety measures. Given various mishaps, cover-ups, and a culture of deceit in the nuclear power industry, there is considerable public unease with this turn of events.[4] The government mandates that every nuclear power plant shut down once a year for an inspection, and in the pre-deregulation era this typically lasted 3 to 4 months. Cost-cutting measures, however, have drastically shortened inspection times to as little as 6 weeks and operators seek further reductions in costly downtime. They are also seeking to extend the shelf life of their plants to 60 years, double what experts thought prudent when they built the plants. In the context of fewer and shorter inspections, and a record of falsifying safety reports, the implications are unsettling in light of the potential harm of an accident.

Rokkasho

In northern Japan the government has established a complex for nuclear enrichment, reprocessing, and waste storage facilities. There were high hopes that the International Thermonuclear Experimental Reactor might be built there, but in 2005 this project was awarded to France.

In 2007, Rokkasho commenced reprocessing of spent reactor waste to reuse as fuel. The reprocessing yields weapons-grade plutonium, raising questions about the growing size of Japan's nuclear-weapons-usable plutonium stockpile, currently estimated at 45 tons, about 20 percent of the global total. There are also environmental concerns about the toxic release of carcinogenic tritium associated with reprocessing nuclear waste. The plant operators have been given permission to release into the ocean 2,800 times the allowed tritium release for conventional reactors.

Even operating at full capacity, Rokkasho will only be able to reprocess about 800 tons of spent fuel per year, less than the 900 tons of nuclear waste currently produced by the nation's 55 nuclear power reactors. Given that it already has 12,600 tons of nuclear waste as of 2006, and new reactors will boost annual waste production to at least 1,200 tons per annum, the reprocessing capacity of Rokkasho is insufficient for the task at hand.

The long-term concern associated with Rokkasho is its nuclear waste storage facility. The projected total capacity for low-level nuclear waste is 3 million 200 liter drums that will be buried under mountains of soil. In addition, canisters of vitrified high-level radioactive waste are also stored there in above-ground facilities for three to five decades, after which they will be placed in an underground storage facility that will require monitoring and safekeeping for several generations. Even if safety assurances are reliable, the huge cost of handling and disposal of nuclear waste underscores just how high the stakes are in pursuing expansion of nuclear power. It is also important to factor in the cost of decommissioning older plants as their shelf life expires, involving dismantling of reactors, disposing of waste, and site clean-up operations. The nation already knows, to its regret, the high cost of improper waste management.

Closure on Minamata

Japan has overcome the toxic legacy of its rapid post-WWII development, symbolized perhaps most viscerally by Minamata disease. For decades beginning in the 1930s a chemical company dumped mercury waste into the bay off this small Kyushu fishing village. It is a long and sordid story involving a corporate cover-up aided and abetted by government officials that prolonged the dumping while the number of victims piled up.[5] Belatedly, Chisso Corporation and government officials acknowledged their negligence for failing to stop the dumping that led to a nightmare of human toxic poisoning, causing serious nervous system damage. Children born to affected women absorbed the mercury, to some extent detoxifying the mothers, but as a result suffered terrible deformities and shortened lives. Lawsuits filed by victims have percolated slowly through the court system since the 1970s and eventually brought incrementally and begrudgingly some measure of justice in the form of financial compensation.

Finally in 2009, the government passed legislation aimed at extending redress and medical benefits to many previously unrecognized victims. Victims, however, are not all pleased with the modality of the settlement and complain that this plan provides inadequate compensation and amounts to a reprieve for Chisso by blurring the company's responsibility. Controversially, the new legislation requires those who receive compensation to give up ongoing litigation and waive any further claims. A court-brokered settlement in 2010 provides benefits to most of the unrecognized victims.

There is no settlement that can truly compensate the victims for what they have endured and it is understandable that many refuse to end their quest for accountability. But this is a triumph of David–Goliath proportions, with citizens finally prevailing against the government and big business. It took a half-century, way too long, to finally reach this more inclusive settlement providing something resembling justice. It is a tribute to the persistence of citizen activists and victims who kept faith against the odds in working through the system to hold the system accountable.

It appears, alas, that the lessons have not quite sunk in. Given the devastating consequences of mercury poisoning in Minamata, and the extremely high concentrations of mercury and PCBs in whales, it is difficult to comprehend why the government is aggressively supporting whaling and trying to boost domestic consumption of whale meat. Purely from a public health perspective alone, this is an irresponsible policy, but there are other reasons to question the wisdom of government-subsidized whaling.

Whaling Wars

Whaling has become Japan's diplomatic scarlet letter, doing significant damage to the nation's international standing while alienating some of its closest allies. No other single government policy provokes such international opprobrium and it is puzzling why the government harpoons its own green credentials, while undermining national interests, over such a marginal issue, one that most Japanese have long stopped caring about.

The battle over whaling has grown more acrimonious since the beginning of the twenty-first century, principally because Japan has become a more vociferous and belligerent advocate for a resumption of commercial whaling. This has been banned since 1986 when Japan and other members of the International Whaling Commission (IWC) agreed to a moratorium because many whale species were on the brink of extinction from overhunting. Japan, however, continues whaling – as many as 1,000 are "harvested" every year – under the cover of conducting "scientific research" as allowed by the IWC. The IWC annual meetings have become increasingly adversarial as advocates and opponents of whaling find little common ground for compromise.[6] Behind the scenes there is consensus that a deal can be made allowing commercial coastal whaling in Japanese waters in exchange for ending or significantly reducing "scientific" whaling elsewhere, but the wider implications for Japan's fishing fleets and access to global fisheries present a formidable obstacle to such an agreement.

Tensions have also mounted over the harassment of the Japanese whaling fleet in the Southern Ocean by eco-activists determined to disrupt the hunt and limit the kill. The *Sea Shepherd* from the US Conservation Society has had some success in this regard, but the confrontations at sea have helped the Japanese government to vilify them as eco-terrorists and rally support for a program most Japanese are indifferent about.[7]

Since 1986, Japan has killed more than 12,000 whales under the guise of its research whaling program. The government issues permits to the quasi-government Institute for Cetacean Research to conduct hunts and it contracts with Kyodo Senpaku, Japan's only whaling company, to provide the vessels and crews for the hunts. The research thus far has only resulted in the publication of a few papers in peer-reviewed, internationally recognized academic journals, fanning suspicions that it is only a figleaf for securing whale meat. DNA samples indicate that some of the whale meat that ends up on supermarket shelves around the country is mislabeled to obscure the fact that it comes from some of the most endangered species that Japan claims not to be hunting.

Japan's image has been further battered by allegations that it is essentially buying votes in the 85-member International Whaling Commission (IWC) via aid programs to island nations in the South Pacific and Caribbean. Curiously, landlocked Mali, Laos, and Mongolia are members of the IWC for reasons that are not obvious, but they vote with Japan.

Acknowledging the high stakes involved in generating considerable ill will by promoting such a low-priority industry, the Japanese government sought to mollify critics by agreeing in 2007 to refrain from hunting the humpback whale beloved of whale watchers for its graceful and enchanting frolicking. It hoped that this gesture would help in its efforts to normalize the IWC, making a concession that might facilitate a return to the founding principles of the organization. For Japan this means managing rather than banning whaling. From Tokyo's perspective, conservationists have hijacked the IWC in order to impose a lasting moratorium on all whaling.

Why is Japan pursuing a foreign policy that carries such heavy costs with so little benefit? How is the national interest advanced in advocating a resumption of commercial whaling? It is important to bear in mind that the pro-whaling lobby in Japan does not represent a consensus view among Japanese, many of who prefer whale watching to eating whale meat. However, the government does favor resumption of commercial whaling and is seeking to end the moratorium that is credited with saving whales from extinction. Given that Japanese whaling operations were at the forefront of exterminating whales pre-moratorium, Japan's eagerness to resume commercial whaling has understandably drawn special scrutiny from conservationists all over the world.

Japan's case rests on culture, national identity, science, principle, and propaganda. Japan's whaling advocates claim that whale consumption is a deeply embedded culinary tradition and assert that anti-whaling activists are guilty of cultural imperialism. To advocates, eating whale meat is an issue of national identity, an identity that is under siege on many fronts due to processes of globalization. They also argue that science is on their side, citing studies that show a strong recovery among certain whale species that would permit a resumption of managed whaling. There is also a sense that Japan has been double-crossed by anti-whaling nations in the IWC. Japan agreed to a moratorium on commercial whaling, not a permanent prohibition, and IWC rules specify that whaling policies should be driven by science. So there is a perception that anti-whaling nations have hijacked the IWC and made it into a vehicle to impose their views on conservation regardless of scientific findings that suggest the possibility of sustainable whaling.

The notion of Japan as victim, always caving into international demands in the interests of maintaining harmony, resonates powerfully among some Japanese. Few Japanese are ardently pro-whaling, but some of the more exasperated are anti-anti-whaling campaigns. Standing up for whaling is projected as a matter of principle, ethnic identity, national pride, and sound science. And this is where the propaganda machine kicks in, hammering home the idea that Japan is the target of double standards. Otherwise urbane and sophisticated Japanese can suddenly morph into sputtering nationalists over the subject of whaling, reflecting a wounded national pride and self-righteous indignation. In some sense, the whaling issue serves as a national pressure valve for a country that believes it is forced constantly to cave in to the demands of other nations. Drawing a line in the oceans helps salve wounded national pride and projects a more vigorous national identity.

How has whaling become a talismanic symbol of Japanese identity and a touchstone of nationalism? Whale meat consumption as a culinary pillar of Japan is an invented tradition. It was traditionally confined to coastal whaling communities and did not become nationally prevalent until after WWII. In the early post-WWII era, whale meat became a major source of protein featured in school lunches. There is thus a certain degree of nostalgia among Japan's aging baby boomers about whale meat, but it is only since the 1986 moratorium that it gained a gourmet cache. These days, however, few people want whale on the menu. *Nikkei*, a business newspaper, conducted a survey in 2008 reporting only 12 percent of Japanese in their 20s have ever eaten whale meat; while in 2006, Nippon Research Center reported that 95 percent of Japanese have never eaten, or very rarely eat, whale meat.[8] Low consumer interest in eating whale, however, has not deterred whaling advocates from trying to create demand for the growing stockpiles of "research" whales that nobody seems to want.

The Institute of Cetacean Research (ICR), funded by the government, is in the business of promoting whaling and also orchestrates a media campaign to convince Japanese that whaling is part of their national identity. They also try to spur whale consumption, but to little avail. The major problem for advocates of whaling is that Japanese consumers are not buying even heavily subsidized whale meat; one-third of the harvest of "scientific research" remains unsold. That is why whale meat prices have fallen dramatically in recent years, about 45 percent between 1994 and 2006, and some is even being processed into dog treats. The trend toward declining whale consumption preceded the 1986 moratorium on whaling and now very few Japanese are eating it even though it is reasonably priced and widely available in supermarkets. What this means is that the proceeds from selling the meat from research whaling do not cover the costs of conducting the whaling. It also means that Japan's stockpiles of whale meat kept in cold storage have increased from 1,500 tons in 1997 to more than 4,000 tons as of 2005.

In sum, Japan's taxpayers are paying more than they realize for this mind-boggling boondoggle, subsidizing research for whaling expeditions that draw international condemnation while funding a research institute that produces little research and also markets whale meat at tax-subsidized prices that most Japanese don't want. The Worldwide Fund for Nature weighed into this debate, reporting in 2009 that Japan has been wasting vast sums of taxpayers' money to sustain a loss-making industry with no prospects of viability without heavy subsidies.[9]

Science is inconvenient in exposing the dangers of whale consumption. There are extremely high concentrations of toxic chemicals in whale meat and pregnant women are warned not to eat any at all to prevent harm to the fetus. While the Fisheries Agency vigorously promotes whaling, Health Ministry officials focus on the harmful effects for everyone of even limited consumption. Advocates have also blamed declining fish stocks on too many hungry whales, the scientific equivalent of blaming ozone depletion on sheep flatulence. Fishery resources have been badly mismanaged, a problem of over-fishing that raises legitimate concerns over the viability of proposals to manage whale stocks. Science also does not require Japan to kill so many whales every year – Greenpeace Japan asserts that 10 whales would be enough to conduct legitimate research – and much of the data can be obtained by non-lethal means.

Whaling advocates argue that since Japan does not condemn Korean consumption of dogs, or Western slaughtering of pigs, cattle, and sheep, it is unfair to single out Japan for its whaling. Isn't this just cultural chauvinism? The problem with this logic is that among these animals only whales are an endangered species. Presumably, if the Chinese started marketing panda burgers, the international outcry would be just as vociferous and include many Japanese.

In the IWC, the vitriolic clash over whaling is intensifying and emotions on both sides continue to trump science and sensible compromises. The acrimonious impasse, and harpooning, look set to continue. In 2009 a compromise deal was put on the table that would have permitted Japanese coastal whaling in exchange for scaling down whaling in the Antarctic Ocean that Australia, with the support of some other anti-whaling nations, has designated as a whaling sanctuary. This is where most of the whaling takes place and where there have been clashes with eco-militants working to disrupt the hunt. However, this compromise is on hold as both sides are reluctant to make any concessions that might embolden their opponents.

In Japan's case, it is also clear that giving up access to distant whaling grounds in exchange for coastal rights would constitute a precedent that might lead to restrictions on its far more important global fisheries industry. Visiting Tsukiji, the national fish market in Tokyo, is to appreciate the scale of Japanese fish consumption and its huge dependence on international fishery resources. Few Japanese consume whale, but almost all are avid consumers of fish that is mostly sourced from distant fisheries. The near extinction of Atlantic blue-fin tuna, and belated efforts to protect this endangered species, are ringing alarm bells in a nation where sushi is a national staple and intrinsic to its culinary identity in ways that whale has never remotely approached. As sushi culture has spread around the world, it has become less sustainable and there are concerns in Japan that it may face restrictions. Agreeing to the whaling compromise is thus not only, or even mostly, about whaling.

The biggest blow to Japan's stance on whaling comes from a former spokesman for the Ministry of Foreign Affairs who frequently defended

Japan against its critics. Tomohiko Taniguchi retired and since 2008 has publically recanted, repudiating his nation's official policy on whaling. He argued that there is no strong cultural or economic justification for continued whaling and laments that it damages the nation's international image at great cost for almost no benefit. He favors abandoning the hunt in the Southern Ocean and focusing on coastal whaling.[10]

So when even the hired apologists are recanting and consumers are shunning whale meat, what drives Japan's pro-whaling policy? Certainly the global fisheries access issue is important, but other significant factors are budget politics and *amakudari*. The Ministry of Agriculture's Fisheries Agency has avidly and effectively cultivated a pro-whaling lobby of parliamentarians within the Diet.[11] These politicians reliably vote appropriations for whaling-related activities. Some are former bureaucrats with the Ministry of Agriculture and as "old boys" loyally vote in line with their institutional interests. Securing larger appropriations for the Fisheries Agency is dwarfed, however, by the importance of creating *amakudari* positions for retiring officials. The industry of promoting Japan's whaling industry offers lucrative sinecures for retiring Fisheries Agency officials. The Institute of Cetacean Research is typical of the type of quasi-government organizations created by related government agencies in order to provide such *amakudari* positions. Thus, the election of the DPJ may be bad news for whaling given its ban on *amakudari* and opposition to subsidies for quasi-government institutions that generate *amakudari* posts. However, during the DPJ's budget-cutting review process initiated in 2009 that targeted wasteful spending across the board, whaling subsidies never came under scrutiny.

The prospects of some eventual accommodation do not seem high given that the conflict within the IWC has degenerated into an acrimonious and intemperate food fight. Conceding coastal whaling rights is unappetizing to anti-whaling advocates, but the alternative of Japan following other whaling nations like Iceland and Norway out of the IWC is less appealing. It is a small cost to pay for IWC-sanctioned restrictions and better than leaving whaling up to the discretion of Japan's hardline whaling lobby. Given awareness that the highest concentrations of toxic substances are found in coastal whale populations can only help promote conservation and sensible public health restrictions. Whaling advocates have tried to promote whale consumption by reintroducing it to school lunch menus around the nation, but this would be more difficult if health officials' concerns about potentially detrimental consequences to children's health are publicized. Traditional whaling communities can be offered the right to engage in coastal whaling and make their own decisions about the wisdom of doing so given the health implications.[12]

Backing down and accepting scaled-down access to the Antarctic Ocean whaling grounds in exchange for coastal whaling would involve a great loss of institutional and personal face among Japanese involved. But not doing so galvanizes opponents and undermines Japan's standing with allies it cares about and needs such as the US, the UK, and Australia. Taking a green stand on whaling offers Japan a way to cut its diplomatic losses and would have few domestic repercussions, because it is only thanks to the government's PR machine that Japanese outside whaling communities care about the international moratorium against commercial whaling. By making concessions Japan can score diplomatic points and make a stronger case for its far more important fishery interests on a quid pro quo basis. Japan is at a crossroads as its aging whaling fleet is badly in need of modernization, meaning substantial new investment in expensive new ships with all the latest technologies. Given Japan's fiscal problems and need to cut spending, allocating budget for upgrading the national whaling capacity is a tough case to make. Similarly, the cost of whaling diplomacy doled out through ODA projects to compliant members of the IWC also faces tougher scrutiny.

Construction State

Japan has been called the construction state (*doken kokka*) because it spends so much on public works projects. Public works at its peak in the late 1990s employed some 10 percent of the workforce involving as many as 6 million workers.[13] A nation the size of California pours twice as much concrete a year as the US and public works spending during the 1990s was on a par with the Pentagon budget. Much of this construction, quite a lot of it unnecessary, is despoiling Japan's environment and scarring its natural beauty. Japan is notorious for its many roads and bridges to nowhere, empty airports, and mountains trussed in cement. More than 60 percent of its coastline is covered with large cement tetrapods that were installed to halt coastal erosion, but turn out to accelerate the problem. Many waterways have been straightened and given cemented banks while dams once planned based on fanciful projections for water consumption needs have been or are being built despite recognition they are unnecessary and are environmentally harmful. Many highways have little traffic because they were built according to the logic of porkbarrel projects and cash-and-carry politics rather than realistic projections. Public works projects have also encroached on wetlands crucial for migratory birds, and it is only due to vigorous grassroots campaigns that some have been saved from becoming garbage dumps, roadways, or parking lots. This enormous investment in public works projects has some merits in a nation prone to natural disasters including flooding, landslides, and earthquakes, but clearly there are many projects that go forward for no useful purpose that harm Japan's environment and wildlife.

During the early years of the twenty-first century under PM Junichiro Koizumi the government scaled back public works spending due to soaring budget deficits and mounting public debt. This downsizing of the construction state meant that fewer unnecessary projects proceeded. Soon after the DPJ came to power in 2009, the government gave momentum to this downsizing by scrapping some high-profile public work projects and trimming the 2010 public works budget by 18 percent. The public overwhelmingly approves such cuts in wasteful spending and welcomes the budget shift away from pouring concrete to badly needed social welfare programs.

The courts have also provided increasing support for opponents of senseless construction projects, issuing a ruling in 2009 canceling a coastal land reclamation and bridge project in the picturesque port of Tomonoura, arguing it would harm the scenery. This is the first time in Japan, but probably not the last, that natural beauty has trumped public works. Future visitors to this captivating UNESCO World Heritage site of traditional wooden houses overlooking the Seto Inland Sea have good reason to be grateful to the Hiroshima District Court judge for exercising common sense and rethinking priorities. Hayao Miyazaki, the acclaimed anime director, applauded the decision and noted that he stayed in Tomonoura while developing the story for his latest blockbuster, *Ponyo on the Cliff by the Sea* (2009). This film, as it happens, focuses on environmental issues, reminding heritage activists just how sweet poetic justice can be.

No doubt there will be many more unnecessary costly projects and the vested interests of the construction state will not meekly slink away, but the logic of shifting priorities, cutting waste, and greater environmental awareness is progressively undermining it.

Conclusion

There are areas where Japan does deserve kudos for its environmental achievements, but as we have seen there are still lots of challenges remaining. Urban pollution, especially air quality, has improved dramatically since I watched newsreels in the mid-1960s showing traffic police in the Ginza wearing gas masks. During the 1970s the government began to cope with the environmental consequences of rapid economic growth with considerable success. Minamata, once synonymous with toxic pollution and corporate negligence, is now a symbol of citizens struggling against the odds to secure justice and eventually prevailing against the powers that be. Whaling is a bleak reminder, however, that public officials are still willing to gamble with the public's health in pursuit of their own interests and don't seem to understand the lessons of Minamata.

Japan has weathered numerous mishaps in its nuclear power program, but has been lucky to avoid a major radioactive disaster on the scale of Chernobyl. Deregulation in the utilities industry and cost-cutting pressures raise legitimate concerns about future prospects given a track record of lax safety and the large number of aging plants. Kashiwazaki is a wake-up call to reexamine design assumptions and calls into question the safety of nuclear power plants in a country with high seismic risk. Rokkasho represents a continuation of Japan's commitment to costly and risky plutonium technology and is destined to be the main dumping ground for Japan's rapidly accumulating high-risk nuclear waste. Safeguarding this repository will be a costly and dangerous burden on several more generations of Japanese into the distant future.

The opportunity costs of focusing on nuclear energy are high as renewable energy sources are starved of support. The reliance on market mechanisms and technological fixes to global warming means that Japan has largely been ignoring the policies that have worked well in Europe where renewable energy sources are growing rapidly and becoming critically important. The one bright spot in renewables in Japan is household adoption of solar panels, something that is spreading because of government subsidies. So it is clear that pro-renewable energy policies can work.

Japan's leadership on the environment depends on a political will that was absent under the LDP. The DPJ-led government appears committed to reducing CO_2 emissions and playing a more responsible role on the environment by pursuing sustainable energy and growth strategies. This is the legacy it can bequeath to future generations of Japanese. But, as Mutsuyoshi Nishimura, Japan's Ambassador for Global Environmental Affairs from 2005 to 2007, argues, the government needs to act more decisively:

> Japan has to shift from the prevailing piecemeal legislation to comprehensive and economy-wide legislation, from enabling and inducing legislation to binding legislation. Another emerging consensus is that the most cost-effective way to abate national emissions is to put a price on carbon and implement an emissions trading system. The EU is doing so and the US is seeking to establish such a system.[14]

Given the imperatives and consequences of global warming, expectations for Japan's leadership and vision run high. Alas, the next chapter examining Japan's immigration policies suggests that political leadership and vision are in short supply.

Chapter 9

Immigration

The rapid increase in the number of immigrants to Japan during the Heisei era has raised anxieties among Japanese about the future of their country, national identity, and how to manage the influx. There is a muted public discourse about this politically sensitive subject against the backdrop of a rapidly aging society and a declining workforce tasked with supporting soaring outlays for retirees' pensions and medical care. This problem is looming as the workforce is projected to decline from about 65 million in 2009 to 55 million in 2030.

There are thus pragmatic reasons for accommodating more immigrants on more favorable terms battling with deep-seated concerns about the implications of a larger non-Japanese population. As in other countries grappling with immigration, xenophobia and prejudice are shaping the debate and complicating policy deliberations. In the early twenty-first century, immigrants in Japan, as elsewhere, are feeling less welcome even as their presence has become more indispensable. Precisely because immigration is such a controversial issue, the government has tackled reform in an *ad hoc*, piecemeal fashion. Several proposals for comprehensive reforms have been tabled and then shelved. Instead, by tinkering at the margins, and not promoting bold, headline-grabbing proposals that would become easy political targets, policy-makers are facilitating incremental increases in immigration. This judicious, step-by-step approach favored by the bureaucracy makes sense in terms of prevailing political realities and public attitudes opposed to immigration, but the absence of a comprehensive approach is also exacting a toll on the interests of immigrants and Japanese society. In short, the rights of immigrants are not well protected and the scale of immigration is too small and slow to meet the needs of the nation.

Japan has relatively few non-Japanese residents, but the numbers in Japan doubled between 1990 and 2008 from 1.1 million to 2.2 million, and they constitute 1.74 percent of the population. While this surge in the non-Japanese population has drawn some shrill commentary in Japan, the percentage remains quite low compared to the UK (5.8 percent), Germany (8.2 percent), and Spain (10.3 percent). The emergence of Japan as a major global economy, labor shortages, and the development of transnational networks (including brokers) all facilitated a surge in foreign migrant workers arriving in Japan from the late 1980s. This rapid increase is largely in urban areas and has been most marked among Chinese and Brazilian immigrants. In the non-Japanese community, there are some 590,000 Japan-born ethnic Koreans, 655,000 Chinese, and 312,000 *nikkeijin* (overseas-born ethnic Japanese from South America). In addition, the number of visa overstayers, mostly from other Asian countries such as Korea, China, the Philippines, Thailand, Malaysia, and Indonesia, grew from 100,000 in 1990 to nearly 200,000 in 1993, prompting a government crackdown following revisions to the Immigration Control and Refugee Recognition Act in 2004. The Ministry of Justice reported 150,000 migrants remaining in Japan beyond the validity of their visas as of 2008.

Heisei era migrants have been recruited because of labor shortages, including unskilled and skilled workers. Their presence is not entirely welcome despite their crucial contributions. It is hard to imagine Japan functioning without its foreign workers, but that doesn't mean this reality is widely acknowledged or appreciated. In the early 1990s there were once 33,000 Iranians in Japan, mostly engaged as construction workers, until most were abruptly sent home in 1992 after the government decided to revoke a visa exemption agreement. The same fate awaited the disposable foreign workers who helped build the facilities for the 1998 Nagano Olympics.

Japan is certainly not as diverse as Europe and the US, but it has become more diverse and in some respects is a multi-ethnic society in denial. Japan as a mono-ethnic, homogeneous nation persists in the collective imagination even if there are jarring signs of change and stealthy transformation. It is telling that the number of international marriages is on the rise, accounting for 6.5 percent of the total in 2006, and one out of 30 babies born in Japan has at least one foreign parent.

Immigration is a touchy issue and a divisive topic that eludes consensus. Current debate about labor migration to Japan focuses on what kind of workers should be allowed in – i.e. skilled workers only or also unskilled workers, how many and from where, and how long they should be allowed to stay and under what conditions.[1] This discourse is also shaped by widespread perceptions that foreigners often resort to crime, although national crime statistics show that in fact foreigners do not commit crimes disproportionate to their numbers and most of their offenses involve visa violations.

Advocates of opening the doors point to Japan's population decline, impending labor shortages, and the need for more taxpayers to keep the national medical and pension schemes solvent. Opponents insist on preserving the current degree of homogeneity and warn against the pitfalls of accommodating large resident foreign communities. These are not only crazed nativists trying to haul up the drawbridges; there is concern that until Japan can put in place laws and regulations that protect the human rights of migrant workers, it should not extend them the welcome mat. The difficult experience of ethnic Koreans born and raised in Japan, commonly known as the *zainichi*, is instructive.

Zainichi

The *zainichi* community of long-term ethnic Korean permanent residents in Japan constitutes the nation's largest minority, one that has not fared that well. The Koreans came to Japan during the wartime years, 1931–45, looking for work or on a coerced basis. With the dissolution of the Japanese empire in 1945 they were stripped of Japanese nationality, but many stayed and raised families here while carrying either South or North Korean passports. Their children and grandchildren may have attended Korean schools in Japan (many don't), but they are fluent in Japanese, culturally socialized, and virtually indistinguishable from Japanese. However, even such assimilated Japan-born "foreigners" face discrimination and tend to have lower levels of educational attainment and income. Facing discrimination in Japanese firms, many have established their own businesses while others have become celebrities, although often hiding their ethnic background. In addition, many yakuza are recruited from the *zainichi* community, reflecting the limited opportunities open to them.

As of 2008, the Immigration Bureau reports that there were 589,239 registered Korean residents in Japan, down from a peak of 688,144 in 1992. This figure does not include the 284,840 Koreans who have opted to become naturalized Japanese citizens. There are nearly 60 Korean schools across Japan, once subsidized by Pyongyang, but now mostly funded through public subsidies and Chongryon, a pro-North-Korean organization in

Japan. Changes in Japanese tax laws, harassment targeting students wearing the distinctive uniforms, and the decision by many *zainichi* to send their children to public schools are creating financial difficulties for many of these schools and their future appears bleak. About 65 percent of *zainichi* are affiliated with Mindan, the pro-South-Korean organization in Japan. Divided ideologically, the two organizations are united in their zeal to sustain a strong sense of Korean identity and oppose assimilation and naturalization.

Koreans in Japan have fragmented identities, living on the margins in Japan and viewed as foreigners in Korea. In recent years there has been an increase in the numbers of Koreans becoming naturalized citizens, some 10,000 a year, due to the advantages this confers, the barriers it lowers, and the inescapable reality for some of having a less resolutely Korean identity rooted in the nation state; identity as a Korean is not, for increasing numbers of young *zainichi*, a matter of passports. There are some 8,000 marriages annually between *zainichi* and Japanese (6,000 with Japanese men and 2,000 with Japanese women); their children automatically gain Japanese citizenship under a 1985 law. Most naturalization occurs at time of marriage or employment, suggesting it is mostly a pragmatic decision, but the implications for the *zainichi* community are ominous as younger generations develop more flexible identity strategies that facilitate their assimilation.

Another reason for *zainichi* to naturalize is because Japan has become decidedly less hospitable to ethnic Koreans despite the incredible boom in Korean popular culture in Japan that was sparked by the joint hosting of the World Cup soccer tournament in 2002 and a massively popular Korean television drama, "Winter Sonata," aired in Japan. This anti-Korean backlash is due to a series of missile tests by North Korea, its nuclear weapons program, and frenzied media coverage of Japanese nationals' abductions by North Korean agents. This has generated a virulent anti-North-Korean groundswell, whipped up by politicians and the media, one that generates pressure on *zainichi* to blend in.

Although there is greater momentum towards naturalization and assimilation, as one *zainichi* found out, assimilation is in the eye of the beholder. In 2005 the 15-justice Grand Bench of the Supreme Court ruled in favor of Tokyo Metropolitan Government (TMG) regulations that exclude foreigners from management-level positions in the civil service, overturning a 1998 high court ruling. The top court upheld the TMG's decision to bar a second-generation *zainichi* from taking an exam that would have qualified her for promotion to a public sector management position. At the time, Chong Hyang Gyun was a public health nurse and there was no possibility that she would be promoted to a national security-sensitive position, but 13 of the justices argued it is reasonable to exclude non-Japanese entirely from the exercise of public authority. The two dissenting justices argued that the ban from all civil service managerial positions based on nationality was not rational.

In essence the TMG is employing *zainichi*, but on the condition they don't expect equal treatment or merit-based promotions. The senior civil service is, like some dodgy nightclubs and baths, Japanese only.[2] The plaintiff, whose mother is Japanese, had argued that this restriction contravenes the constitutional guarantees of equality and freedom of individuals to choose their occupation, but the justices ruled otherwise. *Zainichi* are accorded "special permanent resident" status in recognition of their anomalous circumstances as people born in Japan, but not accorded citizenship unless they choose naturalization. Like other foreigners, *zainichi* are required to carry a foreigner's identification card. The court ruled that TMG is within its rights to bar non-citizens from the upper echelons of the civil service, but from a public relations perspective it did not help that Tokyo Governor Shintaro Ishihara, a conservative nationalist, has made discriminatory and inflammatory remarks about *zainichi*. Many advocates say that loosening immigration restriction is a matter of time as Japan slowly makes a pragmatic accommodation to the growing need for more workers, but the Supreme Court has set a precedent allowing significant restrictions.

Nikkeijin

In 2009, while many *nikkeijin* were losing their jobs and in some cases their housing due to the economic crisis, the Japanese government unveiled a controversial initiative that entailed the government paying each unemployed *nikkeijin* worker a one-time JPY300,000 payment to cover airfare, and JPY200,000 for each dependent, to return home.[3] Initially the government stipulated that anyone accepting the exit bonus would not be able to return to Japan and retain the special working visa status given to *nikkeijin*, rendering it a one-way ticket home. Spain, grappling with even more severe unemployment problems, adopted a similar initiative in 2009, paying unemployment benefits in a lump sum to departees, but exiting migrants always had the option of returning, circumstances permitting, after three years. In the face of widespread denunciation of its plan within Japan and the international media, the Japanese government backtracked, explaining that after three years the *nikkeijin* would be allowed to return. However, since they will have to reapply for the long-term resident visa that has allowed them to work without restriction, it remains to be seen how this policy will work in practice. There are signs that the government will make re-entry tougher for them.

Given bleak job prospects for *nikkeijin* in Japan, mostly unskilled workers, many of whom lack sufficient language skills to enter job training programs or apply for other jobs, the government defended its policy as one designed to promote their welfare while critics asserted that Japan is discarding these unskilled workers because they are no longer needed and have never fit in. Along with the exit bonuses the government also announced language training programs for up to 5,000 *nikkeijin* aimed at facilitating assimilation for those who remain, a belated but inadequate recognition that the government failed the migrants by its indifference, not doing anything to facilitate their social integration since they began arriving in 1990. Unlike in Germany where the government offers immigrants 900 hours of subsidized language and social integration training, the Japanese government has not offered similar programs for the *nikkeijin*, or any other foreigners for that matter. This pennywise approach based on the illusory advantages of shared ancestry tilted the odds against the *nikkeijin* fitting in and becoming accepted. The absence of language skills has kept many *nikkeijin* on the margins of society and trapped them into low-end assembly jobs with few opportunities for training or advancement.

As of 2009, Brazilians account for 317,000 of the estimated 370,000 *nikkeijin* residing in Japan, with Peruvians constituting the next largest group.[4] Most work in manufacturing, frequently in car parts production. This made *nikkeijin* vulnerable to the massive layoffs in the manufacturing sector during 2008–9, especially as the hard-hit automobile industry slashed orders from the subcontractors where many *nikkeijin* were employed. Suddenly many were out of work, local Brazilian schools and other services closed, and unlike in recent downturns, few expected a rebound soon enough to make waiting it out an option. For those fortunate enough to receive unemployment insurance, benefits expire within a year. As a result, even before the government announced its exit bonus plan, many laid-off workers were leaving, sometimes with support from their embassy.

Japan has long maintained a strict immigration policy barring unskilled labor, but in 1990, facing labor shortages, the government revised the immigration law and established a side door that maintained the ban in principle while enabling unskilled overseas ethnic Japanese workers to obtain work visas on the strength of their ancestral blood ties.[5] The law allowed anyone whose parent or grandparent was a Japanese citizen to apply for a long-term resident visa. This visa allowed them to stay for three years and engage in any work, including unskilled jobs, and could be renewed indefinitely provided they kept a clean record. This *nikkeijin* exception was based on what is now regarded as an erroneous assumption that Japanese blood would trump Latin American culture. The government knew companies needed more workers doing undesirable jobs Japanese avoided because of low pay, but also did not want to deal with the problems that they expected from migrant workers. The solution was in the DNA; endowed with Japanese roots, faces and names, *nikkeijin* were seen to have what it takes to fit into a proudly insular society that is closed to outsiders, and would adapt and assimilate seamlessly to working and living in Japan. These high expectations were unrealistic and proved elusive.

Many *nikkeijin* jumped at the opportunity for economic reasons, knowing they could make better wages in Japan. The dramatic influx from 4,000 *nikkeijin* in 1988 to 370,000 two decades on took Japanese small manufacturing towns by surprise. *Nikkeijin* are clustered in 15 towns and cities where local authorities were not well prepared for the new residents, mostly bachelors at the outset, who were seen as temporary guest workers. Local residents also encountered difficulties with their new neighbors and their more exuberant lifestyle. Arriving "home," proud of their heritage, many *nikkeijin* quickly became disillusioned with life in Japan, unable to reconcile their unrealistically high expectations with the realities that awaited them. Dingy towns, cramped living quarters, shabby factories, and a society lacking a sociable zest for good living and fun fueled disappointment. They found the Japanese to be cold, unfriendly, and unreceptive, making the transition all the more difficult.

Many of the *nikkeijin* were employed indirectly through brokers, frequently as contract or temporary workers, and were paid at prevailing hourly wage rates. This meant that in practice the *nikkeijin* were paid less than Japanese counterparts performing the same jobs because they did not receive fringe benefits or bonuses that in many cases are equivalent to five months of wages. Many were also working without medical or unemployment insurance and in some cases brokers received a percentage of their salaries.[6]

Hard as it is, the money is relatively good, so there has been a peripatetic movement back and forth between Brazil and Japan as many migrants work a few years in Japan, return home after a few years with their savings, and then resume their lives as migrant workers. However, more *nikkeijin* began to put down roots in Japan, marrying and raising families and in some cases becoming permanent residents. What initially involved mostly single men morphed into more permanent, family-centered communities with different needs and goals. *Nikkeijin* began staying longer because they had families to take care of and the opportunities in Japan were better than back home. Moreover, due to the prolonged recession, good jobs became scarce and it became more difficult to work overtime and accumulate enough savings to return home. The total number of permanent residents, those foreigners allowed to stay indefinitely, increased 28 percent from 657,605 in 2000 to 911,362 in 2008, while the number of Brazilian permanent residents jumped more than tenfold from 9,062 to 94,400 in the same period. Other *nikkeijin* married Japanese and, as of 2002, 34 percent of Brazilians resident in Japan held a spouse visa.[7] Children born in Japan automatically get citizenship if one parent is Japanese.

Nikkeijin children present significant challenges to small local school boards because of their lack of language skills, but also because as many as one-quarter do not attend any school at all. The government made no provision for teaching Japanese as a foreign language to *nikkeijin* students, meaning they got lost in class, and because school attendance is not mandatory, many dropped out. As a result they lost their chance to gain the know-how and skills needed to give them social mobility. Government indifference, thus, has created pockets of unemployable young people, a recipe for social problems. Some communities have established Brazilian schools, but tuition is relatively expensive and until 2009 these schools did not receive government assistance or funding. Local school boards with limited resources have also responded as best they could in trying to cater to *nikkeijin* needs, offering supplementary language instruction and tutoring, with some success. The high rate of truancy, however, combined with social marginalization has led to problems of juvenile delinquency, reinforcing negative Japanese stereotypes about foreigners' propensity for crime.

Nikkeijin suffer from fragmented identities that render social integration difficult.[8] At home they are an admired ethnic group while in Japan they are stigmatized for being more Brazilian than Japanese. Problematically, because the *nikkeijin* appeared to be Japanese, local people and employers had unrealistic expectations that they would act accordingly. But they were not hardwired to function in Japanese society, and thus many encountered discrimination for not living up to expectations and for acting like the foreigners they were.

Chinese Migrants

Most of the 655,000 Chinese-born people residing in Japan as of 2008 came after the mid-1980s, making them the fastest-growing ethnic community. Between 1990 and 2005, 58,879 Chinese became Japanese citizens, while as of 2008 there were 128,501 Chinese permanent residents, most gaining this status since 2000. Significantly, Chinese are the largest number among foreigners married to Japanese and this trend is increasing. In 2005, over 50,000 Chinese residents in Japan held spouse visas and an additional 35,000 had dependent visas.

Compared to *nikkeijin*, Chinese in Japan tend to have strong language skills and fewer problems functioning in society and in the workplace, but as with other foreigners they do face discrimination. Typically, these migrants start by working at Japanese firms, but leave to start up their own ventures because they find the rules and regimen at Japanese firms oppressive and depressing. In addition, Chinese women confront gender barriers in Japanese companies and so choose other opportunities that don't constrain their careers. Chinese migrants also realize they can't ever really assimilate and don't want to anyway. Instead, they identify and exploit profitable niches as transnational entrepreneurs, tapping into China's economic boom.[9]

Since 2006, China has overtaken the US as Japan's leading trading partner and the China trade has been a major source of growth in the Japanese economy. Bilingual, culturally adept, and armed with contacts on both sides of the East China Sea, Chinese migrants play a key part in building business networks and relationships that are the basis for surging economic ties. They are building bridges in the twenty-first century that help offset the highly contentious disputes over history and territory that have defined and influenced bilateral relations since the late nineteenth century.

More than 80,000 Chinese are studying in Japanese universities, many courtesy of Japanese government scholarships, accounting for some two-thirds of Japan's foreign student population. During the mid-1980s Chinese authorities eased restrictions, making it easier for students to study abroad, an attractive option given the sad state of Chinese universities at that time. Meanwhile, Prime Minister Nakasone (1982–7) promoted internationalization of Japan by setting a goal of attracting 100,000 foreign students by the end of the twentieth century. To this end, the government relaxed procedures and criteria for student visas in 1984 and established scholarship programs. From 1984 to 2005, more than 250,000 Chinese language and university students came to Japan.

Upon graduation many Chinese start their careers at Japanese companies. This influx of white-collar, highly educated migrant Chinese is slowly prompting a reassessment of xenophobic attitudes towards foreigners, at least within government policy-making circles and among human resource managers if not the public at large. Prejudice against Chinese in Japan, however, remains widespread and the government and media fan concerns about their involvement in crime.[10]

Japanese remain dubious about foreigners in general and, in opinion surveys conducted in 2005 and 2006, two-thirds admitted having negative feelings towards China, the highest percentage in two decades and the highest anti-Chinese prejudice in all of Asia.[11] Chinese regularly report housing discrimination and are often stopped for identification checks by police. The media has highlighted the role of Chinese gangs in a spate of robberies, advertising promotes locks that "even Chinese can't pick," while high-profile murders committed by Chinese in Japan cast a shadow over the expatriate community.

There are also reports of widespread abuses involving Chinese who come to Japan under the auspices of a 1993 practical training program that initially allowed three-year working stints and now up to five years.[12] Three-quarters of "trainees" come from China. This is essentially a program aimed at providing cheap, unskilled labor to Japanese small and medium companies where there is little training or technology transfer. Nearly 93,000 trainees came in 2006 alone, including 62,000 Chinese, double the number in 1995, but they are not usually acquiring useful technical skills, and they earn extremely low wages in the range of JPY65,000 a month. This means they have little chance of returning home with either the fruits of technology transfer or significant savings. Given that many of these workers take out loans from job brokers at home, the low pay means they can't pay off their debts when they return.

The Japan International Training Cooperation Organization (JITCO), an organization supported by five government ministries, has been criticized for lax supervision and failing to protect trainees from widespread abuses. The reported abuses included recruiting workers under false premises, forcing them to work excessive hours without overtime pay, withholding pay or underpayment, inflating expenses for room, board, and utilities charged against their wages, seizure of passports, and sexual harassment.

What began as a promising development initiative has become an embarrassment for the government. There have been several lawsuits filed by workers that ensure maximum publicity for what is wrong with JITCO and the foreign trainee program, but it continues to operate while providing plum *amakudari* positions to retiring bureaucrats.

Foreign Caregivers

Japan faces a serious shortage of nurses and caregivers as the number of elderly requiring nursing care is projected to total 7.8 million in FY2025–6, a 1.7-fold increase from FY2006–7. The MHLW calculates that Japan will need an additional 400,000 to 600,000 caregivers and nurses by 2014.[13] The government is partially responsible for the shortage having reduced subsidies to elderly care facilities twice since 2003, causing a decline in already low salaries for caregivers. The annual turnover rate for caregivers is more than 20 percent, and some 500,000 Japanese with licenses have given up working in the field.

Japan's *ad hoc* approach to immigration reform is evident in Japan's Economic Partnership Agreements (EPAs) with the Philippines and Indonesia. These agreements embody the tinkering at the margins approach to the immigration issue, lacking any long-term vision while neglecting the interests of Japan and the migrant workers. These EPAs include provision for accepting 1,000 nurses and caregivers from each country over a two-year period to work in Japan for three to four years, but also set the bar very high for them to remain working in Japan beyond the trial period. These EPAs represent compromises hammered out between various ministries in Japan and with the partner nations to address Japan's massive staffing shortages for elderly care, but stop short of doing enough to alleviate the problem.

Indonesians began arriving in 2008 and Filipinos in 2009. The Japan International Corporation of Welfare Services is coordinating the program. Japan has agreed to accept up to 400 Indonesian nurses and 600 caregivers in 2008 and 2009 as "candidates" for government certification if they pass qualifying exams.[14] In the event, only 104 Indonesian nurses and 101 caregivers, about two-thirds women, began work in 2008, reflecting problems of recruiting suitable candidates. Of the male candidates who passed screening tests, 66 were dropped because they could not secure contracts as male nurses are not in high demand in Japan. In addition, there has been lukewarm interest because of concerns that the time and energy involved in becoming a candidate are not worth it given the high probability candidates will not pass qualifying exams and will be forced to return home after a few years. In 2009, the incoming numbers were also well below target because there is a shortage of jobs at hospitals and care facilities amidst the economic crisis.

Indonesian nurses must have two years' experience while caregivers are required to be graduates of institutions of higher learning or nursing school graduates certified by the Indonesian government. Candidates are given six months' Japanese language and vocational training and then work at hospitals and elderly care institutions. They receive the same salaries as Japanese staff and also get additional living assistance. Nurses are allowed to stay three years before taking national examinations, with three chances to pass, while caregivers have four years and only one chance to pass. Those who pass the exams will be given three-year visas and can renew these a maximum of three times. Given that the pass rate of Japanese is only 50 percent on these exams, there are concerns that the Indonesians and Filipinos will not develop the requisite language skills fast enough to pass. It is not encouraging that none of the Indonesian nurses who took the exam in 2009 passed, prompting the government to offer subsidized supplemental language instruction.

After 5 years of difficult negotiations, the initial 2009 target from the Philippines was 200 Filipino nurses and 300 caregivers, but only a total of 358 arrived, apparently reflecting the economic crisis in Japan and fewer than expected contract offers. Filipino caregivers must have graduated from a four-year vocational course (or nursing program) and be certified, while nurses are required to have three years of prior experience. Under the terms of the agreement, Filipinos who pass their licensing exams in Japan will be allowed to remain in Japan to practice their professions on an unlimited basis.

The problem is that this program is designed to fail and offers no immediate relief to the existing acute shortages of nurses and caregivers in Japan and also no long-term solution. Given Japan's rapidly graying population and rising demand for elderly care services, the EPA model suggests the government does not yet have an appropriate sense of urgency or pragmatism. Sending the nurses and caregivers home if they fail their exams is also a tremendous waste of investment by the employers in the workers, estimated at JPY10 million each over the term of the visas. This is one of the reasons that employers have not extended as many contract offers as had been expected. The program also underutilizes the workers, most of whom are overqualified to perform tasks that are normally the work of hospital orderlies.

Institutions and patients' families remain leery of hiring foreign nurses and caregivers because of concerns about language barriers that might compromise safety and care standards. Clearly, staffing shortages are one of the major risks to patients, and turnover especially in elderly care is very high because of low wages and often unpleasant working conditions. The media has tried to address concerns about maintaining standards by emphasizing that much of what caregiving entails depends on the attitude and kindness of the caregiver, not their aptitude on standardized exams. However, the Japanese Nursing Association and the Association of Certified Caregivers emphasize the threat to standards of service and express concerns that an influx of foreign labor will depress already low wages in this sector. They call on the government to improve working conditions to lower turnover, attract more Japanese applicants, and lure back those who have quit.

There is high demand for Filipino nurses around the world and they express a preference for English-speaking countries; about 18,000 Filipino nurses and caregivers go overseas every year, with the US and Canada as top destinations. NHK broadcast a special about this topic and few of the Filipino participants interviewed expressed a desire to work in Japan.[15] In other countries they are highly sought after and can start work and be earning money immediately, whereas in Japan they have 6 months of language instruction before they start earning wages. In addition, in other countries they are welcome to stay and many prefer Canada because it facilitates naturalization of migrant workers rather than sending them home if they fail difficult certification exams.

Opening the door to foreign nurses and caregivers within the broad framework of an EPA is smart politics. Opposing vested interests are trumped by the ostensibly larger national interests at stake and unable to block labor migration because it is depicted as an unavoidable consequence of negotiations and compromise. Behind the scenes there were pitched bureaucratic battles among relevant ministries ever vigilant about their turf and prerogatives, but a scaled-down and less than optimum plan survived the process and now the nose of the camel is inside the tent. This is a pilot program and, in light of the highly politicized nature of labor migration, a small step that may help break down barriers and provide the foundation for establishing a program better designed to meet the needs of Japanese for good elderly care and improving conditions for the foreign caregivers. Once such a program starts, and sending and receiving institutions are established, bureaucratic inertia favors its continuation.

Rethinking Immigration: A Step Too Far

It is but a drop in the ocean. A single drop that reveals much about how difficult it is for political and economic actors to revise Japan's immigration policy.[16]

During the Heisei era there has been a vibrant public discourse about immigration, with various proposals and counter-proposals but little action or consensus. In the meantime, Japan has adopted a piecemeal approach to immigration policy, mostly tinkering at the margins. As the numbers of immigrants increase, however, there is more urgency to the debate and pressure to revise policies to better manage the foreigners already here and the continuing influx. The *ad hoc* approach has its virtues because it evades political battles, but the absence of a comprehensive overhaul of existing immigration policy means that migrants remain vulnerable and have little recourse when subject to arbitrary decisions. For example, the sudden decision to oust tens of thousands of Iranians after tolerating their presence as illegal construction workers for a few years in the early 1990s was possible because Japan has very strict policies prohibiting unskilled workers, at least when they are enforced. So immigration officials can look the other way when it is convenient to do so and swoop down when the demand for such workers declines. What is often missing from the debate is recognition that Japan is already dependent on foreign workers in many job categories ranging from agriculture and services to manufacturing and IT engineers. Fortress Japan pulling up the drawbridges has a certain appeal, but is not viable and would have adverse consequences for Japanese society.

While promoting the rights and social integration of immigrants has low priority, there is considerable enthusiasm for enhanced monitoring of foreigners. The events of 9/11 provided an opportunity for the Japanese government to enact this long-standing agenda under the guise of cooperating in the war on terror. Bowing to substantial domestic and international pressure, the government abandoned fingerprinting of *zainichi* in 1993 and all other non-Japanese in 2000. However, with the launching of biometric controls at airports around the country in November 2007 requiring the fingerprinting and photographing of all non-Japanese residents and tourists, the government gained considerably enhanced powers of monitoring. The fight against terror has led countries around the world, including Japan, to tighten controls on travelers and visas. The war on terror has also provided political cover in Japan for more intrusive surveillance and monitoring of non-Japanese.

In 2009 the Diet passed legislation overhauling foreign residency rules and concentrating power of monitoring foreigners in the Justice Ministry's Immigration Bureau. The new legislation mandates residential cards (*zairyu*) for non-Japanese and steep fines if they are found not carrying a card. In addition, failure to report changes in personal information can lead to revocation of residential status. This information is stored on the national computer network called Juki Net, an initiative launched in 2002 that centralizes control over all residents' information. In addition, the Ministry of Justice took over control of issuing *gaijin* (foreigner) cards from local government offices. The government crackdown on visa overstayers was being undermined from within as local officials were issuing alien registration cards and providing access to public services to those without proper visas on compassionate grounds. Local officials would issue these crucial documents to undocumented foreigners with "no residential status" typed on them. Now, by taking this discretionary power away from local government officials, the Ministry of Justice controls both the issuing of visas and residence registration, giving it more power and information to keep tabs on foreign residents and enabling it to crack down more effectively on illegal aliens.

The new law also gives the government discretion over revoking spouse visas if there are good reasons to assume that the marriage was a fraud aimed at securing a visa. Somewhat cryptically, and sending shockwaves through the spouse visa holding community, the justice minister now has the power to cancel a spouse visa for those who over a 6-month period fail to conduct without a legitimate reason "activities spouses normally do." What is legitimate and normal is left unspecified, sparking greater interest among foreigners in the married lives of Japanese couples and any applicable bureaucratic standards.

Violators of the new law not granted special permission to stay are subject to detention and deportation, raising concerns about how the government plans to deal with asylum seekers, many of whom are visa overstayers. Thus, when it comes to policing non-Japanese and tightening monitoring of immigration, there is a sense of urgency and purpose that translates into government action. If only immigration was solely a matter of better policing.

The UN helps put the immigration issue in perspective, highlighting the number of migrants Japan needs under various scenarios. According to the UN Population Division:

If Japan wishes to keep the size of its population at the level attained in the year 2005, the country would need 17 million net immigrants up to the year 2050, or an average of 381,000 immigrants per year between 2005 and 2050. By 2050, the immigrants and their descendants would total 22.5 million and comprise 17.7 per cent of the total population of the country. In order to keep the size of the working-age population constant at the 1995 level of 87.2 million, Japan would need 33.5 million immigrants from 1995 through 2050. This means an average of 609,000 immigrants are needed per year during this period. Under this scenario, the population of the country is projected to be 150.7 million by 2050. The number of post-1995 immigrants and their descendants would be 46 million, accounting for 30 per cent of the total population in 2050.[17]

Of course these figures are way beyond what anyone in a position to decide in Japan is talking about or remotely considering, but the scale of the projections casts a disquieting shadow over the debate.

The scope of immigration policy discourse appears more like rearranging the deckchairs on the *Titanic* than a serious and realistic attempt to grapple with Japan's demographic time bomb. The problem is the yawning gap between what is politically realistic and what is essential. People continue to seek refuge in the reassuring scenario of resolving the crisis through more effective use of robots, women, and elderly workers even though this would have little more than a palliative impact. As long as people and leaders put their hopes in such pipedreams, real progress on addressing the various issues of immigration and the demographic time bomb will remain elusive. Postponing action on immigration is a policy that is slowly limiting the range of options and gradually ensuring economic stagnation, a choice that seemingly gambles on pulling a technological rabbit out of the national hat.

Not everyone, however, is burying their heads in the sand. In 2008 a group of LDP lawmakers led by former LDP Secretary General Hidenao Nakagawa submitted a proposal with the backing of 80 colleagues for the admission of up to 10 million foreigners by 2050 and on an annual basis 1,000 asylum seekers and others needing protection on humanitarian grounds. This proposal also includes a target of 1 million foreign students by 2025, 10 times the total PM Nakasone proposed in 1985. This proposal would pave the way for Japan to increase its foreign residents to some 10 percent of the total population, currently projected at about 90 million by 2050 compared to 127 million as of 2009. The lawmakers are trying to overhaul immigration policy in order to address the nation's low birthrate, rapid aging, and depopulation. In order to become an immigrant state, the authors advocate creating something they call a "multiracial symbiotic society" that provides for education and training programs aimed at helping migrants develop language skills and otherwise facilitate social integration. Reflecting the delicate politics of the issue, a provision that would have automatically granted citizenship after 10 years' residence was withdrawn from the final draft.

A 2006 proposal by LDP lawmaker Taro Kono, who served as Vice-Minister of Justice, suggested a lower ceiling for numbers of immigrants, stipulating a 3 percent maximum of the total population. Kono believes the special ancestral visas for the *nikkeijin* are a mistake that should be discontinued, instead favoring immigrants with needed skills and qualifications. Interestingly, rather than portraying immigration as a threat, Kono emphasizes the need to support and protect existing resident foreigners and migrant workers, calling for equal pay and enrollment in social insurance programs. The plan also calls for mandatory education for children and developing language skills as a condition of continued employment, indicating the government is learning from its mistakes with the *nikkeijin*. Reflecting concerns about the growing presence of foreigners, the plan also calls for more extensive monitoring of their activities.

Naturally, like all similar sweeping proposals floated over the past 20 years, the Nakagawa and Kono proposals have been shelved. However, they do mark significant improvements on past proposals and suggest that the terms of the debate have shifted towards a more pragmatic and humanitarian accommodation that balances the interests of Japan and its immigrants. Whereas the government previously emphasized more effective mobilization of elderly workers, retirees, and women to solve expected labor shortages without recourse to immigration, there seems to be guarded recognition that this will be insufficient. Knowing this and acting on this recognition, however, remains a step too far.

Nippon Keidanren (Japanese Business Federation) has also long supported increased immigration to address labor shortages and population decline to revitalize society, but with strict time limits on length of stay.[18] Its proposal also excludes unskilled workers and makes no provision for permanent residency or a citizenship track for migrants. There is thus a desire to tap the potential of foreign workers, but an aversion to assuming the burdens and risks of a permanent foreign community. For most Japanese, this approach is the least threatening and one they can live with even if it does overlook the needs of the growing non-Japanese resident community that is already here.

As former Prime Minister Junichiro Koizumi stated in 2005: "If [foreign labor] exceeds a certain level, it is bound to cause a clash. It is necessary to consider measures to prevent it and then admit foreign workers as necessary. Just because there is a labor shortage does not mean we should readily allow [foreign workers] to come in." He expresses a widespread sentiment that if there is a price to be paid for not allowing sufficient immigration, so be it.

The DPJ has plans to revise the Immigration Control and Refugee Recognition Law by introducing a points system for skilled workers similar to those operating in Canada and the United Kingdom. The aim is to attract highly skilled workers and professionals such as doctors, lawyers, researchers, and entrepreneurs by according them preferential treatment in terms of longer periods of stay and a fast track to permanent resident status. The planned revisions tighten visa eligibility requirements for unskilled workers such as *nikkeijin*, effectively rescinding the 1990 reform that granted visas to overseas descendants of Japanese without employment restrictions. Thus, the window for unskilled workers is narrowing while there are doubts that the green light for highly skilled workers will be enough to lure such professionals given their various options.

The current *ad hoc*, piecemeal approach to immigration reform will persist because resistance to the idea and realities of increased immigration remains strong and widespread. The gap between how things ought to be, and the way things are, is very wide – a chasm that Japanese and immigrants, even among themselves, define quite differently, thus making it a great source of social tension and apprehension. There is support for improving conditions for non-Japanese, but so far few encouraging signs of significant progress. More immigration will happen, but not enough to alleviate the problems of a shrinking workforce, elderly care, and a declining population. This is because public opinion towards foreigners continues to be negative and, if the tradeoff is between economic revitalization depending on more foreigners and economic decline, the people and their leaders, at least through their inaction, seem prepared to accept decline.

As in other countries, immigration has not brought out the best in Japan's politicians, bureaucrats, media, employers, police, or people, and there is little reason to expect much change on this score anytime soon. A stunning level of cognitive dissonance about what is at stake has facilitated inaction precisely because denial is the path of least resistance. Alas, this has also been a prominent feature of war memory in Japan, the focus of our next chapter.

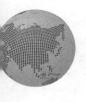

Chapter 10

War Memory and Responsibility

War memory is painful and divisive in any society and especially so when a country considers its responsibility for crimes and atrocities. The examination of what occurred inevitably leads to competing explanations of why such excesses happened, a debate that has eluded consensus in contemporary Japan. There continues to be vigorous disagreement among Japanese about why Japan went to war against China (1931–45) and eventually the US (1941–5). Substantial disagreements also persist about what torments Japan's Imperial Armed Forces inflicted on its neighbors and Allied troops during this period. As a result of Japan's ambivalence about this past, efforts towards reconciliation have been limited because such an agenda depends on agreeing what to take responsibility for and then making efforts to atone.

In this chapter we examine war memory and responsibility in Heisei Japan by focusing on the Yasukuni Shrine and the Asia Women's Fund (1995–2007). Yasukuni Shrine, a Shinto religious site in central Tokyo, symbolizes the nexus of imperial expansion, militarism, and the cult of the emperor during the war years, ensuring that it remains a contemporary battleground over history. The Asia Women's Fund was established in 1995 to compensate the "comfort women," a term that refers to women and girls from around the region who were coerced into providing sex for Japan's military forces. This attempt at reconciliation proved an abject failure for many reasons as we explore below.

Awkward Talisman

Yasukuni Shrine resonates with talismanic symbolism for both its critics and its proponents, and that is precisely why it is so controversial within

Japan and between Japan and its neighbors. For critics, Yasukuni and the adjacent Yushukan Museum represent unrepentant militarism and a vindicating and exonerating historical narrative about Japan's rampage through Asia 1931–45. For proponents, the shrine and museum validate their view that Japan's Holy War in Asia fought in the name of Emperor Showa (Hirohito) was just, motivated by the benevolent desire to liberate Asians from the yoke of Western imperialism.[1] The conflicting meanings of Yauskuni are rooted in the broader historical debate about war memory, responsibility, and reconciliation.[2]

Most Japanese accept Japan's war responsibility and favor atonement, continue to contest revision of the Peace Constitution, and oppose a stronger monarchy – thus acting as a constraint on the more avid nationalists. Nationalism in contemporary Japan is not veering out of control and indeed it seems far more restrained than in either South Korea or China where national identities are rooted in a frequently virulent anti-Japanese nationalism. Governments in both of these countries have nurtured and tapped into this resentment for political purposes in a manner that obstructs reconciliation and undermines regional relations.

Japan, however, bears primary responsibility for handing the hammer of history to its neighbors while they have not been shy about using it time and again. The past still casts long shadows over contemporary Japan, and time has not yet buried memories of the bloody history that continues to divide Japan from its Asian neighbors, because there is a widespread perception, partially accurate, that Japan has shirked its war responsibility. While there is truth in the allegation that the Ministry of Education has encouraged a collective amnesia about Japan's record as imperial overlord and invader in Asia, it is also true that Japanese scholars, educators, politicians, and journalists have robustly challenged such efforts to whitewash the past.[3] And while many Japanese may embrace a keen sense of victimization regarding the Pacific War that baffles its Asian victims, the very public debates about the past have forced the nation to confront inconvenient evidence and memories that undermine the more exonerating versions of this traumatic era. The domestic rift over Yasukuni is part of this larger discourse. The 1990s was a time of reckoning when the past suddenly caught up with the Japanese, largely unprepared by their schooling to confront the unsavory truths of what the imperial forces were engaged in when they were not "liberating" Asians from the yoke of Western imperialism. Although there had been important revelations about this dark past prior to Emperor Showa's death in 1989, this grew from a trickle to a cascade. Equally important has been the sustained pressure applied from the late 1980s by Asian activist groups seeking redress and a more forthright depiction of Japan's sordid past involving abuses and atrocities such as the comfort women system, the slaughter in Nanking, slave laborers, and the chemical and biological warfare experiments at the notorious Unit 731. As a result of these mutually reinforcing domestic and regional developments, during the 1990s the Japanese learned more than they were prepared for about their history. This sudden flood released from the cesspool of Japan's past proved shocking and unsettling to a people accustomed to a less troubling narrative. Understandably there has been resistance to these revelations and efforts to deny, mitigate, justify, and otherwise shift responsibility for the more gruesome tragedies.[4] However, during the cathartic 1990s the self-vindicating narrative that focused on the noble sacrifice and victimization of the Japanese people has been vigorously challenged and in some important respects irreversibly discredited. While many will continue to prefer a more comforting version of their history, the exhumed past is here to stay.

Recrudescent nationalism in contemporary Japan runs the risk of trapping politicians into an escalating war of words and gestures that undermine reconciliation. Former PM Nakasone warns:

> The problem is that a resurgence of nationalism in Japan is bound to clash with the nationalisms of its Asian neighbors. As politicians trumpet nationalism, people tend to follow unhealthy nationalism. As a result, politicians become more responsive to such popular sentiments. This will create a mood of confrontation between the government leaders of the countries involved, as illustrated by Japan's present relations with China and South Korea.[5]

Yushukan and War Memory

Commemorating the war dead at Yasukuni resonates with political purpose.[6] It is an embrace of a war memory that emphasizes that Japan's long war in Asia was justified and fought to liberate Asians from Western colonialism. This vindicating and valorizing narrative on display at the Yushukan Museum adjacent to Yasukuni Shrine makes no mention of Japanese atrocities or its victims. Neither facility enjoys government designation as the national war memorial or museum, but they remain at the heart of Japan's war remembrance and rituals of commemoration. The enshrinement of 14 Class-A war criminals at Yasukuni, the architects of the war under whose authority the excesses were committed, next to the sanitized remembrance displayed at the Yushukan, is an eloquent political statement bristling with historical mischief. The war is depicted as a legitimate act of self-defense and the judgment at the International Military Tribunal for the Far East (IMTFE), accepted in Article 11 of the San Francisco Peace Treaty signed by Japan in 1951, is repudiated. The renovation of the museum in 2002 embellished Yasukuni's image as a symbol of Japan's failure to promote reconciliation by asserting a narrowly nationalistic narrative concerning divisive issues of war memory.

Walking towards the end of 2006 through the Yushukan Museum, I was struck by how terrorism was invoked to justify the Imperial Army's escalating aggression in China back in the 1930s and 1940s. The musty exhibits in the old Yushukan I first visited in 1987 had more the look of a rarely visited, shabby antique shop. The new gleaming version is bursting with slick propaganda, asserting a glorifying and exonerating narrative of Japan's shared history with Asia. This is a post-9/11 museum, one in which contemporary concerns are projected onto the past. We learn that Japan was fighting against Chinese "terrorists" with no mention of invasion, aggression, massacres, or atrocities committed by Japanese troops. Instead we are encouraged to believe that this was a "war on terror" and that Chinese terrorism was the cause of the fighting. Japanese intentions were noble but misunderstood, leading eventually to the US imposing "embargoes to force resource poor Japan into war." Improbably, Japanese suffering is the only suffering on display.

There is resolute silence at the Yushukan about Japanese atrocities and the millions of Asian victims of Japanese aggression. There is no Rape of Nanking, no Unit 731, no comfort women, no indiscriminate aerial bombing of civilian populations by Japanese, no mistreatment of prisoners of war, and no indication that many Okinawan civilians were pressured to commit group suicide by the Imperial Armed Forces. The *kamikaze* are honored for their self-sacrifice with no reference to the fact that many were deceived and pressured into participating or that their sacrifices had so little impact on the course of the war. Here, vainglorious military leaders responsible for the poor planning, logistics, and tactics that subjected so many drafted Japanese soldiers to horrific suffering inexplicably morph into heroes and martyrs.

Just as leaders of the day were routinely misinformed about the extent of Japan's setbacks, visitors are also fed a heavily censored version of events.

In this time machine, it is easy to imagine what life was like under the boot of Japan's military leaders, and indeed, as many older Japanese say, what it must be like in contemporary North Korea.

The Yushukan's one-sided and simplistic explanation of why Japan attacked Pearl Harbor came under fire from George Will, the conservative America columnist, who toured the exhibit and drew attention to the allegation that President Roosevelt conspired to provoke Japan into war.[7] Hisahiko Okazaki, a prominent conservative pundit in Japan, chimed in, publishing an essay in the *Sankei* newspaper also critical of this same explanation of why Japan went to war. Okazaki argued that it discredited the Yushukan and therefore should be revised. He agreed with Will that the exhibit suggesting a US conspiracy to draw Japan into war was "immature in historical judgement, one-sided, cheap, lacking in intellectual integrity," and went on to complain that "this cheap view of history damages the dignity of Yasukuni."[8] This career diplomat insisted on revision of the display criticized by Will, but asserted that the governments of China and Korea have no reason to complain about how their shared history with Japan is depicted at the Yushukan. In fact, they have many good reasons to do so.

The Yushukan has reinforced Yasukuni Shrine's image as a talismanic symbol of Japan's lack of contrition regarding its wartime misdeeds. Yasukuni represents Japan's failure to come to terms with its war history and the futility of attempting to assert a one-sided, exculpatory narrative. The Yushukan spin on history is deeply flawed; depicting Chinese resisting Japan's invasion as "terrorists" is gratuitously insulting to the Chinese people and all those who gave their lives to defend their homeland against Japanese imperialism. The video clip on the capture of Nanjing shown at the Yushukan is equally disingenuous. Viewers see Japanese troops raising their hands in a *banzai* salute atop the walls of the city and then cut to a steaming cauldron out of which a Japanese soldier is ladling soup for hungry-looking Chinese children and elderly. In a triumph of chutzpah over history, visitors are told that the Japanese victory in Nanjing meant that "residents were able to live their lives in peace." The main film shown at the Yushukan puts a spin on Japan's advance into Asia with a female narrator emotionally insisting: "None of the officers and soldiers went to the battlefields for the purpose of cruelly invading and looting. They fought purely for the sake of their families and the state they loved."

As I exited the Yushukan I wondered about the voices of the millions of Asians who died from Japan's "war on terror," the collateral damage of pan-Asian liberation. In this memorial, Japan is the victim, provoked by Chinese "terrorists" and scheming Americans. It is also an object lesson in how the present is imposed on the past. The curators wishfully imagine that artfully invoking "terrorism" will somehow convince.

Just outside the museum is a memorial to Justice Radhabinod Pal who sat on the International Military Tribunal for the Far East, known as the Tokyo Tribunal. He issued a dissenting opinion in which he found the Japanese defendants innocent of war crimes.[9] Eiji Takemae points out that Pal has been invoked ever since by "Ultra-nationalists [who] wielded the accusation of 'victor's justice' in order to obscure the root issue of Japan's war guilt, implicitly justifying their country's wartime record."[10] This is precisely the purpose of the Yushukan.

Paying Tribute

If a single monument can be considered to encapsulate militant nationalism and Japan's failure to offer a convincing repentance for its war record, it is the Yasukuni Shrine. The shrine is controversial not because it is a memorial to 2.47 million subjects of the Japanese empire who gave up their lives for the emperor in past wars, but rather because it is a potent symbol of militarism and veneration of the emperor. Since 1978, 14 Class-A war criminals have also been enshrined there as "gods" and Yasukuni Shrine is now inextricably linked with the men held responsible at the Tokyo Tribunal for Japan's devastating military aggression in Asia.

While Japanese attitudes to Yasukuni are complex, it has undeniably become a focus for an exonerating version of the nation's wartime history. One of the reasons some Japanese give for visiting the shrine is simply to honor all those who died during the war. PM Junichiro Koizumi justified his six visits while in office on the grounds that it is unseemly to discriminate among the dead and thus he honored all equally, including the war criminals. This perhaps reflects a widespread perception among Japanese that the Tokyo Tribunal was a kangaroo court that served up a biased "victor's justice." Conservatives have long chafed under the victor's war narrative that denigrates Japan's pan-Asian aspirations as empty rhetoric justifying its own imperial ambitions in the region. For many Japanese, the Class-A war criminals put on trial were remote from the things of which they stood accused: they were not convicted of actually committing the atrocities, but rather were held responsible for crimes against peace and leading Japan into war. Thus many Japanese consider that their convictions were unjust and that the tribunal failed to recognize Japan's legitimate reasons for going to war, including a variety of Western provocations and colonial domination of Asia. Yasukuni is also a touchstone for domestic controversy because it is a Shinto religious facility and official visits ignore the division between the state and religion enshrined in Article 20 of the Constitution. This is a sensitive issue because, during the war, state-sponsored Shinto was linked with emperor worship and was used as a vehicle to inculcate loyalty to the government and mobilize popular support for the war. Shinto is thus tainted, in the eyes of some Japanese, by its dubious links with imperialism; and Yasukuni, as the focal point of wartime Shinto, is considered the temple of ultra-conservative nationalism where the most regrettable aspects of Japan's military past continue to be venerated. Yasukuni is thus laden with symbolism that reverberates loudly and divisively both within and outside Japan. Powerful right-wing lobby groups such as the War Bereaved Veterans' Family Association (Nihon Izokukai) and the Association of Shinto Shrines (Jinja Honcho) pressure politicians to pay respect to the nation's war dead at Yasukuni in exchange for well-organized electoral support and generous funding. Both have long-standing ties with the LDP, and party leaders regularly serve as the president of Nihon Izokukai.[11] Paying obeisance at Yasakuni is, for such associations, a political litmus test. In 1975, PM Miki Takeo became the first postwar prime minister to visit Yasukuni on August 15, the anniversary of Japan's surrender, albeit in a "private" capacity. His visit occurred shortly after an attempt on his life by a right-wing fanatic. Previously, prime ministers had visited the shrine during autumn or spring festivals. Three years later, in 1978, the 14 Class-A war criminals were secretly enshrined in Yasukuni, ensuring the shrine's future as a potent symbol for unrepentant rightists. Subsequently, prime ministers have walked the Yasukuni tightrope by insisting that any visits they make to the shrine are made in a personal and private capacity. Although such explanations were intended to emphasize the absence of an official government imprimatur, this subterfuge has not succeeded in bamboozling either foreign or domestic critics. When PM Nakasone broke the taboo on official visits in 1985, the subsequent uproar led to an 11-year hiatus in prime ministerial visits.[12] Prime Minister Junichiro Koizumi (2001–6) conducted his six visits amid a media circus and provoked the expected rebukes from Beijing and Seoul. Ongoing efforts to promote reconciliation with the two nations that suffered most from Japanese imperialism were derailed by Koizumi's apparent nonchalance towards historical sensitivities. While his homage to the war dead inflamed international opinion, many Japanese shrug their shoulders about the visits and wonder what all the fuss is about.[13] Some argue that such homage is *atarimae* (natural), because all nations commemorate the sacrifices of their soldiers who have died in past wars.

It would be misleading, however, to assume that there is a national consensus on Yasukuni visits and that those who support, or at least accept, the visits by top politicians knowingly assume all of the attendant historical baggage. It is important to bear in mind that there is considerable domestic opposition to Yasukuni visits. Soon after his election in 2009, PM Yukio Hatoyama of the Democratic Party of Japan signaled that he and his cabinet ministers would not visit the shrine and floated the idea of building a secular alternative for paying respect to the war dead. In addition, New Komeito, a coalition partner in several LDP cabinets, publicly opposes the visits, as does the Japan Communist Party and the Social Democratic Party. The mainstream press also carries considerable critical commentary about Yasukuni. Thus, there is a rich array of countervailing views that belie simplistic notions of the Japanese nation monolithically defending Yasukuni visits and embracing a dangerous nationalism. Unlike in Europe where fringe parties tend to be the standard-bearers for controversial nationalistic sentiments, visits to Yasukuni Shrine have been favored by the LDP, Japan's dominant party from 1955 to 2009.

When Koizumi came to power in 2001, he made an explicit promise to visit Yasukuni Shrine on August 15, the symbolically important anniversary of Japan's surrender. It is intriguing that his political mentor, Takeo Fukuda, was prime minister in 1978 when the 14 Class-A war criminals were enshrined at Yasukuni. The media also revealed that Emperor Showa, the chief priest of Shinto and the man for whom so many soldiers gave their lives, made no more visits to Yasukuni because of the war criminals' presence. His son, Emperor Akihito, maintains this boycott and the unspoken repudiation. For conservatives, this inconvenient symbolism undermines their efforts to promote an unrepentant, glorifying history and highlights that they are acting in defiance of His Majesty's wishes.

Japanese prime ministers need not visit Yasukuni Shrine in order to commemorate the war dead. A viable alternative is the nearby memorial for unknown soldiers at Chidorigafuchi, a secular monument that now looks somewhat forlorn and draws relatively few visitors. Each year on August 15, the government holds a ceremony at Chidorigafuchi expressly to honor the war dead, and it is thus an ideal venue for a prime minister to pay his respects.

There has been a strong domestic reaction to Koizumi's visits. In the wake of his 2001 visit, more than 900 Japanese citizens joined suits against the prime minister across the archipelago, charging him with violation of the constitutional separation of state and religion. This is a sign that democracy is alive and well in Japan and that there are citizens willing to use the courts to hold the government accountable. The government was placed in the awkward position of arguing that the visits were not official and thus the line of separation between religion and state had not been breached. In response to charges that the prime minister had signed the visitors' book with his official title, traveled to the shrine in an official car and laid a wreath bearing his official title, the government disingenuously responded that these gestures were personal and private. In this case, "personal" was certainly a flexible term as Koizumi was accompanied to the site by dozens of other lawmakers and the whole event had been given substantial prior publicity, ensuring a crowd of onlookers and blanket media coverage. The court cases brought against Koizumi drew on similar litigation against PM Nakasone, the last Japanese leader to visit the shrine in his official capacity. In 1992, the nation's three high courts in Tokyo, Sendai, and Osaka all found that Nakasone's official visit in 1985 had been unconstitutional, thereby making it problematic for subsequent prime ministers to follow in his footsteps. Rulings concerning Koizumi's visits were mixed. On September 29, 2005 the Tokyo High Court ruled that Koizumi's visits were private affairs while the next day the Osaka High Court ruled that he made his visits in his official capacity and thus violated the Constitution. Rulings in 2007 skirted the constitutionality issue and instead summarily rejected damage claims by the plaintiffs. However, even with these judicial setbacks, Article 20 continues to cast a shadow over prime ministerial visits, explaining why alternative proposals for paying tribute emphasize a secular option. The politics of Yasukuni ensure that it will remain an important symbol of Japan's militaristic past. Nationalists bridle at suggestions of alternative sites to pay respect to the war dead precisely because the issue is not the souls of fallen soldiers. The issue of the shrine is about national pride and sustaining a more glorious, unapologetic narrative of Japan's past.

In contrast, Ienaga Saburo, a noted historian who led the fight against reactionary distortions of the nation's history for more than four decades until his death in 2002, argued that while the souls of the fallen soldiers must be honored, it should not be by deifying them. In his view, Japan must ensure that the mistakes of the past are not repeated by exposing the crimes of leaders who sacrificed these soldiers as cheap cannon fodder for unworthy reasons; only then will the war dead be truly honored.[14] Ienaga argued that those who support retaining Yasukuni as the *de facto* national war memorial seek to defend an outmoded and reactionary national ideology.

By invoking atavistic symbols of nationalism aimed at reawakening pride in nation, politicians are responding to a sense of fading glory, growing insecurity and a loss of faith in the government. They are also seeking to rally the public and cultivate a sense of shared purpose. In such an atmosphere it is not surprising that some people and politicians seek refuge in reassuring symbols and gestures of nationalism. However, these siren songs from the past sound more like a last gasp than a call to arms.

Koizumi Spotlight

On August 15, 2006 Prime Minister Koizumi made his sixth visit to the controversial Yasukuni Shrine since taking office in 2001, further souring already tense relations between Japan and China and both Koreas. In doing so, he undermined any goodwill generated by his forthright apology to these victims of Japan's wartime aggression on August 15, 2005 – the 60th anniversary of Japan's surrender. Prime Minister Koizumi shrugged off revelations in July 2006 that the Emperor Showa in 1988 confided his misgivings about the enshrinement of Class-A war criminals at Yasukuni to Tomohiko Tomita, the grand steward of the Imperial Household Agency, stating that this is why he discontinued his annual pilgrimages to the shrine.[15] In the wake of this bombshell, public support for shrine visits by prime ministers plummeted to 20 percent.[16]

Predictably, pundits suggested that Koizumi's visits reflect a resurgent nationalism, but what is interesting is that Koizumi was rather isolated on Yasukuni. In 2005, five former prime ministers publicly advised him to refrain from visiting; the head of Keidanren, Japan's leading business federation, urged him not to go; and even the conservative newspaper *Yomiuri Shimbun* weighed in against further visits. Perhaps even more surprising was the statement in 2005 by Makoto Koga, a conservative LDP lawmaker who headed the War Bereaved Veterans' Family Association, suggesting the prime minister reconsider his visit in light of Asian sensitivities. A month earlier, the Japan Association of Corporate Executives (Keizai Doyukai) also urged Koizumi to stop his visits to Yasukuni, terming them the main obstacle to improving bilateral relations with China. Thus, a broad spectrum of conservatives opposed Koizumi's visits to Yasukuni Shrine.

Reconciliation Tango

Japan has shuffled into the twenty-first century still trying to come to terms with its damning past. For every occasion on which a leader apologizes to Japan's neighbors for past misdeeds – and they have done so frequently and with conviction – there is always a bellowing nationalist politician ready to repudiate any demonstrated contrition and undo whatever goodwill was generated. Whether it is a question of denying the Rape of Nanking or publishing textbooks that minimize Japanese atrocities committed against fellow Asians, there is always a sense that Japan is still trying to evade responsibility for its wartime misdeeds while emphasizing the suffering endured by its own people. Given that its invasion and occupation of Asia claimed some 20 million lives, it is startling to other Asians that Japan continues to portray itself not just as victim, but also as liberator of Asia, with little sustained recognition of its role as aggressor. Interpreting the causes of the war, what actually happened during the war, and the aftermath remain divisive questions in contemporary Japan. Just because some groups in society favor airbrushing the inconvenient and unappealing aspects of Japan's wartime record, however, does not mean that this is a widely embraced point of view. The exculpatory junior high school textbook written by the Society for the Creation of New History Textbooks (Atarashi Rekishi Kyokasho oTsukuru-kai) and approved by the Ministry of Education was adopted by fewer than 1 percent of junior high schools both in 2001 and again in 2005, reflecting the good sense that prevails.[17] As much as Japan may deserve the scathing criticism hurled at it by its neighbors, South Korea and China are not above using the memory of wartime excesses for diplomatic leverage. Nationalistic fervor runs high in East Asia, and singling out Japan is a strategy adopted for more than purely historical reasons, justified as they may be. Keeping Japan on the defensive about its past, and its failure to come to grips with its record in the present, has proved to be an effective diplomatic strategy that imposes constraints on Japan's regional diplomacy and security posture.

There is growing Japanese resentment about this "instrumentalization" of history and fierce clinging to old wrongs. Koizumi's shrine visits reflect a desire to end the post-WWII era and move on. Many Japanese are proud of what they accomplished in the second half of the twentieth century and feel that they are not given enough credit for what they achieved and contributed. The constant harping about the past by neighbors is seen to be self-serving, and in the case of China as a way of deflecting criticism about the Communist Party's own checkered record. Breaking out of this pattern of recrimination and distrust requires a level of courage, statesmanship, and vision that has proved far too elusive for too long.

Unfinished Business

In considering the implications of a rising Japanese nationalism, one in which divergent groups embrace disparate dreams but share a visceral pride in nation, it is important to understand both why other nations remain so vexed by such a prospect and why some of Japan's conservative elite remain so obtuse to their neighbors' anxieties. Although Japan has changed considerably since 1945, the unresolved legacies of the wartime era still reverberate in the region. This phenomenon is rooted in a fundamental and unyielding distrust shared by those who suffered from Japan's imperial ambitions, and is fanned by a potent combination of complacency, apathy, and ignorance in Japan about such concerns. Japan is seen to be shrinking from the burden of its history to the extent that it continues to embrace a self-vindicating narrative that casts the nation as victim and relegates competing narratives to the margins. Why have many Japanese clung so tenaciously to a sanitized version of its past and only belatedly recognized – and that tentatively and intermittently – their nation's role as victimizer? Surely Japan would gain stature in the eyes of the world, and facilitate its own regional integration, if it came clean about its devastating wartime record and stopped caviling about details that make it look eager to evade responsibility. The reasons for continuing denial are various. For many Japanese, the vilification of Japan and ceaseless demands for apologies reflect a double standard; many countries have committed horrible crimes on an enormous scale that they minimize or ignore. For younger Japanese, the burdens of history seem unfair and irrelevant; grandfather did those things and that is his problem. For many older Japanese, the exoneration of Emperor Showa has clouded the issue of war responsibility; if the man in whose name a sacred war was waged was never held accountable, why should anyone else be? For pragmatic government officials, there are worries that the tab for compensation could prove very expensive.

There is also concern, based on several incidents, that confronting ultra-nationalists over the past could provoke violent retribution. In the post-WWII era, the US alliance and access to US markets effectively insulated Japan from the demands of its neighbors and made regional reintegration a choice rather than an imperative. In contrast, war-ravaged West Germany faced the Soviet menace to the east and had no alternative to a reintegrated future with Western Europe. West Germany thus needed to facilitate reintegration and could only do so by paying the price that history exacted. For Japan, the stakes of regional integration have been lower. Under the auspices of the US, Japan could ignore the dictates of reconciliation and escape some of the heavier burdens of its past. Its reckoning with China was postponed until the 1970s because of Cold War policies dictated from Washington that blocked normalization of relations with the nation that suffered most from Japanese aggression. However, with the end of the Cold War and the rising threats in a more dangerous neighborhood, especially those emanating from North Korea, this approach is ripe for reconsideration. Moreover, the specter of China as the regional hegemonic power, and its role as the great frontier for Japanese business interests, is raising the potential rewards of reconciliation. Thus, like Germany, Japan may also find that the cost of ignoring the burdens of history is too expensive while the potential benefits of reassuring past enemies prove a compelling spur to change. Recognizing that Japan must assume the burdens of its past for its own interests and rehabilitation as much as for regional reconciliation, in 1995 the government launched the Asia Women's Fund, a first attempt to address the controversial legacy of the comfort women.

Asia Women's Fund (AWF)

The AWF also is an awkward talisman, a symbol of Japan's continuing failure to promote reconciliation with its neighbors. For decades after WWII, the Japanese government remained determinedly oblivious to the comfort women system, but this travesty ended in the early 1990s when researchers gathered evidence from the archives that established the military's involvement in recruiting comfort women and establishing and running comfort stations throughout Japan's theater of operations, beginning in 1932 and continuing until surrender in 1945. It has not been possible to reconstruct a complete picture of this tragic saga because many people had an interest in destroying evidence, but over the past two decades researchers have gathered considerable documentary evidence and oral testimony to ensure that there is no doubt that the comfort women system existed and that Japan's responsibility is incontrovertible.

In the face of mounting evidence, finally in 1993 the government issued the Kono Statement, named after then Chief Cabinet Secretary Yohei Kono, which admits state responsibility for the comfort women system, acknowledges coercion was involved, expresses remorse and promises to pay further attention to this blot on the nation's record. The full text of the Kono Statement reads as follows:

The Government of Japan has been conducting a study on the issue of wartime "comfort women" since December 1991. I wish to announce the findings as a result of that study.

As a result of the study which indicates that comfort stations were operated in extensive areas for long periods, it is apparent that there existed a great number of comfort women. Comfort stations were operated in response to the request of the military authorities of the day. The then Japanese military was, directly or indirectly, involved in the establishment and management of the comfort stations and the transfer of comfort women. The recruitment of the comfort women was conducted mainly by private recruiters who acted in response to the request of the military. The Government study has revealed that in many cases they were recruited against their own will, through coaxing, coercion, etc., and that, at times, administrative/military personnel directly took part in the recruitments. They lived in misery at comfort stations under a coercive atmosphere.

As to the origin of those comfort women who were transferred to the war areas, excluding those from Japan, those from the Korean Peninsula accounted for a large part. The Korean Peninsula was under Japanese rule in those days, and their recruitment, transfer, control, etc., were conducted generally against their will, through coaxing, coercion, etc.

Undeniably, this was an act, with the involvement of the military authorities of the day, that severely injured the honor and dignity of many women. The Government of Japan would like to take this opportunity once again to extend its sincere apologies and remorse to all those, irrespective of place of origin, who suffered immeasurable pain and incurable physical and psychological wounds as comfort women.

It is incumbent upon us, the Government of Japan, to continue to consider seriously, while listening to the views of learned circles, how best we can express this sentiment.

We shall face squarely the historical facts as described above instead of evading them, and take them to heart as lessons of history. We hereby reiterate our firm determination never to repeat the same mistake by forever engraving such issues in our memories through the study and teaching of history.

As actions have been brought to court in Japan and interests have been shown in this issue outside Japan, the Government of Japan shall continue to pay full attention to this matter, including private research related thereto. (August 4, 1993)

This forthright statement was welcome by victims and their supporters, but has been challenged and repudiated by those who continue to deny or minimize state responsibility for the comfort women system. These apologists argue that it was no different than long-established practice by other military forces and they seek to focus debate on questions such as exactly how many comfort women there were and where they came from rather than what they experienced. Ikuhiko Hata, a revisionist historian, disputes the commonly cited figures of between 50,000 and 200,000 comfort women, estimating that there were fewer than 20,000, and he also denies the scholarly consensus that most were Korean.[18] There is also, however, a rich scholarship about the comfort women that depicts their recruitment, life in the comfort stations, and the ongoing attempts to deny or minimize the existence of this system.[19]

In 1994, the comfort women were mentioned for the first time in school textbooks, putting into action the spirit of the Kono Statement. The inclusion of comfort women in textbooks was a call to arms for revisionist historians who established the Tsukurukai with the specific aim of writing a history text that would instill national pride among young Japanese. The comfort women represented an especially damning stain on Japan's history, one that highlighted exactly what conservatives could not acknowledge. A nation that coerces and deceives tens of thousands of teenage women into providing sex for the troops was not consistent with the type of national identity they sought to cultivate. Nor could many conservatives accept the establishment of the AWF because paying consolation money and providing medical care for elderly survivors constituted an admission of guilt, one they could not abide.

The political cross-currents in Japan during the early 1990s ensured that the AWF was a controversial compromise, one largely viewed as inadequate by advocates and victims. Victims, their advocates and many Japanese who wanted the state to take legal and moral responsibility and atone for the abuses of the comfort women system were disappointed that the AWF was a quasi-public entity limited to assuming moral responsibility. The AWF did offer financial compensation, an apology, and health and welfare support, but did not involve the state admitting its criminality, providing direct compensation, or offering an unequivocal apology. Supporters realized that this was the best they could achieve given the strong political forces aligned against them, and were eager to move forward even with this flawed effort towards reconciliation before the former comfort women died. Conservative critics thought that merely establishing the AWF conceded too much even if it fudged state responsibility.

In the end, the AWF was a joint project of redress by the state and the people with funding from both. A national appeal raised some JPY550 million from private donors, money that was used to directly compensate individual victims, while the state covered medical and welfare programs and the administrative costs of the AWF. Victims received a JPY2 million solatium payment drawn from private contributions and an additional JPY1.2–3 million in medical and welfare support from Japanese government funds. Successive prime ministers signed letters of apology to those who accepted compensation, but they were carefully worded to avoid conceding criminality and legal responsibility. This less than unequivocal apology and the fact that the government disbursed funds at arm's length through the AWF proved a public relations disaster. In the court of public opinion, the AWF was judged insufficient and failed to convince people that Japan was assuming full responsibility or sincerely atoning, meaning it had limited success in promoting reconciliation.

Money and letters of apology were distributed until 2002 to victims from South Korea, the Philippines, and the Netherlands. Compensation to Indonesia was collective in the form of nursing homes rather than individual compensation, ending in 2007 when the AWF was shut down. The AWF did not compensate any victims from China, Burma, Malaysia, Singapore, Indochina (Vietnam, Laos, and Cambodia), East Timor, Papua New Guinea, or North Korea.

In South Korea, comfort women advocacy groups lambasted the AWF and actively discouraged victims from accepting the offered compensation. There was no inclination to let Japan off the hook of history by allowing the AWF to atone, especially in such an imperfect manner. Soh argues that vilifying Japan over the comfort women enables Korean society to overlook its own complicity in the Korean women's trauma.[20] The Korean Council, an advocacy group for former comfort women, pressured those women to renounce the AWF's gesture of contrition, while the Korean government offered them compensation provided they refused the Japanese money. Those who accepted faced public ostracism and humiliation. Korean nationalism, in Soh's view, has thus tainted the redress movement, one that shades the truth while demanding justice.

Requiem for Reconciliation

On March 1, 2007, the anniversary of the Korean uprising against Japanese colonial rule in 1919, Prime Minister Shinzo Abe rekindled controversies about Japan's shared past with Asia by quibbling over the degree of coercion used in recruiting the comfort women. Abe said that there was no evidence that the recruitment of comfort women had been "forcible in the narrow sense of the word." A few days later in a Diet committee debate, he repeated this statement, adding that to be "forcible in the narrow sense of the word" the system would have had to have involved "officials forcing their way into houses like kidnappers and taking people away." Abe, however, admitted that the recruitment of "comfort women" was forcible "in the broad sense of the word." Whether at bayonet point or due to deception or intimidation, there is evidence the comfort women system was established at the behest of the Imperial Armed Forces and was an institutionalized system of sexual subjugation, violence, and abuse.

Abe's comments contradict the letter and spirit of the Kono Statement, but in trying to dampen the firestorm of criticism he ignited within Japan and the world, he subsequently reiterated support for the declaration and under duress expressed his remorse for their suffering. He learned the hard way that he cannot unilaterally assert a history to his liking or downplay the torments inflicted on these women. Abe, and likeminded colleagues in the LDP, are critical of the Kono Statement, and until his remarks went international, Abe thought it perfectly okay to disavow it. He retracted his comments under intense pressure, but tarnished Japan's image all around the world while souring relations with neighbors by insulting the dignity of the comfort women.

This was certainly a strange and sad way to bid sayonara to the AWF, an organization that paid a total of $19 million compensation and medical care expenses to 364 former comfort women between 1995 and 2007.[21] The Japanese public contributed about $5 million to the AWF, lending some credence to the government-orchestrated subterfuge that it was a private organization, one subsidized with some $31 million in government money.

Pulling the plug on the AWF ends a fumbling attempt by the Japanese government to atone for the suffering endured by the comfort women. The politics of the comfort women controversy highlight the difficulties Japan faces in coming to terms with its past and advancing reconciliation. Clearly, many well-intentioned officials associated with the AWF feel they were burned and this setback for the government has complicated further reconciliation initiatives.

Conservatives who favor a glorious narrative of the Pacific War feel vindicated by the AWF's failure and remain steadfast in their rejection of apology diplomacy and what they call masochistic history. These reactionaries have never accepted the Kono Statement and are committed to retracting it. They opposed the establishment of the AWF and forced the government to adopt the awkward quasi-government arrangement that watered down the state's responsibility and undermined the AWF from its inception. They have also opposed the inclusion of references to comfort women in middle school textbooks and, in the most recent editions, have succeeded in doing so.

Japan prevents reconciliation by making itself hostage to history in trying to rewrite it. Reconciliation is based on unequivocal recognition of war responsibility and sincere gestures of atonement that restore dignity to victim and perpetrator alike. It is also based on the victims accepting such gestures. The AWF has been a disheartening experience for the majority of Japanese who do accept responsibility for the atrocities committed by Japanese soldiers and believe more should be done to atone for them.

Prospects

Although the signs of renascent nationalism in Japan are hard to miss, there is a risk of exaggerating their significance. Regrettable as Koizumi's visits to Yasukuni Shrine may be, it is folly to assume that they signal a consensus in Japanese society about how to honor the war dead, indicate support for the war criminals enshrined there, or betoken an unqualified embrace of the ultra-nationalists' agenda. The nationalistic whitewashing of history in a government-approved textbook, lamentable as it may be, must be balanced against its nearly universal rejection by school boards all over the country.

One of the main obstacles to Japan's reconciliation with its neighbors is that the Japanese people are divided over war memory. Competing narratives about the past that divides Japan from Asia send mixed signals, muddying war memory, vitiating gestures of contrition, and thus preventing reconciliation based on a shared view of the past. The divisions over history among Japanese have developed over six decades and the ongoing debate has polarized positions. A forthright reckoning acceptable to China and South Korea involves acknowledgement that it was a war of aggression in which the Imperial Armed Forces committed widespread atrocities, but this is unacceptable to conservatives in Japan who reject such a narrative as masochistic history. In these circumstances, under the LDP the prospects for "solving" the history problem were remote. Under the DPJ, however, these prospects have improved as it favors assuming war responsibility and pursuing reconciliation initiatives.

The Yasukuni problem is just as intractable because it revolves around the same issues. The Yushukan Museum fails to acknowledge that Japan fought a war of aggression and continues to assert a narrowly nationalistic narrative of war memory that will continue to irritate China and Korea. There is virtually no chance that the Yushukan will come to embrace a forthright reckoning on Nanjing, comfort women, chemical weapons, vivisection experiments, and systematic abuse of POWs and other slave laborers, because to do so would negate the meaning of Yasukuni for those who run it and those who invoke it for political purposes. To not do so will sustain the current divisions over history that animate public discourse within Japan and between it and its neighbors in East Asia.

In some ways, the spotlight that PM Koizumi focused on Yasukuni has been a boon to conservatives, sparking interest in the shrine and exposing a far wider public to the Yasukuni narrative. And yet, in other ways, pushing Yasukuni into the limelight has flustered and embarrassed many conservatives who seek a pragmatic accommodation with neighbors over the past in order to get on with the future. Many in the establishment disavow Yasukuni precisely because it is an awkward talisman for a nation that has done much to redeem itself since 1945. They do not see any reason or hope in making this history, undeniably a tragedy for the nation and its neighbors, a touchstone of national identity. Many of Japan's cosmopolitan elite understand and agree that Yasukuni is a symbol of Japan's failure to assume the burdens of history.

Yasukuni remains useful, however, to stimulate a vibrant public discourse about Japan's shared history with Asia. Stirring controversy generates a debate that forces the media, academia, politicians, business-men, and the public to confront this tragic era over and over. Yasukuni places Japan's failed efforts to come to terms with this history in the lime-light at home and abroad and in that sense serves as a powerful reminder about the nation's unfinished business. For those who believe that the Japanese need to remember the past, Yasukuni is a godsend. The clumsy and biased history featured there eloquently undermines the credibility of revisionists and encourages people to seek a more balanced narrative. This attempted hijacking of history galvanizes domestic opponents who remain vigilant and determined to prevent such a view gaining sway while generat-ing unwelcome criticism overseas.

The Yasukuni dilemma involves shifting the focal point of official war remembrance away from the shrine. Various proposals to somehow "cleanse" Yasukuni and render it an acceptable venue for paying tribute to the war dead by removing the spirits of the 14 Class-A war criminals, depoliticizing it, or making it into a secular memorial won't work. Yasukuni's image has been cast and no amount of artful repackaging will obscure its indelible links with Japan's discredited imperial ideology or the excesses it exhorted and sacrifices it extracted. Whether it is at Chidorigafuchi or some other site, the dictates of reconciliation require that Japan adopt a secular war memorial where people and officials can pay respect to the war dead free from political agendas and historical baggage. A facility for dignified homage to those who made the ultimate sacrifice is what these spirits, other war victims, and the Japanese people deserve. Solving the Yasukuni dilemma will not resolve Japan's overall history problem, but it is a necessary step towards doing so.

Similarly, regaining national dignity by restoring dignity to the comfort women remains unfinished business. The AWF was a flawed attempt to bring closure that began and ended in controversy. Clearly the Japanese government is frustrated that powerful civil society organizations in Korea and Japan have worked to prevent reconciliation on the terms offered by the AWF. It would be easy to use this opposition as an excuse for inaction, but that is not a promising tack for reconciliation. The burden is on Japan to keep trying and to rework the terms and conditions to accommodate the concerns of the remaining comfort women and their advocates. It is also important to broaden the scope of reconciliation efforts to include victims from countries that were not party to the AWF efforts and to do more in Japan to honor the Kono Statement and ensure that history is not distorted or airbrushed in vain attempts to instill pride in nation. A pride that rests on trampling the dignity of others offers little to the agenda of reconciliation or the honor of Japan.

Next we examine the reign of Emperor Akihito, Japan's symbolic head of state, who has arguably done more for regional reconciliation than anyone else in Japan.

Part IV
Institutions at Risk

Chapter 11

The Imperial Family

A prolonged economic malaise defines the first two decades of Emperor Akihito's reign, the Heisei era. Shortly after he ascended in 1989 to what is known as the Chrysanthemum Throne (a reference to the flower that constitutes the family crest) the economic bubble of the late 1980s burst. Signs of the gloom that still envelops Heisei Japan are hard to miss, evident in the shuttered shopping streets of provincial towns, homelessness in the cities, relatively high unemployment, record levels of bankruptcies, swelling welfare rolls, and a public consensus that Japan's best days are behind it. Even though Heisei (literally it means "peace everywhere") has come to mean recession at home, by virtue of its pop culture and trendy designs Heisei Japan has become a nation admired internationally for its gross national cool, an image upgrade from the stoic salaryman stereotype that prevailed in much of the post-WWII era.[1] In contemporary Japan's cutting-edge vibe of hip and modern, it is easy to understand why many traditions are fading, creating new challenges for the imperial family.

Heisei has also come to represent a time of belated regional reconciliation as Emperor Akihito has accepted war responsibility and made significant gestures towards atonement. Under Emperor Showa (1925–89: known as Hirohito when he was alive, but now by his reign name posthumously), despite considerable efforts to reinvent him as a man of peace, it was never quite possible to escape the taint of wartime atrocities committed during his reign. However, as the victims and perpetrators pass from the scene, the imperial institution has achieved a stature and legitimacy under Emperor Akihito that could never have been possible under his father. He has made a difference by operating effectively within the confines of the Imperial Household Agency (IHA), a government bureaucracy that manages all matters related to the monarchy, and constitutional restraints on any political activity. Compared to his post-1868 restoration modern era predecessors, Emperors Meiji (1868–1912), Taisho (1912–26), and Showa (1926–89), Akihito has been far the most benevolent and visionary, leaving a legacy untarnished by aggression overseas or repression at home. His initiatives promoting reconciliation and modernization of the imperial system while attending to those in need of consolation or support are sowing the seeds of a positive legacy and will leave him remembered as the people's emperor.[2]

Relevance

The imperial family is a richly symbolic institution representing a reassuring continuity for many Japanese. The swift pace of change in post-WWII Japan has challenged and transformed established customs, beliefs, and norms in profound ways that generate considerable anxieties. In this context, traditions and culture are appealing precisely because national identity is at stake. In searching for a national identity in a globalizing world, the imperial institution is distinctive and quintessentially Japanese, a touchstone of tradition that animates the core of the country's collective consciousness. Certainly many Japanese, especially the younger generations, do not seek an identity grounded in the emperor system, nor do they view it as a reassuring bridge to the past. Some question the need for an imperial system while others are indifferent to an institution that seems distant and irrelevant, one that faces more risk from fading into oblivion than concerted opposition. However, for some Japanese the imperial connections with the past and myths of origin continue to resonate powerfully and others argue that the monarchy exerts a unifying influence that offsets democracy's divisive struggles. Moreover, Emperor Akihito does command widespread respect and has brought the Chrysanthemum Throne closer to the people in many important ways. Public opinion polls indicate that 75–85 percent of the public support retention of the monarchy even though many feel it is remote from their lives; typically less than 10 percent demand abolition of the monarchy while even fewer advocate enhancing the powers of the emperor.

Akihito is credited with doing much to atone for the ravages of colonialism and war that define the legacy of his father. His reconciliation diplomacy in Asia is also supported by public opinion polls indicating that the majority of Japanese believe the government should do more to acknowledge its war responsibility and atone for it. He avoids overt political actions and gestures due to constitutional constraints, but within these confines he has made an impact on how Japanese regard their shared past with Asia and has also distanced himself publically from conservative activists who advocate their own nationalistic agendas in his name.

The media has covered the imperial family's tribulations, especially the estrangement of Empress Michiko from Crown Princess Masako and the rift between the Crown Prince Naruhito and his younger brother, in ways that generate sympathy for the monarch. His prostate cancer surgery in 2003, and his scaling back of duties at the end of 2008 due to exhaustion, have elicited considerable sympathy and also reflect just how much more open the imperial institution, and society, has become during his reign. At the end of the Showa era, cancer was still a taboo topic, something almost shameful that doctors were usually reluctant to discuss with patients and relatives. And so, as Emperor Showa slowly wasted away, his terminal illness was never openly diagnosed as cancer even though everyone knew.

Democratic Reconciler

Since acceding to the throne as the 125th emperor, Akihito has been a model constitutional monarch. Only 3 days after his father's death, while addressing a national television audience on January 10, 1989, Akihito used informal language to express clearly his support for the Constitution, setting a far more populist tone than his predecessor. Overseas, especially in Asia and the United States, Akihito appears to have won respect through his diplomacy. In 1990, when the Korean president visited Japan, Akihito became the first prominent Japanese to make a public apology for the suffering Japan inflicted upon Korea during the colonial period 1910–45. In 1991 he won kudos in a tour of Southeast Asia, and in the following year when he visited China he expressed his "profound regret" at the "many and great sufferings" inflicted by Japan on China. These significant gestures may not have resolved his father's bloody legacy in the region, but did help change perceptions in countries victimized by Japan's Imperial Armed Forces and demonstrate his personal commitment to healing the wounds of the past. Most Japanese welcome these initiatives, while conservatives are decidedly unhappy with his apologies for wartime aggression and reject what they see as a masochistic view of history. Emperor Akihito has also maintained his father's embargo on visits to Yasukuni

Shrine that began in 1978 when 14 Class-A war criminals were enshrined there.

Subsequently, during occasions marking the 50th and 60th anniversaries of the end of WWII, the imperial couple visited the atomic bomb memorials in Hiroshima and Nagasaki, and in 1993 visited war memorials in Okinawa Prefecture where the brutal battle waged there continues to be the focus of bitter recrimination among Okinawans towards the imperial Japanese government who they feel used them as sacrificial pawns at a time when the war was already lost. It is telling that Emperor Showa never visited Okinawa because he was never welcome.[3] In 2005 the emperor and empress also traveled to Saipan, the first visit by an emperor to an overseas battlefield site, to pay respect to all those who gave their lives in battle, making offerings and prayers for Japanese soldiers and civilians, Korean laborers, local people, and US servicemen. In 2009 the imperial couple paid their respects at a cemetery in Honolulu where many of the war dead from the attack on Pearl Harbor are buried. Thus, for two decades he has criss-crossed the region to make amends, a sustained goodwill mission that has brought a measure of redemption to a nation that has too often shirked the burdens of the past.

Conservatives' Fading Hopes

Akihito has been a disappointment to conservatives precisely because he has distanced himself from their agenda and repudiated some of their key projects. Conservative opponents of contemporary Japan's downsized and democratized monarchy may only constitute a tiny minority, but are politically influential and lobby for a reassertion of imperial prerogatives and symbols. They seek to invoke the emperor for neo-nationalistic purposes, while shoring up voter and donor support among the large membership of the Shinto Shrine Association. This association is eager to restore state recognition and support for Shinto shrines, including the Sun Goddess's Shrine at Ise, the Yasukuni Shrine for the war dead located in Tokyo, and several thousand smaller shrines across the nation that at one time were bastions of the imperial cult. As a result of the separation of religion and the state in the 1947 Constitution, Shinto shrines have become dependent on private support, leaving many in desperate circumstances.

Akihito's enthronement rites sparked considerable controversy among many Japanese, ranging from Buddhist organizations to communists and ordinary citizens, who objected to using public money to conduct Shinto religious rituals. The Daijosai, as the crucial ritual is known, was conducted in November 1990 despite heated opposition from various liberal groups, who protested the US$80 million state funding for a ceremony that breached the constitutional separation of state and religion. This sum was almost equivalent to the entire annual budget of the IHA. The Daijosai is a mystical rite that celebrates the emperor's unique relationship with the Sun Goddess including his symbolic rebirth as a woman and impregnation by the gods, an act that confers divine qualities.

Conservatives welcomed the Daijosai for exactly the same reason so many opposed it; this ceremony highlighted the fundamental continuity between the pre- and post-WWII imperial institutions. Despite denying his divinity in 1946, Emperor Hirohito continued to perform the very rituals that defined him as a deity and the high priest of Shinto. Paradoxically, the first truly democratic emperor, Akihito, performs these same symbolically powerful rites today, demonstrating his role as guardian of tradition and, at least to some eyes, an undiminished divinity.

Divisive Symbols

In 1999, the government legally recognized the national flag known as the Hinomaru (the rising sun) and the national anthem entitled Kimigayo (Your Majesty's Reign) as symbols of the nation. The crimson disk in the field of white on the flag symbolizes the rising sun, representing the Shinto Sun Goddess Amaterasu. The anthem's lyrics date back to a Heian era (794–1185) poem and are a paean to the emperor. The LDP pushed the flag-and-anthem bill through the Diet despite widespread public misgivings and a range of economic and social problems demanding urgent government attention. The flag and anthem have long been *de facto* national symbols, but passing a bill giving legal sanction to this status pleased conservatives while provoking liberals in a nation still divided over its wartime past and lingering religious vestiges of the imperial system. The sun flag is not much of an issue for most Japanese, but many consider that Kimigayo is a throwback to the era when the emperor was an absolute monarch and as such incompatible with the postwar Constitution. Moreover, for many the song is a reminder of when Japan was waging war throughout Asia in the name of the emperor and how little it has done to atone for this past. Passage of the bill in the Diet by an overwhelming majority demonstrated the influence of conservative political forces, that on this issue and on war responsibility has been out of tune with public sentiments.

In 1992, revised national curricula guidelines for schools were implemented nationwide that instruct teachers to sing Kimigayo while standing and facing the Hinomaru during official school ceremonies. Those who do not abide by the guidelines risk reprimand by their local education boards. From the outset the teachers' union has opposed the guidelines, arguing that they violated the Constitution. These guidelines sparked a national controversy when a high school principal in Hiroshima committed suicide in 1998 after failing to resolve a conflict between the board of education, which demanded mandatory singing of the anthem, and the teachers, who opposed the local edict.

Subsequently in 2003, the Tokyo Metropolitan Government issued a directive mandating singing of the anthem while standing and facing the flag. This directive came at the behest of Governor Shintaro Ishihara, an unabashed nationalist, and sanctioned punishments on teachers refusing to abide by the orders. As a result, hundreds of teachers have been reprimanded, including salary cuts and other administrative sanctions. The Organization of Reprimanded Teachers for the Retraction of the Unjust Punishment Involving Hinomaru and Kimigayo represents many teachers who have filed lawsuits demanding that the metropolitan government retract the order, arguing that it violates Article 19 of the Constitution that protects the freedom of conscience.

The emperor weighed into this political controversy unexpectedly while hosting a large autumn garden party at his palace in October 2004. A conservative member of the Tokyo Metropolitan Board of Education approached the emperor and brought up the flag-and-anthem issue. In a conversation reported in the mass media the official said: "Making teachers and students to raise the national flag and sing the national anthem in unison at schools across the country is my job." In response the emperor simply said, "It's not desirable to do so." Stunned by the frank imperial censure the official replied, "Of course, it should not be, sir. Thank you so much for giving me such wonderful words." The following spring the emperor repeated his opinion that it is "desirable not to force" teachers and students across the nation to venerate the Hinomaru flag while singing the Kimigayo anthem, indicating that it is a matter for individual choice. Given the constitutional strictures against the emperor intervening in political matters, his words reverberated powerfully through the top echelons of government, sending an unmistakably clear and inconvenient message repudiating a key conservative initiative. The government spokesmen scrambled to explain to the media that the emperor's comments should not be misinterpreted as conveying a political message, confirming inadvertently that indeed they had.

In its ruling in September 2006 on one of the lawsuits filed by teachers, the Tokyo District Court agreed with the plaintiffs that the flag and anthem represent Japan's militaristic past. The judge wrote, "It is an undeniable historical fact that the Hinomaru and 'Kimigayo' were the spiritual props of imperialism and militarism from the Meiji Era (1868–1912) until the end of World War II," adding that the two are not yet unbiased symbols. The judge affirmed that teachers are not obliged to sing the anthem and music teachers are not obliged to play the piano accompaniment. The court asserted that the anthem and flag should not be imposed on people, but should rather be supported spontaneously, and that notices or orders that force school staff to sing the anthem before the flag amount to an unwarranted control over education.

The education ministry has since published a revised education curriculum guideline in 2008 for elementary and junior high schools that calls for promoting patriotism and for making children between the first and sixth grades sing the Kimigayo. The revised guideline takes effect in elementary schools from 2011 and the following year for junior high schools. This revision to the education guideline is the first since the Fundamental Law of Education was revised in 2006 by the administration of former Prime Minister Shinzo Abe aimed at instilling patriotism in classrooms. The revised guideline states: "Moral education shall be aimed at nurturing respect for [Japan's] tradition and culture, and sentiment of loving our country and our homeland that have cultivated them ... and at cultivating morality." The new guideline also urges elementary schools to teach pupils to sing Kimigayo in all six elementary school grades.

However, many teachers remain adamantly opposed to mandatory singing of Kimigayo and venerating the Hinomaru national flag at public ceremonies because of their association with Japan's militaristic past. These conscientious objectors suffered a setback in March 2009 when the Tokyo District Court rejected a lawsuit filed by teachers who had been penalized for refusing to sing Kimigayo at school ceremonies. The court ruled that the 2003 flag-and-anthem directives of the Tokyo Metropolitan Government do not violate teachers' constitutional rights and rejected demands by the plaintiffs that the sanctions be rescinded.

Thus the courts have sent a mixed message about efforts by the government to instill patriotism by requiring flag veneration and anthem singing. The emperor made his opposition to such measures clear, and in so doing pleased liberals and gave moral support to objectors. Although he undermined conservative loyalists by openly repudiating their efforts, he has not prevailed. Ironically, efforts to revive the imperial symbols of flag and anthem displease the monarch, but the ardor that animates this conservative movement remains undiminished.

Korean Ancestry

His Majesty has also proved troublesome to conservatives in his efforts to promote improved ties with Korea. Relations between Japan and Korea are close, but often antagonistic, never quite escaping the shadow of their shared history when Japan colonized Korea (1910–45). Disputes over history and territory percolate uncomfortably and ceaselessly. Politicians in Korea are wont to play the Japan card when their popularity sags, knowing that if there is one thing all Koreans can agree on it is the horrors of Japanese colonial rule and an infuriating denial in Japan about these excesses. In this context of frayed and fractious relations, the decision by FIFA to designate Korea and Japan as joint hosts of the World Cup soccer tournament in 2002 was a gamble. There had been little political vision or leadership in Japan concerning the troubled state of bilateral relations, and prospects for using the tournament to forge better relations seemed unpromising.

Emperor Akihito, as he has done on numerous occasions, seized the opportunity to weigh in on the issues that divide, showing the way forward by unflinchingly looking at the past and emphasizing fraternal ties as the basis for building a more fruitful relationship. In his annual message in December 2001, Emperor Akihito caused a muted stir by publicly acknowledging for the first time that Japan's imperial line descended from Korean ancestors. By confirming to the Japanese public what scholars have long known, Akihito was trying to set the tone for an improvement in bilateral relations by challenging the basis for ethnic chauvinism; they are we. Interestingly, among the major newspapers, only the *Asahi*, a relatively progressive newspaper, carried this part of his message and thus many Japanese, caught up in the end-of-year celebrations, were blissfully unaware that the emperor had spoken of his dynasty's Korean lineage. However, his forthright admission garnered praise in the Korean press. (Most Japanese must have been mystified by subsequent reports of Korean praise for Emperor Akihito since the Japanese media largely ignored the ancestry comments that were so welcome.)

The World Cup final held in the Yokohama Stadium proved a memorable "Kodak moment" in bilateral relations as Emperor Akihito sat next to South Korean President Kim Dae Jung while watching the match between Brazil and Germany. This was an improbable image, one resonating with layered meanings. The former democracy activist and political prisoner, once abducted in Japan by Korean agents sent to assassinate him, was now the honored guest of an emperor committed to reconciliation and laying to rest the ghosts of the shared past. Ironically, those in Japan who most strongly support a revival of the imperial system, a motley collection of extremists, ultra-nationalists, mobsters, mainstream conservative politicians, and pundits, are also those most opposed to this emperor's agenda of healing. His emphasis on promoting a more humanitarian and pacifist sense of nation predicated on assuming responsibility for the past and demonstrating contrition clashes with their hopes for using him as a focus of a more emphatic nationalism.

Clearly, Akihito's poignant gestures towards Korea are in line with a series of reconciliation initiatives towards past enemies and regional victims. The Lost Decade of the 1990s was a time when Akihito demonstrated courageous leadership in tackling the unfinished business of WWII that has impeded improvement in Japan's regional relations. Akihito has stepped forward as assertively as possible, and helpfully, to undo the accumulated harm of neglecting, denying, and minimizing past wrongs committed during his father's reign. His efforts to draw a line under Japan's inglorious past in a manner acceptable to past victims stands in contrast to the inaction of hesitant bureaucrats and opportunistic politicians who have failed miserably in coping with the contemporary repercussions of past misdeeds.

Guilty?

The Women's International War Crimes Tribunal (WIWCT or Tokyo Women's Tribunal) convened in Tokyo in 2000 represented a belated attempt by Japanese and international jurists to hold Emperor Showa accountable for his role in Japan's escalating war in Asia between 1931 and

1945. The tribunal was aimed at rectifying the silence of the International Military Tribunal for the Far East (IMTFE, 1946–8) regarding the emperor's war responsibility and to delve into the experiences of women caught up in that maelstrom. The tribunal attracted protests by right-wing groups eager to keep a lid on this past and considerable media attention, including a subsidiary of Japan National Broadcasting (NHK) that negotiated the rights to film the proceedings.

In 2005, the *Asahi* newspaper, based on reports by a whistleblower, alleged that NHK censored its 2001 documentary covering the Tokyo Women's Tribunal because of political pressure from senior politicians in the Liberal Democratic Party. Four presiding judges declared that Japan's system of military sexual slavery, known as the "comfort women" system, was not only a war crime but a crime against humanity; they further found Emperor Showa guilty, and the Japanese government to have incurred state responsibility.[4] The TV program's producer stated, "We were ordered to alter the program before it was aired. I would have to say that the alteration was made against the backdrop of political pressure."[5] The censored version of the documentary that was aired eliminated testimony by soldiers and references to the verdict finding Emperor Showa guilty of allowing the comfort women system to operate.

On January 30, 2001 NHK screened a 40-minute segment, part two of a series entitled "How to Judge Wars," that featured the proceedings of the Tokyo Women's Tribunal. This tribunal was convened in December 2000 to examine issues involving violence against women in war, most notably the comfort women system. Presiding over the court was an international team of prosecutors and judges, some of whom had participated in the Bosnian and Rwandan war crimes trials.

The Tokyo Women's Tribunal was established because there had been no previous judicial determination of responsibility for acts of violence committed against women in Asia during WWII. Organizers believe that the IMTFE did not go nearly far enough in assessing Japan's war responsibility, letting too many Japanese off the hook for heinous crimes they committed, especially those involving women. The controversy over the tribunal and the NHK documentary provides insights into the fundamental fault-line of post-WWII Japanese history that divides Japanese: unfairly condemned for challenging an international order that subjugated Japan and other Asian nations; or, guilty of justifying, minimizing, and shirking responsibility for extensive war crimes committed by Japan's Imperial Armed Forces acting at the behest of the emperor.

In the Treaty of Rome (1998) an International Criminal Court was established and empowered to try genocide, rape, and sexual slavery as major war crimes. Animated by similar concerns, the Tokyo Women's Tribunal represents an attempt by civic groups to judge past crimes and determine state responsibility for them. Since the early 1990s, when victims finally came forward and researchers found archival evidence proving state and military involvement in recruiting the comfort women and running the comfort stations, debate in Japan about the entire issue has been highly charged and controversial. The battles have been fought over whether to include reference to the comfort women in school texts and to what extent the state should bear responsibility and atone. In 1993, as we noted in the preceding chapter, Yohei Kono, the chief cabinet secretary at the time, acknowledged state responsibility, proffered an apology and promised to make amends, riling right-wing groups opposed to acknowledging Japan's wartime crimes much less atoning for them.

NHK aired the documentary film on the tribunal on its educational channel, one that typically attracts less than 1 percent of all TV viewers, so it is only because of the censorship scandal that many Japanese actually became aware of the tribunal's finding and the degree to which NHK is politicized. The documentary was subject to a last-minute in-house editing process at a time when NHK was besieged by right-wing protestors and sound trucks demanding the entire program be cancelled. During this phase of editing, NHK incorporated the critical comments of a prominent conservative historian, Ikuhiko Hata, well known for his apologist views regarding the comfort women system. Then, shortly before the film was shown, a meeting was allegedly held between senior executives of NHK and two prominent LDP politicians, Shinzo Abe, then deputy chief cabinet secretary and later prime minister, and Shoichi Nakagawa. Following this meeting, major changes were then made, only hours before the broadcast. This final cut deleted all reference to the emperor's guilt even though this was the main finding of the tribunal.

Abe and Nakagawa were members of the Association to Consider the Future Path for Japan and History Education. This organization, founded in 1997 with 107 Diet members, embraces an exonerating narrative about Japan's wartime past totally at odds with the tribunal and its conclusions, not to mention Japanese public opinion. Political intervention involving media coverage is forbidden by both Article 21 of the Constitution and Article 3 of the Broadcasting Law, but it is standard procedure for NHK executives to meet with Diet members because politicians must approve NHK's annual budget.

Abe defended his meeting with NHK executives, saying he had heard that the tribunal was biased and was naturally concerned about possible misrepresentations. He explained, "Because I was told that the mock trial was going to be reported in the way that the organizers wanted it to be, I looked into the matter. I found out that the contents were clearly biased and told [NHK] that it should be broadcast from a fair and neutral viewpoint, as it is expected to."[6]

The NHK censorship controversy ended up in the courts. The Supreme Court in June 2008 reversed a lower court ruling and dismissed a suit filed in 2001 by one of the seven NGOs that organized the tribunal, Violence Against Women in War-Network Japan (VAWW-NET Japan). The NGO demanded that NHK and two affiliated production companies pay compensation for altering the documentary and deleting discussion of the emperor's responsibility for the comfort women system. The NGO claimed cutting this crucial conclusion constituted breach of trust.[7]

The top court ruled the three media firms involved were not obliged to produce a documentary in accordance with the plaintiff's expectations because broadcasters are free to edit their productions. It also rejected the plaintiff's complaint that NHK had betrayed their trust and expectations since the public is aware that TV programs are normally edited. At issue, as the court defined it, was whether NHK and the two production companies were obliged to explain to VAWW-NET Japan about the changes they made before the program was broadcast. In the court ruling, Justice Kazuko Yokoo, the presiding judge, said legally protecting the trust and expectations of people who become the subjects of broadcast productions would impinge on press freedoms.

Although NHK was exonerated in the courts, the censorship scandal and the appearance of kowtowing to conservative politicians about the emperor's war responsibility has further tarnished a reputation already suffering from a series of embezzlement scandals. Significantly, in 2009 the Broadcasting Ethics and Program Improvement Organization criticized NHK's handling of the documentary, stating that for the sake of independence and autonomy NHK should cease the practice of consulting with senior government officials about program content. This ethics committee specifically criticized NHK for the meeting with Shinzo Abe prior to airing the program, but refrained from concluding that political meddling influenced the editing process. The panel's surprising recommendation that NHK stop consulting politicians over specific programs is not legally binding, but does carry moral authority within the industry and the public at large. So just as it thought that the issue had been resolved to its satisfaction, NHK found that its journalistic ethics and editorial independence are still questioned. Certainly the millions of Japanese who refuse to pay their mandated dues to NHK are not doing so because it covered up the emperor's war guilt, but it does provide them with a convenient reason to claim conscientious objector status.

Just as the NHK imbroglio exposed to what extent the government works to buff the image of the imperial family, a new more fundamental threat has emerged that shows the IHA at its meddling worst.

Family Discord and Succession Politics

In 2004, Crown Prince Naruhito vented his frustrations with treatment of his wife, Crown Princess Masako, publically stating, "There were developments that denied Masako's personality." This was a thinly veiled reference to the oppressive restrictions on her activities imposed by the IHA and her mental breakdown attributed to the stress of adjusting to life in the palace where clothes, food, press conferences, and a heavy schedule of ceremonial duties are dictated by the IHA mandarins. When the couple was engaged, he vowed to defend her and to his credit he made a stand, but the repercussions within the family have been divisive. His father expressed bewilderment at the nature of the complaint, his younger brother suggested he owed an apology, while the IHA claimed innocence and suggested it was all a misunderstanding.

The roots of this family squabble have fueled tabloid speculation and, given how closely drawn the Chrysanthemum curtain is, it is hard to separate fact from fiction.[8] Crown Princess Masako was a reluctant bride and the courtship was prolonged because she was ambivalent about giving up a promising career at the Foreign Ministry and living the life of a princess in the imperial court. She and Crown Prince Naruhito first met in 1986, but it was not until 1993 that they were engaged, apparently only after his third proposal. Finding anyone willing to marry the prince and live in the imperial fishbowl was never going to be easy, and clearly the IHA preferred someone younger and less cosmopolitan, but in the end the prince had his way.

The royal wedding was held later that year in June 1993 with great fanfare, and briefly Masako graced the imperial family with some of the glamour that Princess Diana bestowed on the House of Windsor. However much the people and press may have yearned for this glamour, and valued her potential as a charming multi-lingual ambassador of goodwill given her background and intelligence, the IHA had other plans. The British royals and the endless scandals and gossip were an object lesson of what had to be avoided at all costs to maintain the dignity of the imperial family and palace decorum. At their first joint press conference, Masako spoke longer than her prince, a *faux pas* that apparently invoked the ire of the IHA handlers whose job is focused on protocol, etiquette, and proper deportment which they define as they see fit. Japan might have been at the cusp of the twenty-first century, but the IHA sees its role as maintaining tradition, invented or otherwise, and thus patriarchal prerogatives; a wife waxing more eloquently than her spouse is a familiar sight, but not in the imperial household where women are expected to be more circumspect, deferential, and self-effacing. It is thus not surprising, given her free-spirited ways and troubled marriage, that no Japanese royal attended the funeral of Princess Diana in 1997.

Masako caused another stir in off-the-record comments following a 1996 press conference in which she said she enjoyed reading the novels of Nobel laureate Kenzaburo Oe, a staunch critic of the imperial system who once turned down an imperial decoration saying it was unsuited to democracy. Perhaps she has a mordant sense of humor and sought to retaliate against her handlers, but given the influence and power of the IHA she remains vulnerable to their control of her schedule, her overseas visits, the purse strings, and media access and information.

Masako's principal duty was to produce a male heir to ensure a smooth succession scenario given the 1947 Imperial Household Law excluding women from reigning. There have been eight empresses in Japanese history, but the post-WWII law specifies a male monarch. Thus, as the months and years passed without pregnancy, the crown prince was reduced to repeating that they were still waiting for the stork to visit. This was not a happy time for the royal couple as the pressures to produce an heir mounted and overseas visits by Masako were curtailed by the IHA, ostensibly so she could concentrate on conceiving. In 1999, alas, her first pregnancy ended in miscarriage. In 2001, after eight years of marriage and fertility treatment, Masako, a fortnight shy of her 38th birthday, finally gave birth to a baby girl, Princess Aiko, delighting her family and the nation, but leaving the issue of an heir unresolved.

The 1,100 strong staff of the IHA does not always get its way, but does control the purse strings. Unlike the British monarchy, Japan's royal family has no money or assets of its own and is entirely dependent on public money. The UK's Prince Charles lamented: "If they have to look to the state for everything, they become nothing more than puppets and prisoners in their own countries. That's what happened to the Japanese royal family. They can't even go on holiday without asking parliament." Actually they can, but the point concerning their absolute dependence on the government for their living allowances is correct and overseas travel is at the discretion of the IHA. Many of the high-ranking staff of the IHA are seconded from other government ministries and their brief is to manage the imperial family. Given their background and training as bureaucrats, and role as guardians of the modern, largely invented traditions of the court, it is not surprising that they have a conservative outlook that at times seems to chafe with the emperor's desires to modernize the monarchy and bring it closer to the people.[9] Never was this more apparent than when the chief of the IHA publically called on the royal couple to have a second child; unsaid but understood was the admonition to bear a male heir.

The media scrutiny and speculation about a royal heir added to the IHA pressures, apparently causing Masako to have a nervous breakdown and largely withdraw from the public eye from late 2002. She was diagnosed with an "adjustment" disorder and appears to suffer from mental depression. She left a cosmopolitan lifestyle and the rigors of negotiating trade issues for a life within a very rigid monarchy where her duties comprise presiding over ribbon cutting events and an endless array of public ceremonies. Her talents have thus gone untapped by her IHA handlers who focused obsessively on her heir-bearing duty.

With no male heir on hand and Masako already 41 years old, Prime Minister Junichiro Koizumi appointed a panel to investigate the issue of amending the 1947 Imperial Household Law to allow for a woman to inherit the throne. In 2005 the panel endorsed revision of the law to permit a female succession and in January 2006 Prime Minister Koizumi pledged to submit legislation accordingly. Public support for allowing a female succession was overwhelming, with nearly 80 percent indicating support for this reform in public opinion polls. Conservatives were aghast and one royal suggested bringing back the concubine system to ensure a male heir, an idea that was widely ridiculed.

In February 2006 the announcement that Princess Kiko, wife of the younger Prince Akishino, was pregnant shelved efforts to amend the succession law. In September she gave birth to her third child, Prince Hisahito, the first male born in the imperial family in 41 years. Conservatives breathed a collective sigh of relief that male primogeniture remains intact. However, even as they welcomed the new heir, press editorials uniformly endorsed continuing the debate over female succession, suggesting that almost everyone else in twenty-first-century Japan is fine with the idea. And, pundits pointed out, one male heir does not really resolve Japan's succession crisis.

Upstaging the crown prince by producing the coveted male heir has sparked media speculation about a sibling rift between Naruhito and Akishino. It has also fueled speculation in some quarters about whether Crown Prince Naruhito might abdicate in favor of his younger brother in order to spare Masako the added scrutiny and duties of being empress and facilitate a smooth succession.

Masako's relations with her in-laws are strained despite the fact that her mother-in-law also suffered bouts of depression in the 1960s as she "adjusted" to the stressful life of being the daughter-in-law in the imperial family. Common problems, however, have not led to mutual understanding. In 2008 the IHA even publicly chided the crown prince's family for their infrequent visits to the emperor and empress, maneuvering him to promise to be more attentive. In April 2009, in a NHK television special commemorating the emperor's 50th wedding anniversary, a show carefully scripted by the IHA, Masako was notable for her absence. Crown Prince Naruhito was also marginalized, only appearing when he was a child and teenager, but unlike his younger brother, never as an adult.

The sad saga of Masako inevitably has put the IHA in the limelight and it has not fared very well, its inept handling of the media and orchestrated attacks backfiring. In essence, the IHA is accused of bullying Masako and trying to make her conform to their dictates and in doing so they have ignored her potential. With Masako essentially on strike, refusing to assume her normal duties, the IHA has clipped her wings, virtually banning foreign travel, and arranges selective press leaks designed to portray her unfavorably. For example, it is widely believed that the IHA is behind press reports in 2008 about Masako's occasional dining out at restaurants that draw attention to her spending as much as JPY10,000 ($100) on these meals. Media restraint and tolerance regarding the ailing princess quickly degenerated into condemnation and accusations of malingering, indicating just how poorly mental depression is understood in contemporary Japan. While her dining tabs were expensive compared to what many people spend for dinner, in Tokyo such prices are fairly standard for good restaurants and far less than is commonly spent by those in political and business circles. Certainly by the standards of European monarchy, Masako is not living a lavish, jet-setter lifestyle, but even such minor indulgences rub up against the self-conscious austerity of the imperial family; the emperor still drives a 1994 Honda Accord around the palace grounds. Many Japanese sympathize with her plight and few envy her position under the thumb of the arrogant IHA martinets.

Prospects

The imperial family has not, in many respects, enjoyed a promising beginning to the twenty-first century. The emperor's reconciliation diplomacy has been overshadowed by the travails of Crown Princess Masako, controversies over his father's war guilt, and concerns about the succession. Crown Prince Naruhito has come to his wife's defense and in so doing embarrassed officials in the IHA, and the tension has sowed discord within the family. In addition, Emperor Akihito's prostrate surgery in 2003 and brief break from official duties at the end of 2008 due to exhaustion raise concerns about his health. The greatest danger to the imperial family, one the IHA seemingly ignores, is maintaining relevance in a rapidly changing world. The IHA is also a danger to the legitimacy of the monarchy because its clumsy manipulation of the media and very prominent tethering of Crown Prince Naruhito risk a *Wizard of Oz* scenario. His powerlessness to protect his wife and promote a more modern and relevant role for her that makes use of her talents has made the IHA's power all too clear and this does not serve the interests of the throne. The power of the court's symbolism depends on illusions that the IHA is inadvertently undermining by its heavy-handed tactics; as in *bunraku* (traditional Japanese puppet theater), the audience focuses on the puppets that are brought to life precisely because the deft movements of the puppeteers dressed in black who the audience barely notices sustain this illusion if they are adept at their art. Nobody accuses the IHA of being adept or subtle in asserting its prerogatives.

However, sources of continued support for the Chrysanthemum Throne remain powerful and the "people's emperor" has arguably broadened the court's constituency and bridged the gulf between the palace and the public. The Heisei era may be best known as a period of prolonged economic stagnation, but Akihito's legacy will draw on his numerous gestures of atonement aimed at facilitating reconciliation in the region. Akihito has quietly but relentlessly served his nation and contributed compassionately to addressing the grievances of those who have suffered, whether from Hansen's disease (leprosy) or natural disasters at home or the depredations of Japanese expansionism under his father. His successor has a hard act to follow and will be hard-pressed to maintain the public support and status of the monarchy while carving out an appropriate role in twenty-first century Japan. Making the transition to the twenty-first century is also challenging another traditional institution, organized crime (yakuza), but as we see in the next chapter it has been considerably more resourceful and flexible in adapting to the risks it faces.

Chapter 12

Yakuza

The yakuza (organized crime syndicates) are Japan's mafia, controlling various illegal and profitable rackets ranging from drugs and prostitution to gambling, blackmail, loan sharking, and extortion based on their core strengths in violence and intimidation. The yakuza have a long and rich tradition in Japan dating back to the seventeenth century, although contemporary gangsters have little in common with their forebears beyond initiation rituals and a penchant for violence. The yakuza are also quite distinct from the mafia. In its heyday the mafia in the US numbered some 5,000 while even the greatly downsized yakuza of the twenty-first century have more than 40,000 core members and as many non-regular members. Another significant difference, until recently, has been the high-level, visible access of yakuza bosses reaching right up to the top of the political and business establishment and a symbiotic relationship with law enforcement. Until the twenty-first century the yakuza, unlike their mafia counterparts, could operate quite openly and maintained cordial relations with police with whom they would frequently share information.[1]

The Lost Decade led to significant changes in Japan and also within the yakuza and in their relations with the establishment. The economic turmoil of the 1990s is often dubbed the yakuza recession because they are blamed for pushing many lenders to the edge of bankruptcy by not repaying large loans, thereby damaging the overall economy. The yakuza, like most other investors at the time, suffered tremendous losses from the dramatic drop in asset values, but unlike other borrowers, they were in a good position to renege on their loans. The scale of non-performing loans linked to the yakuza is stunning, indicating that regulators and bankers could not have been in the dark as to the nature of who was borrowing such extraordinary sums.

The yakuza like to portray themselves as keepers of Japan's traditions, men of virtue who help the vulnerable and regulate crime. The reality is quite different. These avatars of tradition are thoroughly adapted to modern ways and conduct their operations ruthlessly with scant compassion for those who do not comply with their demands. They are violence specialists who tap modern niches and constantly reinvent themselves to stay a step ahead of the police and to develop lucrative new business lines. The stereotypical images of the yakuza projected in film, anime, manga, and novels are mostly way out of date. The punch-perm hairstyle has given way to the moussed look, tattoos and missing pinkies are not quite so common, and few wear the flashy clothes of yesteryear.

The yakuza are also adjusting to vastly different operating conditions. Law enforcement has become hostile and is cracking down, forcing the yakuza to adapt accordingly. In addition, the prolonged recession, rapid aging, and labor shortages that are causing havoc in Japan are similarly bedeviling the yakuza. While the yakuza may be experiencing a microcosm of the ills facing all of Japan, they are pioneers in rapidly and effectively adapting to these challenges. Some pundits predict their demise, but as we examine below, it is premature to count the yakuza out.

Flexible Business Model

The yakuza remain at the cutting edge of business, responding nimbly and resolutely to new challenges and constantly reinventing their organizations and methods to deal with those they face and those they anticipate. Their motto, if they had one, would be "by any and all means necessary." They are a lesson in how to successfully adapt to a rapidly changing world. The yakuza, of course, have the added problem of pursuing many dubious if not illegal activities while the state is ratcheting up pressures on them to go out of business. Paradoxically, in a society that values harmony and peace, these violence specialists belonging to very visible crime syndicates have managed to survive by nurturing a symbiotic relation with mainstream Japan. But times are changing.

The yakuza's problems are exactly those of Japan as a whole: they are rapidly aging, have trouble recruiting and retaining a young cadre, face hungry international competitors and an unfavorable regulatory market, are downsizing while merging to gain efficiencies while cutting costs, and are trying to reinvent themselves and adapt their core strengths to new market niches, all amidst a stagnant economy. Like their upper-world counterparts, underworld bosses are pruning their core labor force and relying increasingly on non-regular workers and outsourcing. Harvard Business School is not likely to make them a case study, but it ought to.

The yakuza have long faced adversity since they began operating in the seventeenth century and would have faded long ago if they couldn't respond quickly and effectively. It is worth bearing in mind that the term *yakuza* is derived from the name for a losing hand in cards that requires a player to skillfully judge opponents in order to overcome the odds.

For many yakuza, the odds are steep indeed. They are rapidly aging and their profligate lifestyles are catching up with them. Gambling, prostitution, drugs, public works bid-rigging, and usury – the mainstays for the yakuza – are not as lucrative as they once were and the police are not as tolerant. The police crackdown beginning in the early 1990s has forced the yakuza to diversify, and many operations that were once openly practiced have been driven underground. In the old days the yakuza would hand over criminals to the police and favored knives and swords, but in recent years they have been having shootouts with the cops and even gunned down two mayors of Nagasaki. The cozy and collusive cooperation between the state and the yakuza, always oversimplified and overstated, is not nearly as symbiotic as it once was, one of the many transformations in contemporary Japan.

Like corporate Japan, crime syndicates are worried about attracting and retaining sufficient labor, and both see possibilities in tapping the talents of foreign workers and developing alliances with foreign operators. They also have to contend with a new breed of Japanese who have higher expectations, more options, and less patience about paying their dues to rise in the mob hierarchy. The reluctance of young Japanese to enter the yakuza means that organized crime is aging even more rapidly than the general populace, a huge problem given that their operations ultimately rely on intimidation and credible threats of violence.

Membership

The police estimate the ranks of the core yakuza at some 43,000 as of 2007, down from 91,000 in 1991 and a peak of 184,000 in the early 1960s. This is still a large number compared to the 5,000 "wise guys" working for the US mafia at its peak. An additional 40,000 gangsters are quasi-members, reflecting the yakuza response to a harsher legal and economic environment that bears some resemblance to the expanding Japanese corporate reliance on part-time and temporary workers during the Heisei era. The shrinking numbers of yakuza are a response to the new laws that create incentives for groups to expel members with criminal records (or at least pretend to do so) or run the risk of being designated a "dangerous group" subject to various sanctions. In addition, members who are not performing well or those who fall in arrears on their tribute payments have been expelled.

The three biggest syndicates, the Yamaguchi-gumi, Sumiyoshi-kai, and Inagawa-kai, have between them around 61,100 members, or nearly three-quarters of the total mob population of 84,000. The Yamaguchi-gumi alone employs nearly half of this total. If listed on the stock exchange, the Yamaguchi-gumi would be the Toyota in its sector, a juggernaut besting all its rivals. Robert Feldman, chief economist at Morgan Stanley Japan, calls it the "largest private equity group in Japan."

The yakuza are employers of last resort, employing and imposing discipline on poorly educated, marginal young men prone to violence and crime who have few, if any, other options. Many are juvenile delinquents and some are recruited from motorcycle gangs.[2] Koreans and *burakumin* (a hereditary outcast group subject to persistent discrimination despite legal strictures) are overrepresented in the ranks of yakuza due to exclusion from many other career options. The National Police Agency estimates that some 10 percent of the Yamaguchi-gumi is *zainichi* (ethnic Koreans born and raised in Japan) while 70 percent of its members are *burakumin*.

The new breed of yakuza that has emerged during the Heisei era is not all about brawn and violence. The core strength of yakuza remains "protection" and that depends on a credible threat of violence. However, as yakuza have diversified their interests and moved into legitimate business activities, usually through layers of front companies, other skill sets have become valuable. Yakuza are less concerned about maintaining a flashy image and are more inclined these days to adopt the corporate camouflage of business suits and blend into the world of legitimate business. In the twenty-first century, they also need good computer and management skills, knowledge of the law, and financial savvy. The yakuza's core competence remains rooted in intimidation, ruthlessness, opportunism, and violence, but more than ever smooth, intelligent, and presentable operators are guiding the yakuza through a tough and prolonged period of transition as they reposition operations and adapt to new realities.

The key problem facing the yakuza is a rapidly aging leadership and core membership. Geriatric hoods are just not as intimidating as they need to be. To some extent yakuza are outsourcing, cultivating symbiotic relationships with foreign gangs and bringing in Chinese mobsters to provide the muscle on certain types of jobs such as armed robbery and human trafficking. As legitimate businesses all know, however, there are limits to outsourcing and dangers in nurturing tomorrow's competitors. It is indicative that yakuza groups have resorted to placing classified ads, a sign of desperation that is unlikely to address the key problem: younger people have other options, the marginalized are not so hungry anymore, and few have the patience to put up with the strict discipline and hierarchical structure of the yakuza. Moreover, for new recruits the rewards are less than they used to be and the police are more hostile and more inclined to arrest and imprison gangsters.

Construction State

Japan has an enormous public works budget and the yakuza have earned considerable sums from their involvement in construction projects and bid-rigging, just as organized crime exploits sand and gravel contracts in other nations. The nexuses of massive construction projects, bureaucrats, politicians, businessmen, and yakuza are as revealing about Japan as they are about Italy and Russia. In Japan, the yakuza cut on construction projects is estimated at 3 percent, a vast sum that keeps them afloat, given that during the 1990s the public works budget was on a par with the US Pentagon's budget and remains quite high despite huge cutbacks.

During the bubble era in the late 1980s, yakuza came to provide a crucial service for real-estate developers and construction companies by clearing large plots of land of tenants and small landowners. These *jiage* operations involved thugs intimidating and threatening people living on or adjacent to sites designated for development to sell out, thereby creating a large plot of land needed for some of the expansive real-estate projects that characterized the tasteless excesses of the bubble at its worst. This was a frightening experience for many of the older people living in central Tokyo, and cast yakuza in the role of hoods bulldozing aside the weak and vulnerable at the behest of the powerful, hardly the Robin Hood image the yakuza are keen to promote. Anyone visiting Tokyo these days can see these huge gleaming new shopping centers and condominium projects all over the city where there had once been vibrant neighborhoods and tightly knit communities of mom-and-pop stores, small business operations, and traditional wooden family homes.

For their work, these violence specialists got a 3 percent commission on the value of the land cleared at a time when land values were skyrocketing in the late 1980s. This lucrative business led many yakuza to plow their illicit earnings into land speculation and stock investment, believing like everyone else that asset prices would continue to soar. These significant underworld investments in legitimate enterprises involved them much more extensively in the establishment where their existence has been tolerated because they provided services in demand that others were unable to carry out as effectively. In doing so, the yakuza were setting themselves up as competitors and blurring distinctions, making them increasingly unwelcome in the mainstream, a theme we return to later in the chapter.

Following the crash in land prices at the beginning of the Heisei era, the *jiage* business dried up and the yakuza were bleeding from the implosion in asset values. Their investments had soured big time and they could no longer service loans many had taken out. However, unlike other borrowers, the yakuza could rely on their ruthless reputation to keep creditors at bay while scrambling to find new lucrative business opportunities.

Recession Management

The new businesses were adaptations of old staples: debt collection, bankruptcy management, and protection. In Japan's distressed economy, these were highly profitable growth markets for violence specialists. Yakuza normally charge a 50 percent commission on whatever they collect from debtors, but could easily supplement their earnings by adding expenses and working both sides of the deal. Approaching a debtor, the yakuza could negotiate a favorably low settlement, collect half of it from the creditor, and then also net a handsome "tip" from the grateful debtor for having drastically reduced their debt. The creditors played along because it was better than nothing and only the yakuza had the ability to convince deadbeat debtors, often colleagues, to ensure partial payment. In some respects it is an elaboration of the protection racket where the yakuza sell protection from the threats and inconveniences that only they themselves pose. They were collecting from underworld debtors only they would dare approach and only they could make pay.

Another lucrative market involved obstructing the auction of foreclosed properties. By inveigling in various ways to take some form of possession of a distressed property, or occupy it, the yakuza could make life miserable for the creditor trying to sell the property. By making it clear to potential buyers that buying the property also meant buying into an unwanted connection to the yakuza, the yakuza could drive away buyers and depress the price. They could then turn around and buy the property at a much reduced price or wait for the creditor to make them a generous offer to leave. Either way, they stood to profit. The reason the yakuza manage to survive under adverse circumstances is because they have many arrows in their quiver.

Sokaiya

One of the more lucrative rackets involves corporate extortion by *sokaiya*, professionals specializing in information.[3] *Sokaiya* ferret out, or invent, information about embarrassing corporate or executive misconduct and threaten to expose this to the public unless they are paid large sums of hush money. Police estimate that this has been a key source of yakuza income because firms, including a who's who of corporate Japan, are determined to keep their secrets. Although this extortion is illegal, it persists. Companies are vulnerable and pay precisely because reputation and image translate into financial performance; inconvenient revelations can hammer a company's share price. Society, and perhaps more importantly the market, value good reputation, sound and ethical business practices, decorum, and harmony. These would all be at risk if the yakuza publicized indiscretions, malfeasance, or incompetence.

Clearly this racket depends on the yakuza reading the cards, understanding exactly what corporate executives fear most and what they are prepared to do to make their nightmares go away. There are different permutations of the squeeze, ranging from threats to disrupt annual shareholder meetings by asking embarrassing questions or surrounding corporate headquarters with sound trucks blaring out the juicy details. Alternatively, yakuza might publish their research in special magazines and offer management the opportunity to buy the entire print run to bury the story, or enroll them as subscribers to expensive newsletters as a quid pro quo for not spreading the secrets. Occasionally the yakuza researchers feed some stories of corporate misconduct to the media just to remind "subscribers" about the advantages of keeping up with their subscriptions.

Ironically, *sokaiya* were initially hired by companies to protect them from such threats. One of the most infamous cases involved the Chisso Corporation that hired *sokaiya* for its annual shareholder meetings to intimidate and shout down the questions by victims of mercury poisoning caused by effluent from its factory in the fishing village of Minamata. Savvy *sokaiya* quickly learned just how valuable their intervention and information could be, whether defending corporations or shaking them down. In the booming days of the bubble in the late 1980s, firms flush with cash proved easy and lucrative targets.

As times got tough in the 1990s and paying the *sokaiya* to go away became an apparently dispensable luxury, some companies stopped paying. As a result, executives were threatened with violence and targeted for reprisal. An executive of Fuji Film was stabbed to death on his doorstep, a warning to others about the dangers of not paying. It is difficult to know with certainty about the scope and nature of *sokaiya* activities, but their ruthlessness suggests that the state's determination to limit this practice faces a tough hurdle.

In fact the government initially tried to tackle the *sokaiya* problem in 1982 by prohibiting the use of corporate (but not personal) funds for payoffs, but the *sokaiya* modified their tactics, establishing *uyoku dantai* (fake right-wing groups) who harassed companies with their loudspeaker trucks until paid off. The government also mandated holding annual shareholder meetings on the same day, making it more difficult for *sokaiya* to disrupt them. However, cracking down on *sokaiya* while respecting shareholder rights puts the government in a tight legal bind because ostensibly they enjoy the same rights and legal protections of any citizen.

Close ties with yakuza groups, legal shortcomings, and adaptability have kept the *sokaiya* in business. Not only are they creative in elaborating new scams, they have an ace up their sleeves: executives' reluctance to cooperate with police because they fear exposure of corporate wrongdoing.

Public Image

If it was up to the yakuza, they would try to keep public attention focused on how they set up the first soup kitchens for survivors of the Kobe earthquake in 1995. This stands as their greatest public relations triumph of the Heisei era, one that highlighted the government's dawdling and bumbling response in contrast to their selfless, generous, and timely provision of assistance to ordinary citizens hammered by a massive natural disaster. Nothing could have been more humiliating to the government and more flattering to the yakuza. But a reputation is not made on a single event and overall the yakuza image has taken a well-deserved pummeling during the Heisei era, largely a consequence of self-inflicted wounds.

During the Heisei era, increasing numbers of non-combatants have been caught in the crossfire of gang battles while there have been more citizens victimized by predatory gang operations. This has created a groundswell turning public opinion against the yakuza. As long as gangsters engaged in crimes of a consensual nature such as gambling and prostitution, the police averted their eyes, but as *minbo* (extortion) operations targeting citizens expanded during the 1990s, the yakuza were setting themselves up for a backlash.

One of the more notorious cases involved film director Juzo Itami whose 1992 film *Minbo No Onna* (*The Anti-Extortion Woman*) satirized the yakuza and made them look foolish. In the film, a hotel vying for an important conference contract is targeted for extortion by yakuza that decide it makes a good place to hang out unless they get paid to leave. Naturally their uncouth presence undermines the ambience that the upscale hotel wants to project. The hotel staff is useless in trying to deal with the yakuza until a woman lawyer specializing in such matters begins to advise the hotel on how to get rid of the unwanted guests. In the film the yakuza come across as weak and foolish bullies who are all bark but no bite and, most embarrassingly, no match for this clever woman. In retaliation for all the laughs at their expense, real-life yakuza from the Gotogumi exacted revenge on Itami by brutally beating him and slashing his face. This violent attack on a popular actor and director shortly after the film's release led to harsh media coverage and calls for action. In that same year, coincidentally, the Diet passed the *botaiho* (anti-yakuza) legislation targeting yakuza organizations and their activities.

Thus in the 1990s the yakuza could only blame themselves for destroying all the glamorous and noble myths they had been promoting for so long with notable success. The myths had power and considerable currency not because they were true, but because people didn't know better. Once people began to understand the seamy and nasty nature of the yakuza and their operations, the cozy image faded rapidly. Yakuza may claim to be agents of social control who keep the streets free of crime, but citizens observe the reality of their ruthless violence increasingly reported in the press and government white papers on organized crime. Based on their track record, they are now seen and depicted as a threat to safety and social harmony rather than as guardians of traditional ethos and values.

The once symbiotic relationship with the police, a lingering image that vastly oversimplifies the situation pre-*botaiho*, was always a partial truth that is fading rapidly. Now that the state has declared war on the yakuza and treats them as a social evil, vestiges of cooperative relations between authorities and gangsters have receded.

Nonetheless, the yakuza do maintain close ties with politicians and until the 1990s saw no reason to hide such relations.[4] Some politicians depend on yakuza campaign donations and support in canvassing, and rumors suggest much more. In return, yakuza are always eager to develop networks of powerful and influential friends who can give them an inside track and put in a timely word. But working with politicians carries the risk of scandal and media attention.

The Sagawa Kyubin scandal that erupted in 1992 revealed the sleazy nexus of ties linking yakuza, businessmen, and politicians. Most attention focused on this parcel delivery company's large illegal donations to Shin Kanemaru, an LDP political heavyweight. A police raid on his home uncovered a stash of gold ingots, cash, and bank debentures worth several million dollars. But this was no ordinary cash for favors scandal. Kanemaru, it turns out, had asked executives at Sagawa Kyubin to arrange a meeting with Susumu Ishii, the head of the Inagawa-kai. The purpose of the meeting was to ask for Ishii's help in stopping right-wing sound trucks from harassing Noboru Takeshita as he was campaigning for support to become the Japanese prime minister. The right-wingers were embarrassing Takeshita with effusive and excessive praise (*homegoroshi*), just the kind of support and ties he was not eager to embrace or advertize. Kanemaru persuaded Ishii to intervene, the volume was turned down, and Takeshita became prime minister (1987–9), one who owed the mob.

While many Japanese suspect that politicians' links with mobsters are extensive, never has the highest-ranking politician found himself in the spotlight in such a compromising situation, at least since 1960 when Prime Minister Nobusuke Kishi unleashed yakuza goons on left-wing demonstrators protesting the security treaty with the US. And almost never again, except in December 2000 when the media published an old photo of PM Yoshiro Mori drinking in an Osaka bar with a former top-level gangster. It was one of many good reasons why he was ousted from the premiership, but since then he remains an influential player in the LDP and the Diet.

Apparently mobster friends in political circles are not as taboo as some would imagine or hope.

The public, however, is not amused that gangsters seem to have excellent access to the corridors of power, a situation most would believe is a problem in Italy or contemporary Russia. Imagining that the yakuza can pull strings is somewhat different than actually watching them doing so. It appears odd, for example, that Japan still lacks a racketeering law akin to the RICO (Racketeer Influenced and Corrupt Organizations) Act in the US that has been a key to anti-organized crime efforts there, fueling speculation that the fix is in.

One of the key problems is that most yakuza no longer lead the good life because they can't afford to. Budgets no longer stretch to designer clothes, expensive cars, and posh watering holes except for privileged members of the relatively well-off Yamaguchi-gumi and higher-ranking members of other groups. Losing the appurtenances of wealth and power, and leading a less flamboyant lifestyle, have lowered the yakuza's cool quotient and also help explain why fewer youth aspire to join.

Yakuza Recession?

During the economic bubble of the 1980s, the yakuza plunged into legitimate ventures, borrowing from banks and their affiliates with abandon to fund them while often diverting chunks of the loans into other dubious schemes. Banks were desperate to lend money because their established corporate customers were not borrowing and instead were raising easy and cheap money on the frothy stock market. Bankers were thus not as fussy about who they lent to and yakuza could borrow large sums using land as collateral based on madly inflated values. Many yakuza-related loans were channeled through *jusen*, real-estate lending affiliates of the major banks. In 1996 the *jusen* went belly-up under the weight of massive non-performing loans. It is the yakuza connection to Japan's massive bad debt problem in the 1990s, and its role in deepening and sustaining Japan's economic nosedive, that led many commentators to dub this the yakuza recession.[5]

The *jusen* were lightly regulated and not covered by the Ministry of Finance's 1990 belated restriction on banks' real-estate-related lending, issued with impeccable timing just as the bubble was collapsing. The *jusen* were known for lax lending standards and no risk assessment, often lending more money than the collateral was worth. During the early 1990s they were lending into a highly risky market in a tailspin and went bankrupt as a result of this folly. The banks and the Ministry of Finance all knew about *jusen* activities, but chose to look the other way; the banks were trying to make money on higher interest rate spreads on *jusen* loans and the government wanted to help banks through what was then thought to be a rough patch.[6] It ended in a colossal financial disaster requiring an unpopular bank bailout as the *jusen*'s non-performing loans reached some US$81 billion. As a result, in 1996 the government liquidated seven jusen.

The large volume of loans to yakuza presented creditors with special challenges and dangers not usually associated with foreclosure. The yakuza had lost heavily in the collapse in asset values while banks faced the unanticipated problem of the land used as collateral guaranteeing the loans being worth a fraction of bubble era values. To the extent that the banks took over the land posted as collateral, assuming they could do so, and sold it off to recover some of their money, they risked sparking a further downward spiral in land prices that would further undermine their already distressed balance sheets. But foreclosing on the yakuza was never going to be easy.

The murders of two bank executives in 1993 and 1994 highlighted the risks of recovering debts owed by yakuza. Sumitomo Bank adopted an aggressive strategy of recovering the loan collateral and in yakuza-related cases hired other gangsters to spearhead such loan collection efforts. The yakuza responded by fatally shooting a Nagoya-based Sumitomo Bank officer involved in these efforts. Subsequently, the Ministry of Finance granted Sumitomo Bank permission to write off some JPY500 billion of yakuza-linked non-performing loans, suggesting that it was not oblivious to institutions under its supervision having mob connections. Other banks also lined up for permission to write off what were euphemistically designated "hard-to-recover" loans, totaling some JPY20 trillion by 1997.

Official estimates of the bad loan problem of banks and non-bank financial institutions were relatively small, but in 2002 Goldman Sachs estimated the total as high as JPY237 trillion. Yakuza exposure, directly and indirectly, was estimated at 40 percent of this bad debt mountain. When the government acted to clean up the mess it established the Resolution and Collection Corporation in 1999 that purchased non-performing loans to take them off bank balance sheets. By its own reckoning nearly 20 percent of the loans purchased by the RCC were believed to be yakuza linked. Foreign investors buying up distressed assets would often purchase a basket of mortgages at a fraction of their face value. Based on their due diligence they estimated that about 30 percent of the mortgages involved yakuza and priced their offers accordingly. Rather than trying to get the yakuza to pay, they would then forgive their debts and concentrate on the more readily recoverable loans.

It's not every day that you get a riveting post-WWII social history of Japan from the perspective of a yakuza, but Manabu Miyazaki, a former member of Japan's underworld, has risen to the task.[7] Among other things, he seeks to set the record straight on the yakuza recession. Unexpectedly, he waxes philosophical about the hysteria and greed that gripped Japan during the booming bubble era at the end of the 1980s. This all may seem odd coming from a man who made ends meet and then some by busting heads and elbowing in on land speculation. Here, however, he settles scores against the Japanese establishment "wimps" who he accuses of forgetting how to act like men. The crime? Getting in bed with the yakuza to enlist their help and then betraying them. This is not how everyone sees it, but Miyazaki thinks the yakuza have been unfairly blamed for causing the Lost Decade, also known as the yakuza recession.

Miyazaki recalls his life as a *toppamono*, one who bulldozes his way ahead regardless of the consequences. He rescued his family's fortunes, telling his older brother to carry on the legitimate side of the construction business while offering to secure contracts in any way possible. Here we learn about the art of bid-rigging, price-fixing, and the web of corruption in the *doken kokka* involving yakuza, politicians, bureaucrats, and businessmen.

Miyazaki also recounts the artful way gangsters were able to shake down banks for massive real-estate-related loans that they didn't repay. In popular lore, these deadbeat borrowers pushed the financial system to the verge of insolvency. He argues, however, that the real villains were the bankers and that the yakuza became convenient scapegoats. In his version, the bankers were desperately pushing loans to gangsters speculating on real estate, all with the knowledge of the Ministry of Finance.

Yakuza as victims? Well as it turns out when the bubble burst and the music stopped it was the bankers who were without a chair, the nation's best and brightest outmaneuvered and fleeced, mistakenly thinking they could play with the players. Miyazaki has a point in fingering the bankers and bureaucrats for their negligence, but surely the yakuza worked the relationship for all it was worth and did commit crimes in carrying out the dirty work. In Miyazaki's version, the establishment was not amused by the yakuza muscling in on legitimate businesses, although happy to avail of their services when needed. The establishment responded by cracking down on the yakuza, passing new legislation aimed at putting them out of business and in their place.

Miyazaki makes a convincing case that the Iron Triangle of big business, the bureaucracy, and politicians has much to answer for in creating the bubble and prolonging its messy unraveling. In his view, they shifted blame for the consequences of their incompetence and neglect onto the yakuza, helping turn public opinion against them.

The Tide Turns

Public tolerance of the yakuza was based on the misperception that their activities involved largely victimless crimes of mutual consent such as gambling and prostitution. However, the expansion of *minbo* (extortion) operations in the 1980s meant an increase in victims and rising public discontent with this situation. Media coverage of those victimized by *jiage-ya* (eviction specialists) and *sokaiya*, various other frauds and scams, not to mention violent gang wars lowered public tolerance of yakuza operations and ratcheted up pressure for more concerted state action.

In Heisei Japan, the yakuza are facing a two-pronged challenge – economic and legal.[8] The collapse of the bubble economy in the early 1990s and the prolonged recession since then hit the yakuza hard by saddling them with investment losses and reducing lucrative opportunities. The weak economy and a shrinking pie generated greater competition among the yakuza groups that has erupted in violence and intensified turf wars that have inflicted collateral damage on ordinary Japanese citizens. With more civilians caught in the crossfire, corporations complaining of systematic shakedowns in the form of *sokaiya*, and facing international pressures to join in the "war on drugs," the government was forced to abandon its averted eyes approach to organized crime. As a result, in 1992 the government passed legislation, revised and expanded several times since (1993, 1997, 2004), targeting the yakuza and their ways of making money.

Botaiho, the organized crime legal countermeasures, target the grey zone of yakuza activities by criminalizing them and subjecting blacklisted crime syndicates to various sanctions. *Minbo*, including the various scams, squeezes, extortion, loan sharking, bankruptcy management, evictions, dispute resolution, and shakedowns by the yakuza, rely on implicit threats of violence. For most citizens an encounter with a yakuza is fraught with peril and anxiety precisely because they know what might happen if they don't comply with the demands. The yakuza, through his demeanor, way of speaking, casual presentation of a card indicating his gang affiliation, or display of a tattoo or severed pinky, is threatening without actually voicing a threat. This meant that yakuza in the pre-*botaiho* era could get what they wanted without explicitly threatening people, thus avoiding a criminal offense.

Under the *botaiho*, a Public Safety Commission can blacklist certain groups who meet various criteria. To blacklist a syndicate the PSC must determine that: (1) it has considerable influence and power as an organization; (2) it has many members with a criminal record; and (3) it has a tightly knit structure of command and control. The PSC can issue injunctions prohibiting certain activities by members of blacklisted syndicates. Violations of the injunctions are subject to small fines and/or short prison terms. Members of a blacklisted group are prohibited from making demands or gaining some financial advantage by invoking or otherwise using their gang affiliation. By broadening the definition of what constitutes a threat, focusing on institutional affiliation, and essentially declaring yakuza organizations a social evil, the government changed the rules of the game, cutting off yakuza from some lucrative scams and giving the police more power and citizens more protection.

In addition, the government established Centers for the Elimination of Boryokudan, staffed by retired police officers, designed to raise public awareness about the threats of yakuza to society and advise people and communities on how to respond. The yakuza have relied on their glamorized image and quiescent, fearful communities. Now, communities affected by yakuza activities are learning how to organize, mobilize media coverage, and fight back in the courts.

By international standards, these countermeasures are relatively tame in terms of both scope and penalties. Designating certain activities as illegal does not necessarily discourage yakuza persisting in such activities, especially if they know that the odds of detection are low and the penalties relatively light. The countermeasures' value is in reducing, at least to some extent, "yakuza intervention in the private and business affairs of law-abiding members of society."[9] Now the state has more power and citizens can seek legal redress in response to predatory activities.

The shortcomings of laws targeting the yakuza hamper effective enforcement. The countermeasures, by proscribing certain yakuza activities, drive yakuza into other scams in a criminal version of whack-a-mole, a game center staple where hammering a mole in one hole is followed by it popping out another. In addition, out of respect for constitutional guarantees, the government has not outlawed gang membership. More importantly, there is no conspiracy law like the RICO Act used in the US to put mafia dons in prison, and Japanese prosecutors cannot offer immunity and witness protection/relocation as inducements to testify against fellow mobsters.

In 1999, however, the government upped the ante by passing new laws that target the yakuza where it hurts. Now in cases of "serious crimes" (chiefly involving drugs and guns), the police have wider scope to engage in wiretapping and sting operations. These new laws are crucial for gathering evidence to prosecute yakuza. The government has also increased penalties for serious crimes and allows seizure of gangsters' assets. Again, every initiative elicits a response, but this expansion of police powers gives them new weapons to make life harder for organized crime.

The first wiretap under this law, which took effect in 2000, was not conducted until 2002. Wiretapping remains limited, but in 2008 the police conducted 11 authorized wiretaps that led to the arrest of 34 suspects. The government says that none of the wiretaps lasted more than 30 days and all focused on mobile phone conversations, mainly in connection with illegal drug sales and gun possession. Thus far, the impact appears limited, but as police, prosecutors, the media, and the public become more accustomed to such surveillance, the probability of expanded use, and more successful prosecutions, is high.

The crackdown may be a mixed blessing. If the expanded police powers become more effective in weakening the major crime syndicates, who will oversee and encourage a degree of stability in the criminal world and prevent competition from overheating into intensified turf wars? By targeting the Big Three oligopoly that now manages organized crime, the police may unwittingly spark a free-for-all among new contenders for domination in battles that will put a premium on demonstrating ruthlessness and the skills of violence specialists, meaning higher risks for non-combatants.

Red Queen Syndrome

In Lewis Carroll's *Through the Looking Glass*, Alice encounters the Red Queen who runs ever faster just to stay in the same place. Biologists use this as a metaphor to describe evolution evident in the contest between a host and a virus, with the host's defenses constantly adapting to new mutations in the virus. Like the Red Queen running faster just to stand still, the government countermeasures against the yakuza elicit a response that requires a new round of actions and adaptations, a flurry of activity that sustains an evolutionary arms race with the parasite. In Japan, this seems a race that the police are destined to lose.

The yakuza have responded to legal reforms by modifying their institutional structure, insulating bosses from criminal activity, slashing membership by ousting those with criminal records, abandoning gang offices, cutting ties with police, and otherwise lowering their profile. Yakuza groups have adopted varied strategies, and they are evolving all the time, but have worked to avoid intra-gang wars that could create opportunities for a police crackdown, not always with success, and sought to lessen the victimization of ordinary citizens.

The countermeasures have also sparked consolidation of yakuza syndicates. Many smaller groups disbanded and forged ties with or merged with the Big Three – the Yamaguchi-gumi, the Inagawa-kai, and the Sumiyoshi-kai. The Yamaguchi-gumi, with a total of some 40,000 soldiers, is based in the Kansai region with headquarters in Kobe. However, it has steadily expanded operations in the Kanto region during the twenty-first century and through alliances and sheer power has grown to some 3,000 affiliated gangsters in Tokyo. Although it has cultivated cordial ties with Kanto-based Inagawa-kai, this infringement on the turf of the Tokyo-based gangs that began in 1991 has sparked a series of violent gang conflicts and killings that have intensified since 2004 with Sumiyoshi-kai. Yamaguchi-gumi has taken the risk of expanding into Tokyo because there are more attractive opportunities in the capital where economic power is concentrated than in the Kansai region. By sparking gang violence the Yamaguchi-gumi is providing police the pretext they need to crack down and thus there are strong pressures to pursue diplomacy with its rivals. However, the impulse to grow is irresistible.

The legal changes restricting *minbo* activities have also generated increased inequalities among yakuza, mirroring one of the controversies animating public discourse in the early twenty-first century. The widening income gap among ordinary Japanese is also evident among yakuza, as those with good networks and financial savvy are doing well while those with more limited skills and contacts are facing tougher times. These "lumpen yakuza" have responded by moving into less sophisticated operations involving drug peddling, especially amphetamines, organized robbery, illegal dumping, Internet pornography, credit card fraud, and various phone scams.[10] These are all good earners, but the barriers to entry are not high and competition from non-yakuza operators is stiff because yakuza have no insuperable comparative advantage as they do in other fields.

Miyazaki, the gangster writer, reminds us, however, that the yakuza are the ultimate entrepreneurs, constantly reinventing themselves, flexibly adapting their core strengths in intimidation and violence to new niches and angles. Despite the new laws, hostile public attitudes, and more aggressive law enforcement, he remains hopeful about the future of the yakuza. Ultimately, if one believes that human nature involves "traits of violence, pleasure-seeking, and dissipation," smart money is on the yakuza.

International

The yakuza have not been content to rest on their laurels at home and have expanded aggressively throughout Asia and also made inroads in Europe and the US. They are involved in gambling, prostitution, human trafficking, drug and gun smuggling, and money laundering as well as corporate extortion. They also invest in real estate, buy art and antiquities, and establish legitimate businesses. The Yamaguchi-gumi is the major international player among the Japanese crime syndicates, drawing on its experiences in organizing sex tours and drug deals in Southeast Asia in the 1960s and 1970s. With slimmer pickings in Heisei era Japan, diversifying into international markets has made sense, at least to the mob.

At home too the yakuza have been involved with foreign crime syndicates, especially from China and Korea, but also from Russia. There has been a degree of media sensationalizing the foreign peril, focusing on cases where foreign criminals have preyed on Japanese ranging from Korean pickpockets to trafficking, robberies, and murder involving Chinese criminals. In reality, the yakuza is partnering with foreign crime syndicates operating in Japan and outsources some jobs to them. For example, some of the heists attributed to foreign gangs could not happen without the inside information supplied by the yakuza. By co-opting foreign gangs and involving them in operations that don't pose a threat to core operations, the yakuza tap new sources of income, insulate themselves from prosecution, and also thwart police unable to deal with non-Japanese criminals speaking a variety of foreign languages and dialects. Thus, rather than the Japanese streets being taken over by foreign gangsters, the yakuza are shrewdly bringing in hired help who are boosting profits.

In the world of international crime, money speaks louder than history, as gangsters from countries with long-standing enmities like Japan, Korea, China, and Russia have put aside the past and focus on raking it in. Russian and Japanese government relations are chilly due to disputes over Russian control of northern islands that Japan claims, but that hasn't stopped a brisk trade in poached seafood netted from northern waters for sale in Japanese markets by arrangement between the yakuza and their Russian counterparts. Russia has also been a lucrative source of prostitutes and hostesses as statuesque blond-haired, blue-eyed beauties command a premium in Japan, while the trade in second-hand cars exported from Japan to the Russian Far East has thrived, at least until 2009 when the Russian government imposed prohibitive import taxes. It is clear, however, that international cooperation among criminal syndicates has been mutually rewarding and will continue as long as this is the case.

Citizens Fight Back

Japanese, widely known as deferential to authority, inclined to harmony, politically apathetic, and averse to lawsuits, are undermining these stereotypes by taking the mob to court. Japanese courts, often depicted as protectors of the wealthy and powerful, have now become a weapon of the weak; gang bosses are now being hit with civil suits by victimized citizens demanding compensation. In 2008, fed up with a two-year-long succession battle between rivals featuring bombs, sub-machine-guns and seven deaths, 1,500 residents of Kurume, a small city on the island of Kyushu, decided to fight the yakuza in the courts. They are suing to shut down the head office of a blacklisted organized crime organization located in their neighborhood. Whether or not they succeed in driving the mobsters out of town, this case is a watershed in yakuza history as they have now become the target of NIMBY (not-in-my-back-yard) activism. It has inspired Japanese elsewhere as residents of the posh Akasaka district in Tokyo filed a similar case in 2009 to bar a gang from moving in.

Glamorized in film and manga, the yakuza are now on the defensive, forced to fight back with lawyers rather than their weapons of choice. The people are trying to take back the streets and oust the violence specialists through non-violent means. Much of the ire directed against the mob is due to their killing of non-combatants. In the Kurume war, in an incident that shocked the nation, a gangster walked into a hospital ward and fatally shot a man he mistook for a rival, putting the yakuza in an unwanted and unflattering media spotlight.

The gang in Kurume, however, is wealthy and well entrenched in the town, so even if the residents push them out of their area, they can just move to another neighborhood and continue conducting business as usual. The problem in fighting organized crime is that society and the police have become resigned to their presence and are not confident they can be eliminated, for the very good reason that the yakuza are constantly adapting.

The 2004 anti-yakuza legislation makes gang bosses responsible for injuries or losses caused by gangland wars, allowing victims to sue them for compensation. The law states that when any member of a blacklisted syndicate has killed or injured a citizen or damaged their property as a result of gangland conflict or internal strife, the leader of that syndicate is liable for damages. There are some two dozen blacklisted syndicates, including the Yamaguchi-gumi, so designated by the Public Safety Commission because they routinely encourage acts of violence. Each of these groups runs a pyramid-like network of subsidiaries and affiliates that pay it large amounts of tribute and protection money.

Previously gang bosses were immune from responsibility for the actions of their rank-and-file members, but now they are liable. And, as ordinary gangsters usually cannot afford to pay much compensation, the new legislation benefits victims and puts a financial squeeze on the bosses. The new law also lowers the bar for plaintiffs who previously had difficulty in gathering evidence and proving a command–supervision, boss–subordinate relationship.

It is a sign of the times that, in 2009, two top members of a crime syndicate agreed to pay nearly JPY100 million in compensation to the relatives of a man fatally shot by yakuza in Maebashi, Gunma Prefecture, acknowledging their liability as employers in a court settlement. In the settlement, the bosses also agreed to apologize to the relatives. The victim was a customer at a bar who died in the 2003 shooting when three yakuza entered and tried to kill the ex-boss of a rival group. The attackers also killed a former gangster and seriously injured the ex-boss along with another ordinary citizen.

The three gangsters are all appealing death sentences while their bosses, unexpectedly, are paying off plaintiffs.

The first case under the 2008 law holding gang bosses liable for their underlings' actions was actually filed by a Thai restaurant owner in Tokyo in 2009, claiming that when she refused to continue paying protection money, the mob came in and busted up her joint. She is suing Kenichi Shinoda, kingpin of the Yamaguchi-gumi, for JPY15 million in damages stemming from the alleged assault and robbery carried out by gang members who beat her with wooden swords. With even foreigners suing them, the yakuza must be wondering what's next.

These disparate cases stretching from Kurume to Tokyo and Maebashi are the tip of the iceberg, demonstrating that the yakuza have alienated the public, and now citizens are willing to risk taking them to court to hold them accountable and curtail their operations. Yakuza believe that the police are orchestrating these lawsuits, but even if this is true it is clear that ordinary citizens, foreigners, and the lawyers representing them have crossed a line that nobody in his right mind would have considered 20 years ago. Anybody taking gangsters to court then would have been deemed suicidal, but now this is a rational response given tremendous changes in laws, attitudes, and context.

In pushing greater accountability, the government is also trying to help insulate citizens from the yakuza by including a provision in the lay judge system enacted in 2009 that allows prosecutors to petition for permission not to try certain serious cases involving yakuza under this quasi-jury system.[11] This opt-out clause addresses concerns that yakuza might attend trials involving associates and identify, otherwise intimidate, or exact revenge on the citizen judges. Given that polls in 2009 show lukewarm support for the new lay judge system, making sure that those who do participate are safe from mob retribution is good public relations.

Clearly, the yakuza remain scary violence specialists, and their adversaries remain wary, but they have worn out their welcome and are finding powerful and persistent adversaries among citizens, courts, police, and media.

In Transition

The yakuza's high-profile ties within the corridors of political power during much of the latter half of the twentieth century until now are remarkable. Politicians have relied on the yakuza to help battle left-wing radical groups while also using them in election campaigns for fundraising, voter organizing, and digging up dirt on rivals.

In general, however, the Japanese establishment is now repudiating the yakuza and trying, with episodic commitment, to put them out of business. Gone are the days that the yakuza could operate openly and ostentatiously, comfortable in the knowledge that the police tolerated them and the public bought into the myth of their chivalrous *samurai* spirit. Gone too are the days when they were treated as valued customers by major securities companies such as Nomura and Nikko who lent them billions of yen and helped ramp share prices to their benefit.[12]

As with many other aspects of contemporary Japanese society, what were once considered ineradicable verities are now yesterday's news. Now the government has passed a series of laws that make the yakuza more vulnerable while the prolonged Heisei recession has slashed revenues from gambling, loan sharking, and prostitution, traditional core businesses. To offset these setbacks the mob has been developing new rackets involving cybercrime, financial scams, and stock manipulation. Grossing an estimated $21 billion annually, and probably far more, organized crime remains a major industry, one that is increasingly efficient with a much smaller workforce.[13] Thus, it's a bit early to be lamenting their plight and betting on their demise. After all, they are prominent stockholders in listed companies and have a web of front companies that provide lucrative opportunities in legitimate business to go along with some of their more traditional recession-proof "entertainment" operations. But there are some powerful demographic trends working against them.

The aging crisis is a significant threat to the yakuza, many of who develop lifestyle-related health problems at relatively early ages. After all, older violence specialists can't take care of business like they used to. Aside from engaging in risky businesses and enduring stressful situations, most yakuza are hedonists who love heavy drinking, smoking, and carousing. This takes a physical toll, especially on livers, and there is a big need for transplants in a country that banned such operations until 1997. Since then, organ transplants remain rare and are strictly regulated.

A doctor at UCLA hospital helped out by performing four liver transplants for gangsters between 2000 and 2004, including a prominent gang boss named Tadamasa Goto in 2001.[14] Since known gangsters are routinely denied visas to the US, clearly someone had put in the fix – the FBI as it turns out. In exchange for revealing inside information to FBI agents about yakuza operations in the US, especially money laundering, the FBI helped arrange the visas and liver transplants. The FBI had long suspected that the yakuza were actively using US gambling casinos to launder their illicit earnings, and maintains that such deals are an effective way of getting necessary information for effective law enforcement. Critics maintain the FBI got little valuable information in exchange for aiding and abetting some dangerous crooks that now have a new lease on life. The transplants also sparked controversy because the yakuza jumped the queue and got preferential treatment despite long waiting lists. While the good doctor was stitching up the mob, in each of the years from 2000 to 2004 more than 100 patients died awaiting liver transplants in greater Los Angeles. Now, even as yakuza lifestyles remain dissolute, all the negative publicity has closed mob access to US healthcare options.

Even if the yakuza can sort out their ailments, the real demographic challenge is recruiting and retaining productive members amidst a looming labor shortage. The marginal and dispossessed will remain a key pool of recruits, but their lack of education and twenty-first-century skills makes them ill-suited for some of the mob's important new lines of business in finance and cybercrime. And, Japan has become a more affluent society, raising everyone's expectations and hopes, meaning that getting in on the ground floor of the yakuza hierarchy, never all that appealing, is even less so, especially given that the money, perks, and prospects aren't what they used to be.

The yakuza have addressed this problem to some degree by outsourcing, but foreign crime syndicates have been relegated to non-core operations. There is always some danger that partners today might turn into tomorrow's ruthless competitors, but foreign crime syndicates remain dependent on inside contacts, networks, and information that only the yakuza can provide. So the yakuza does not look in danger of being pushed off Japan's streets by the international competitors; but by the same token they can only solve the yakuza's manpower problems at the margins. The yakuza have also taken to hiring a handful of foreigners to work as members, but again this is not a panacea for the aging problem. In the end, aging violence specialists have a limited shelf life and the yakuza will need to restructure and streamline operations in the best traditions of corporate downsizing.

In some respects, however, the aging problem may be exaggerated. It is worth recalling that the mafia membership in the US peaked at 5,000 in a much bigger and more populous country and did okay for themselves until aggressive law enforcement, legal reforms, and political will turned the tide. A more compact yakuza focusing its core strengths on maximizing returns will mean reducing some of the labor-intensive retail protection rackets, but that is where quasi-members can fill the void.

For all the gloomy news about economic recession and an establishment backlash, the yakuza continue to work profitably in the mainstream because in certain lines of business they are peerless. The *jiage* business, for example, still thrives even if it is a pale shadow of the booming bubble days. In 2008 it was revealed that a formerly listed company, Suruga Corporation, employed gangsters between 2003 and 2007 to evict tenants from properties that Suruga had acquired and wanted to develop. The company explained that gangsters are good at what they do, producing speedy and cost effective results that were key to its business strategy, results that could not be achieved by legitimate means. In the five buildings targeted, tenants were ousted within 12 to 18 months, a process that could drag on for several years through legitimate means without the desired outcome, given strong legal protection of tenants' rights in the courts.

Mob involvement with major companies in Japan is also highlighted in the 2008 police white paper on organized crime. The police assert that the yakuza are major players in security trading and have invested in hundreds of listed companies. This raises concerns about corporate governance and stock manipulation, factors that will give foreign fund managers pause as they consider their options. The yakuza have also bilked many corporations, even blue-chip firms, of large sums of cash in artful cons launched from front companies that conceal their involvement. Thus, Japan does have a treacherous business operating environment if one falls in with the wrong crowd. The problem is that identifying them is not as easy as it used to be and has generated a brisk business in due diligence.

Prospects

The long-term future for the yakuza appears grim due to incremental legal reforms, tougher enforcement by the police, and judicial support for these initiatives. Moreover, Japanese society is rapidly changing in various ways that are shrinking the social and economic space that has allowed the yakuza to thrive for so long. Citizens are aroused against them and working collectively to bring pressure on law enforcement to act. Judicial and quasi-judicial remedies are increasingly taking over dispute resolution and arbitration, areas where yakuza have been profitably active. Greater transparency is also shining a light on the darker recesses where yakuza thrive and making operations involving establishment players more difficult.

Successful law enforcement targeting the major criminal syndicates carries its own risks. Rather than eliminating organized crime, weakening the stabilizing influence of the current yakuza oligopoly could spark greater violence as new contenders emerge and make it more difficult to restore law and order. A less centralized yakuza could well become more dangerous and more difficult to police. But a weaker and divided yakuza with fewer resources could also be a boon precisely because they would have less potential to conduct criminal activities. This is the gamble the police are taking.

But betting against the yakuza seems like a losing gamble. The yakuza were on the ropes in the 1930s under military-dominated governments when state actors took over the operations of violence specialists.[15] As we know, they recovered quickly following WWII and became major players in cahoots with the Iron Triangle (business, bureaucracy, and politicians), expanding their influence most dramatically during the bubble era in the late 1980s. The subsequent recession has been tough on business, but crisis has created new opportunities and the yakuza are reinventing themselves, staying a step ahead of law enforcement, maintaining their underworld rackets, and straying further into mainstream pursuits. It is worth bearing in mind that the new yakuza are ruthless investment bankers, intimidating guys in Armani suits and Gucci shoes with a penchant for violence and a gift for lucrative frauds, manipulating stocks and hiding their illicit activities behind legitimate front companies. Rumors circulate that a yakuza front company even conned Lehman Brothers out of nearly $350 million only months before the once venerable investment bank went bankrupt, and similar sophisticated scams have involved other blue-chip firms. Ultimately, the continuing demand for yakuza services by the mainstream world, and the primordial impulses of violence, greed, thrill-seeking, and sex, mean that the yakuza are likely to survive even the most concerted actions by authorities to wipe them out. Make no mistake, the yakuza will not go gently into the night.

Part V

Postscript

Chapter 13

Prospects

The previous chapters detail many of the serious challenges Japan faces in the twenty-first century, but this crisis also carries opportunity for significant reforms precisely because the situation is so desperate. The first two decades of the Heisei era have been a time of tremendous upheaval and turmoil reverberating throughout the archipelago. We are witnesses to this transition, and this book chronicles and analyzes some of that process and what it may portend. Japan may not be able to "solve" its many problems, but I suspect it will pragmatically manage and mitigate the consequences. In a messy, incremental, and fitful manner Japan will somehow manage to muddle through, cobbling together policies and adjustments on an *ad hoc* basis, and in so doing avert some of the worst case, doom-and-gloom scenarios that abound in contemporary Japan. Muddling through remains the most likely scenario and, given the grim circumstances that prevail, not such a bad one.

Public opinion polls show that most Japanese think their nation's best days are behind it and they are pessimistic about future prospects. Who wouldn't be after two decades of an economy locked in the doldrums and political, bureaucratic, and business leaders seemingly at a loss about how to promote recovery? The cascade of scandals since the late 1980s has shaken confidence in Japan's governing class and exposed far more chicanery and corruption than even the most jaded observers could have imagined. The Lost Decade was much more than an economic catastrophe; it was the requiem for Japan, Inc. and its ways and means. The myths and beliefs that had sustained social cohesion in post-WWII Japan have faded along with job security, stable families, and the social contract.

There is a pervasive social malaise in contemporary Japan, and talking to students these days is to understand how tough it is just to even find a full-time job let alone nourish dreams or get on with their lives. When I arrived in 1987 it was a completely different vibe with the economy buzzing and people feeling confident and upbeat, proud of their nation's achievements and fully aware that the rest of the world was envying their success. Japan was on top of the world and *pax Nipponica* seemed much more than a pipedream. Students exuded a brash and exuberant style, were confident of getting job offers, and expressed a degree of hope for the future that now seems unimaginable. On a more encouraging note, contemporary students seem to be much more aware of social problems than in the past, and in their essays and presentations are far more likely to examine contemporary ills such as poverty, homelessness, unemployment, domestic violence, and human trafficking. Interest in civil society organizations is higher and more students these days are well informed about Japan's troubled past with Asia. This greater social and historical consciousness is a profound change I have observed among an unrepresentative sample of young Japanese, but encouraging nonetheless.

Clearly, there is considerable work to be done on fine-tuning and managing the greater degree of risk in twenty-first century Japan. However, none of the risks detailed in this book are unknown to Japanese and it is because they are prominent in public discourse that one can be guardedly optimistic that episodically and gradually politicians, policy-makers, employers, the media, civil society organizations, unions, and citizens will collectively and separately figure out reasonable responses that will help society better manage risk and its consequences than is now the case. By forcing people to reconsider their relationship with the state and employers, the rising risk, and efforts to improve risk management, is generating reform and greater public involvement under greater media scrutiny.

The ouster of the LDP from power after nearly a half-century is an encouraging sign about the prospects for Japan's renewal. The DPJ won impressive victories in the upper house elections of 2007 and the more influential lower house elections in 2009, signaling that the people had lost faith in the party that has dominated Japan since it was established in 1955. In 2009 the rallying cry for the DPJ was *seiken kotai* (political change) and the people responded by handing it a landslide victory, mostly because they blamed the LDP for the foundering economy and introducing greater risk without preparing for the foreseeable consequences. The people repudiated *jiko sekinin* and the LDP policies that led to widening income disparities and a society of winners and losers that left the vulnerable in the lurch.

In electing the DPJ, voters expressed their strong support for reform, and their hopes for significant changes in the way that Japan is governed.

The DPJ is asserting cabinet control over the bureaucracy and imposing its agenda by shifting budget priorities away from public works to greater emphasis on social welfare programs. This is what voters want and is also what will help alleviate some of the serious consequences of a higher-risk society. The strengthening and expansion of the social safety net and investing more in social welfare programs are important initiatives marking a break with the LDP's emphasis on individualism and self-responsibility. But, the LDP dug a deep fiscal hole with a public debt to GDP ratio of 200 percent that will constrain the DPJ's options and slow progress on its reform agenda. Cleaning up the mess the LDP left behind and restoring public confidence in those who govern are essential but difficult tasks. The persistence of money politics and corruption in the DPJ, a party that promised to hit the reset button on politics as usual, renders this agenda even more elusive. Voters are impatient for results and along with the media are more feisty and critical. Having finally thrown the bums out of office, they are ready to do so again if they don't see tangible progress. As elsewhere the urgent desire for real political reform among the people confronts the unseemly realities of mainstream politics, generating disaffection and cynicism.

While keeping the hurdles in mind, it is also important to appreciate the great strengths that the DPJ inherits as it pursues its renovation agenda. The social, institutional, and physical infrastructure of Japan is in very good shape. Even if social cohesion is frayed and disparities are widening, many countries would love to have Japan's set of problems. Japanese are also highly educated and enjoy a very good medical system. The economy for all its problems is still one of the top three economies in the world and many of its companies are global leaders in their sectors. Japan is also a leader in technological innovation and produces excellent products that are in high demand around the world. It is well positioned to tap into the growth of China and India and is already benefiting from expanded links with both economies with significant room for continued expansion. The government's fiscal woes are massive but manageable because institutions within the country hold most of the public debt. The government has massive foreign exchange reserves and Japanese companies have forged overseas partnerships and made large overseas investments that are delivering healthy returns. Relations between politicians, business, and the bureaucracy are close and cooperative, making it easier to act. Japan's problems are also driving reform by generating a sense of urgency that facilitates policy innovations and implementation. In addition, Japan's civil society organizations are expanding in numbers and capacity and will benefit from the shifts in spending and attitudes ushered in by the DPJ. It is worth recalling that the surge in social welfare programs and spending during President Lyndon Johnson's Great Society initiative in the 1960s led to significant growth in the capacity and influence of US NGOs. Given fiscal constraints, it will make sense for the DPJ to rely more extensively on NGOs to realize its agenda, putting wind in their sails and money in their budgets. Problems and issues reflecting the concerns of citizens that LDP-led governments have not addressed are now more likely to get attention.

All this is to say that there are some good reasons to believe that political change can improve Japan's future in some significant ways, even if faith in the DPJ is waning. There are no magic wands or panaceas, but brick by brick, slowly and incrementally, Japan's quiet transformation is proceeding and has gained momentum from the DPJ's emergence and the heightened political competition this signifies. Whether or not the DPJ continues to lead this transformation is an open question, but clearly voters support more wide-ranging reforms than the parties are offering. Attracting and retaining voters' support depends on enacting reforms that produce changes they can believe in and benefit from.

There are six key policy areas that will serve as a barometer of Japan's progress on its renewal agenda that bear close monitoring over the coming years. Innovative policies in these areas can propel and shape Japan's transformation while neglect will deepen and prolong crisis.

1   *Risk.* Improving risk management can be achieved by striking a viable and more compassionate balance between risk and security that takes into consideration the benefits of competition and need for productivity growth. Expanding the safety net and job retraining programs are crucial to mitigate the consequences of risk, while equal pay for equal work, standard in Europe, is key to enhancing the security of Japan's growing precariat, giving them hope and shoring up social cohesion.

2   *Family.* Family-friendly policies by companies and the government are crucial to help working couples achieve a better work–life balance that facilitates sharing household responsibilities so that women can better balance careers and family rearing duties. Such policies involve shorter working hours for both fathers and mothers and flexible work schedules. Providing more flexible daycare and universal access is crucial to support families and encourage couples to have children. Families are also burdened by care for the frail elderly and need more professional assistance and access to assisted living options. Japan stands to gain

considerably from tapping women's potential more fruitfully and family-friendly policies are crucial to doing so.

3 *Immigration.* Immigration is one of the key policy questions facing the government and, like elsewhere, one that is very divisive. How it decides to manage immigration will have a major impact on Japan's overall economic prospects and how it copes with labor shortages and the challenges of a rapidly aging society.

4 *Civil society.* Civil society can, as elsewhere, play a crucial role in partnering with government agencies in many areas, including expanding the safety net and providing other social welfare programs more efficiently and cheaply than the bureaucracy. This could increase their capacity and benefits to society.

5 *Governance.* Improving governance means promoting greater transparency and accountability. More open government will be able to regain the trust of jaded citizens while curbing corruption, cronyism, and opaque decision-making. Limiting the discretionary and regulatory powers of bureaucrats can curb the rule *by* law. By reducing *amakudari* and trimming wasteful spending the government can restore public trust. Improving governance also depends on judicial reform to nurture a more open and accessible judiciary, and the transition to the rule *of* law.

6 *Environment.* Making the transition to a viable low-carbon society is high on the government's agenda. There are formidable obstacles to doing so, but also great opportunities that are all the more appealing due to the urgent need for reduction of CO_2 emissions. Japan is well positioned to be a global environmental leader given its green technologies, and can help other nations reduce their emissions by exporting know-how and equipment, generating green-collar jobs that can help make this a sustainable transition.

Looking ahead 20 years, it is hard to imagine any really bright scenarios for Japan, but one suspects the apprehension that envelops Japan today may overstate the downside risks and overlook the opportunities to reshape priorities, improve governance, boost transparency and accountability, shift from the rule *by* law to the rule *of* law, and otherwise create a more dynamic polity, one more in tune with the aspirations of twenty-first-century Japanese. After all, who looking around them in 1950 would have expected the subsequent economic miracle, and who at the time of the oil shock in 1973 would have expected the economic boom at the end of the 1980s? And in 1989 at the height of the bubble, who other than Bill Emmott would have imagined that Japan's economic crisis would be so sudden, severe, and long lasting?[1] I am continually astonished to see how much has changed in terms of attitudes, inclinations, taboos, expectations, policies, priorities, and norms in the past two decades. This transformation has been stunning in scope and speed and, precisely because of Japan's massive challenges, the ongoing reforms and reshaping of Japan will probably be even more profound. As a result, Japan in 2030 may not be in nearly as bad shape as most Japanese now anticipate.

Glossary

Amakudari (descent from heaven) A reference to the common practice of retired senior bureaucrats moving to well-paid sinecure positions in firms that they dealt with in the course of their government duties. Often criticized as a source of collusive relations between bureaucrats and the firms they hope to join upon retiring.

Article 9 The article in the Japanese Constitution that bans the establishment of military forces and the resort to war to settle international disputes.

ASEAN Regional Forum (ARF) This organization focuses on security issues in the Asia-Pacific area.

Asia-Pacific Economic Cooperation (APEC) APEC was established in 1989 as an informal dialogue group in response to the dynamism, growth, and accelerating integration among member economies. Over the years APEC has developed into the primary regional vehicle for promoting open trade, investment, and economic cooperation.

Association of Southeast Asian Nations (ASEAN) A regional organization established in 1967 including 10 nations of Southeast Asia: Brunei, Cambodia, Indonesia, Laos, Malaysia, Myanmar (Burma), the Philippines, Singapore, Thailand and Vietnam.

Atarashi Rekishi Kyokasho oTsukuru-kai Society for the Creation of New History Textbooks, a conservative group of pundits and scholars responding to more critical assessments of Japanese expansionism 1931–45 that emerged after Emperor Hirohito's death in 1989. This group published an exculpatory history textbook in 2001, but it and subsequent editions were adopted by less than 1 percent of Japanese school boards.

Aum Shinrikyo Supreme Truth Sect, a new religion centered on the teachings of Shoko Asahara. It staged an attack on Tokyo subways in 1995 using sarin gas; its leadership has been prosecuted and some received the death penalty.

Baby boomers The first baby boom and largest population cohort in Japan, numbering 7 million, was born between 1947 and 1949. The second baby boom was their children, born between 1971 and 1974.

Big Bang Financial deregulation program initiated by the government of Prime Minister Ryutaro Hashimoto in 1996, often characterized by the media as the "little whimper" for failing to meet expectations for sweeping liberalization.

Botaiho Anti-organized crime legislation that criminalizes various yakuza activities and empowers the government to subject designated crime syndicates to various sanctions.

Bubble economy Period in the late 1980 when prices of land and stocks suddenly skyrocketed only to implode in the early 1990s, ushering in the Lost Decade and prolonged recession.

Bunraku Traditional Japanese puppet theater in which men in black deftly manipulate large puppets on stage and blend in so as not to distract the audience from the drama.

Burakumin (hamlet people) Discriminatory term used to refer to some one million Japanese today. Visually indistinguishable from other Japanese, they suffer discrimination in jobs, housing, marriage, etc. because they are identified as being members of this class. During the Tokugawa era (1603–1868) this class became hereditary and was linked to "polluting" activities such as slaughtering animals.

Choiwaru oyaji (cool older man) Refers to stylish and wealthy elderly men targeted by upscale brandname fashion industry and regaled in mass media.

Chongryon Pro-North Korean Association of *zainichi* (ethnic Koreans) in Japan.

Class-A war criminals Refers to 28 Japanese leaders prosecuted at the International Military Tribunal for the Far East (1946–9) for crime against peace, of whom seven were sentenced to death by hanging.

Daijosai Mystical rite that celebrates the emperor's unique relationship with the Sun Goddess including his symbolic rebirth as a woman and impregnation by the gods that confers divine qualities. This rite was most recently conducted in November 1990 despite heated opposition from various liberal groups protesting state funding for the ceremony.

Dekichatta kekkon Marriage between couples after the woman becomes pregnant, an increasing phenomenon in Japan accounting for some 25 percent of all marriages, ones with a much higher than average risk of divorce.

Diet The parliament in Japan that is composed of elected upper and lower houses.

Doken kokka (construction state) A reference to the vast spending on public works projects with implications of environmental devastation, wasteful spending, spiralling budget deficits, and political corruption.

DPJ (Democratic Party of Japan) Launched in 1996, this party grew through mergers of small parties and defections. Represents a broad political spectrum ranging from conservatives to progressives and maintains close ties with labor unions. Gained control of the upper house in 2007 and the lower house in 2009.

Enjo kosai Compensated dating, usually between junior or high school girls and middle-aged men, often involving sex.

Freeters Refers to job-hopping youth employed as part-time or contract workers who face bleak economic futures because their jobs are low paid, have no benefits, and offer no security.

Fukoku kyohei Literally "rich nation, strong military." This was the rallying slogan of the Meiji era government (1868–1911).

Gaiatsu (foreign pressure) Refers to the pressures put on the Japanese government by other governments to modify various policies. In some cases, such pressures are actually welcomed and orchestrated as a way to overcome a domestic political impasse that is preventing necessary reforms.

Gaijin Foreigner(s).

Gengo The imperial system of periodization based on making the first year of an emperor's reign Year 1 and so on. Official dates in Japan and even rail passes are commonly based on this system.

Giri An obligation one incurs due to one's formal relationship with another or to reciprocate someone's favor or kindness.

Gyosei shido (administrative guidance) A reference to the informal manner in which bureaucrats wield their broad regulatory and discretionary powers to ensure corporate compliance with government goals and policies. Implicit is the threat to use those powers in a manner harmful to those who do not comply.

Habatsu Factions within the LDP.

Haken mura Temporary tent village providing housing and food for unemployed contract workers who lost their jobs at the end of 2008, set up by non-profit organizations and unions at the beginning of 2009 in Hibiya Park in downtown Tokyo.

Heisei era From 1989 to the present, a period of "achieving of peace" or "peace everywhere" under the reign of Emperor Akihito.

Hinomaru The national flag with a red circle in the middle of a white background.

Honne Inner feelings, usually unexpressed because they do not conform to social norms and expectations.

Ie The patriarchal family system that denied women independence and legal rights. The Constitution sought to correct this bias, with decidedly mixed results.

Ijime Bullying, a pervasive practice in Japanese society that is aimed at imposing conformity within a specific group and ostracizing those who do not conform or meet expectations.

Imperial Household Administration (IHA) A government bureaucracy that manages all matters related to the monarchy.

Iron Triangle The nexus of power involving big business, the bureaucracy, and the Liberal Democratic Party (LDP) that controlled Japan in the post-WWII era.

Japan, Inc. A term coined to characterize the close relationship between the government and big business in Japan and the government's focus on economic issues.

Jiage Land clearance operations involved gangsters intimidating and threatening people living on or adjacent to sites designated for development to sell out and leave.

Jiko sekinin (self-responsibility) A concept used to justify a shifting of greater risk onto individuals by the state and employers that has reduced their burden as guarantors of security.

Jinja Honcho Association of Shinto Shrines, a conservative religious organization that pressures politicians to pay their respects to the war dead at Yasukuni Shrine and otherwise lobbies to promote a vindicating and exonerating history of Japanese aggression 1931–45. In exchange it provides campaign funds and well-organized electoral support.

Joho kokkai Information disclosure permitting citizens access to official documents, thus promoting transparency and accountability.

Jusen Real-estate lending subsidiaries of banks that incurred massive unrecoverable loans in the wake of the bubble, threatening the collapse of the Japanese financial system in the mid 1990s.

Kakusa shakai The income gap society of disparities, a term symbolizing growing discontent with neo-liberal economic reforms that have widened disparities and the income gap in society, creating "winners" and "losers."

Kankan settai Lavish wining and dining of central government bureaucrats by prefectural officials as part of budget-related lobbying efforts.

Kanson mimpi Bureaucratic arrogance towards the public.

Kara shucho Claiming expenses for fictional business trips, which became standard operating procedure for bureaucrats throughout the nation.

Kazokukai Families of Abductees Association, organization of relatives of Japanese abducted by North Korean agents in the 1970s and 1980s that lobbies government to pressure Pyongyang for a full accounting about the fate of the missing abductees prior to any moves towards normalization of bilateral relations.

Keiretsu Bank-centered industrial conglomerates that dominate the Japanese economy, many of which have strong links with the pre-WWII *zaibatsu*. The exclusionary business practices and conflicts of interest within the *keiretsu* suppress competition and have come under scrutiny as a source of trade friction.

Keizai Doyukai Japan Association of Corporate Executives, a private, non-partisan lobbying organization that conducts policy-oriented research on the economy.

Kimigayo (Your Majesty's Reign) The national anthem, controversial because of the apparent reference to the days when the emperor was an absolute monarch, making it a divisive political issue between conservatives and progressives.

Koenkai Local political support organizations that mobilize voters and funds for politicians.

Koseki A family register maintained over the generations with information about births, deaths, marriages, etc.

Kozo oshoku Structural corruption in Japan's political system.

KY (*kuuki yomenai*, unable to read the situation) Refers to someone who is clueless.

Lehman shock The sudden global economic crisis beginning in the autumn of 2008 precipitated by the subprime mortgage debacle that caused Lehman Brothers, a venerable investment bank, to collapse.

LDP (Liberal Democratic Party) Formed by a merger of the Liberal Party and the Democratic Party in 1955. It is the conservative political party that dominated post-WWII Japanese politics until its ouster from power in 2009.

Minbo Range of extortion scams perpetrated by organized crime against individuals and companies.

Mindan Pro-South Korean Association of *zainichi* (ethnic Koreans) in Japan.

Narikin The nouveau riche who emerged during the bubble at the end of the 1980s and engaged in conspicuous and often garish consumption fueled by wealth generated by spiraling land and stock prices.

Nenko The seniority employment system that has determined wages and promotions, but is now no longer sacrosanct as firms shift towards a more merit-oriented system.

Nihon Izokukai War Bereaved Veterans' Family Association, a conservative group of descendants of soldiers who fought in WWII that pressures politicians to pay their respects at Yasukuni Shrine and promotes a vindicating and exonerating historical narrative regarding Japan's aggression 1931–45. In exchange, it provides campaign funds and well-organized electoral support.

Nikkeijin Descendants of Japanese immigrants to South America, mostly Brazil, who came in large numbers to Japan during the 1990s following a revision of visa regulations that facilitated their entry as unskilled workers that was implemented to ease labor shortages.

Nippon Keidanren Japanese Business Federation, a big business lobbying association that nurtures strong connections with political and government leaders to influence policy.

Nopan shabushabu Notorious restaurants featuring beef, mirrored floors, and waitresses wearing short skirts and no panties. The entertaining of Ministry of Finance bureaucrats at such establishments by businessmen provoked public outrage in the 1990s and became symbolic of the unseemly collusion between corporate Japan and the government.

Nure uchiba (wet leaf) Reference to retired husbands who are dependent on their wives and annoy them by clinging to them.

Omoiyari yosan (sympathy budget) A reference to the money the Japanese government pays to base US troops in Japan, amounting to more than $2 billion a year.

On A personal sense of social debt or obligation created in a relationship by a benevolent act.

Rachi mondai (kidnapping problem) Refers to dozens of Japanese abducted by North Korean agents in the 1970s and 1980s. A number of these missing Japanese remain unaccounted for and this has become a significant political issue in Japan preventing normalization of bilateral relations.

Red Purge The US-controlled SCAP and the conservative Japanese government initiated a crackdown beginning in 1947 on left-wing activists, radicals, unions, etc. as a consequence of the Cold-War-inspired reverse course. The purge was a response to shared concerns that prevailing socio-economic conditions left Japan vulnerable to the appeal of communism, a prospect feared by the US and their conservative allies in the Japanese government.

Reverse course After 1947, the US Occupation in Japan became influenced by the Cold War between the US and the USSR. Punitive policies were replaced by an emphasis on rebuilding Japan into a showcase for American-style democracy and capitalism.

Rinban Government buying back government bonds as a monetary easing policy.

Rosu gene (lost generation) Refers to young people who have lost hope in Japan during the prolonged Heisei recession as it has become difficult to secure regular jobs, forcing many to the employment periphery, thereby swelling the ranks of the working poor.

Safety net Social programs targeting the working poor, unemployed, and vulnerable, aimed at maintaining a basic standard of living and providing training programs to facilitate employability. The inadequacies of Japan's safety net became a focus of political discourse in 2009 due to a spike in need for such support.

Salarymen (sararimen) Salaried white-collar workers who are often the subject of both mockery and respect. They are seen to be hard working, extremely loyal company employees who place greater emphasis on work than on the family and personal desires.

SCAP (Supreme Commander of the Allied Powers) General Douglas MacArthur served in this capacity during the US Occupation of Japan (1945–52) and as the *de facto* leader of what was nominally a multilateral institution that governed the country and sought to realize the goals of demilitarization and democratization. SCAP also refers to the institutions of the Occupation and is often used interchangeably with GHQ (General Headquarters).

SDF (Self-Defense Forces, *in Japanese* Jietai) The military forces of Japan.

Seiken kotai (political change) Defining DPJ slogan of the 2009 election campaign that refers to the snowballing disaffection among voters with the LDP that gave the DPJ a landslide victory in the lower house elections.

Shinjinrui (new species) A negative reference by older people used when criticizing the various presumed failings of the younger generation.

Showa era From 1926 to 1989, a period of "enlightened peace," the era in which Emperor Hirohito reigned.

Soapland An establishment where men pay for sexual services.

Sodai gomi (large garbage) Expression used to refer to retired husbands who hang about the house and annoy their wives.

SOFA (Status of Forces Agreement) Refers to the regulations, provisions, and stipulations that govern the presence of US military forces in Japan and specify the terms under which they are allowed to operate.

Sogo shoku Career track in employment system that involves full-time work and regular rotation within the company, imparting general, firm-specific skills.

Sokaiya Corporate extortionists linked with the yakuza that threaten to expose company secrets and disrupt shareholder meetings unless they are paid substantial sums. The government and firms have tried to curb this widespread practice.

Tanshin funin Common employment practice involving dispatch of male workers to a firm's distant branch offices for a rotation of a few years where the employee will live apart from his family while it continues to live in the same residence, often in order not to disrupt children's schooling.

Tatemae Public behavior conforming to acceptable norms.

Yakuza Organized crime syndicates in Japan.

Yasukuni Shrine Shinto religious facility in downtown Tokyo that is a talismanic symbol of an unrepentant view of Japan's wartime aggression and where 14 Class-A war criminals are enshrined. Visits by Japanese politicians, notably Prime Minister Junichiro Koizumi, have harmed relations with China and South Korea.

Yoshida Doctrine The policy of Prime Minister Shigeru Yoshida (1946–7, 1949–54), emphasizing the need of Japan to concentrate resources on economic recovery as a way to deflect US demands that it rearm in the early 1950s.

Yuai Fraternity, the rallying ideal of Prime Minister Yukio Hatoyama in the 2009 elections that drew attention to growing disparities and individualism and promised a reinvigoration of community.

Zaibatsu Family-owned industrial conglomerates that dominated the pre-WWII Japanese economy. During the Occupation the ownership and structure of these conglomerates was transformed and they became the post-WWII *keiretsu*.

Zainichi Ethnic Koreans born in Japan who are descendants of Koreans brought to Japan during the colonial period (1910–45) as Japanese subjects, many as forced laborers.

Zombie companies Bankrupt and uncompetitive firms that stay in business because their banks continue to lend them money to avert bankruptcy and loan defaults. These firms contribute to deflation by lowering prices to boost sales and symbolize inefficient use of capital.

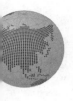

Notes

Chapter 1 Transformations After World War II

1   For a detailed examination of the US Occupation and its legacies see: John Dower, *Embracing Defeat*, New York: Norton, 1999; Eiji Takemae, *Inside GHQ*, London: Continuum, 2002.

2   John Dower, *War Without Mercy*, New York: Pantheon, 1987.

3   Herbert Bix, *Hirohito and the Making of Modern Japan*, New York: Harper Collins, 2000.

4   On Japanese politics see: Gerald Curtis, *The Logic of Japanese Politics*, New York: Columbia University Press, 2002; J. A. A. Stockwin, *Governing Japan: Divided Politics in a Resurgent Economy*, 4th edn., London: Wiley, 2008; Ian Neary, *The State and Politics in Japan*, London: Polity, 2002.

5   The other Nixon shock was in 1971 when the US unilaterally terminated the direct convertibility of the US dollar to gold, thereby unraveling the Bretton Woods system of international financial exchange that had prevailed since WWII. This heralded the shift away from fixed currency values pegged to the US dollar to floating exchange rates.

6   Chalmers Johnson, *MITI and the Japanese Miracle*, Palo Alto, CA: Stanford University Press, 1982.

7   Jeff Kingston, *Japan's Quiet Transformation*, London: Routledge, 2004, pp. 4–12.

8   Richard Katz, *The System that Soured*, Armonk, NY: Sharpe, 1998.

9   Ibid., pp. 55–60.

10   Heisei is the reign name for Emperor Akihito who succeeded his father in 1989.

11   Glenn Hook and Hiroko Takeda, "'Self-Responsibility' and the Nature of the Postwar Japanese State: Risk through the Looking Glass," *Journal of Japanese Studies*, 2007, 33 (1), 93–123.

Chapter 2   The Lost Decade

1   Non-regular workers do not enjoy job security or employment benefits, whereas regular workers are full-time, with associated social insurance benefits, and have an open-ended, secure employment arrangement. The category of part-time is related more to status, pay, and perquisites than actual hours of work or responsibilities, which can be similar to full-time workers. In 2007 the government adopted legislation that calls for lessening disparities between part-time and full-time workers, but these guidelines do not cover other categories of non-regular workers. Temporary workers have fixed-term contracts, often directly with the employer, while dispatched workers are hired indirectly on fixed-term contracts through job placement agencies. Contract workers also work on fixed-term contracts.

2   Richard Koo, *The Holy Grail of Macroeconomics: Lessons from Japan's Great Recession*, London: Wiley, 2009.

3   For more on these pathologies see Jeff Kingston, "Downsizing the Construction State," *The Japanese Economy*, Winter 2004–5, 32 (4), 36–95. Also Chapter 5 in Jeff Kingston, *Japan's Quiet Transformation*, London: Routledge, 2004.

4   Philip Seaton, *Japan's Contested War Memories*, London: Routledge, 2007.

5   See Chapter 2 in Jeff Kingston, *Japan's Quiet Transformation*, London: Routledge, 2004.

6   Randall Jones, "Income Inequality, Poverty and Social Spending in Japan," Economics Department Working Papers no. 556, June 12, 2007, Paris: OECD.

7   Ibid., p. 26.

8   Jeff Kingston, *Japan's Quiet Transformation*, London: Routledge, 2004.

Chapter 3   Defusing the Demographic Time Bomb

1   For a succinct and incisive analysis of the various issues see Florian Coulmas, *Population Decline and Ageing in Japan: The Social Consequences*, London: Routledge, 2007.

2   John Campbell and Naoki Ikegami, *The Art of Balance in Health Policy: Maintaining Japan's Low Cost, Egalitarian System*, Cambridge: Cambridge University Press, 1998.

3   See John Campbell, Paul Hewitt, and Chikako Usui, *The Demographic Dilemma: Japan's Aging Society*, Woodrow Wilson International Center for Scholars, Asia Special Report no. 107, 2002.

4   Glenda Roberts, "Balancing Work and Life: Whose Work? Whose Life? Whose Balance?," *Asian Perspectives*, 2005, 29 (1), 175–211.

5   OECD, *Economic Survey: Japan*, Paris: OECD, September 2009, p. 91.

6 Asbestos is another leading cause of lung cancer. It was still approved for use in Japan until 2006, two decades after being banned in other countries because of health risks.

7 Mark Levin, "Tobacco Industrial Policy and Tobacco Control Policy in Japan," *Asian-Pacific Law & Policy Journal*, Winter 2005, 6 (1), 44–70.

8 Naoki Ikegami and John Campbell, "Health Care Reform in Japan: The Virtues of Muddling Through," *Health Affairs*, May/June 1999, 305–14.

9 Figures and analysis from review by John Campbell of David Wise and Naohiro Yashiro (eds.), *Health Care Issues in the US and Japan*, Chicago: University of Chicago Press, 2006, in *Journal of Japanese Studies*, 2008, 34 (1), 136–40.

10 Olivia S. Mitchell, John Piggott, and Satoshi Shimizutani, "Developments in Long-Term Care Insurance in Japan," Australian School of Business, University of New South Wales, Research Paper no. 2008 ECON 01, January 2008; John C. Campbell and Naoki Ikegami, "Long-term Care Insurance Comes to Japan," *Health Affairs*, 2000, 19 (3), 26–39; Tadashi Fukui and Yasushi Iwamoto, "Policy Options for Financing the Future Health and Long-Term Care Costs in Japan," NBER Working Paper no. 12427, 2006; Naoki Ikegami, "Japan's Health Care System: Containing Costs in a Stagnant Economy," Presentation for The Wharton School, 2003.

11 For a critical analysis of health reform in Japan see Hideaki Hiratate, "Patients Adrift: The Elderly and Japan's Life-Threatening Health Reforms," *Japan Focus*, March 11, 2008, no. 2693. Also see a riposte from John Campbell, "The Health of Japan's Medical Care System: 'Patients Adrift?,'" *Japan Focus*, April 26, 2008, no. 2730.

12 This practice has been widespread and is often called "social hospitalization," meaning stays that are extended for social reasons rather than medical necessity in what amounts to high-cost terminal care.

13 International Longevity Center (Japan), *A Profile of Older Japanese*, Tokyo: ILC, 2009.

14 For a discussion of this trend see Naohiro Ogawa, Robert Retherford, and Rikiya Matsukura, "Demographics of the Japanese Family: Entering Uncharted Territory," in Marcus Rebick and Ayumi Takenaka (eds.), *The Changing Japanese Family*, London: Routledge, 2006, pp. 19–38. The assumption that women will serve as the primary family caregivers is based on the observation that 85% of family caregivers are women. The media lavishes attention on cases of Japanese men taking on the caregiving role precisely because it is relatively uncommon. Norms and values are changing in contemporary Japan, but patriarchal attitudes remain robust and a caregiving system that relies on male relatives serving as primary caregivers does not seem viable.

15 Japan's pension system is complex and there are different schemes depending on one's employment status. This 40% pension delinquency rate in 2008 is for the National Pension Plan (Kokumin Nenkin).

16   Under this system, three professional judges and six citizens adjudicate serious criminal cases that could involve imposition of the death penalty.

17   In contrast, the police took action against 121,165 juveniles in 2007, about 10,000 less than the year before. Juveniles often view shoplifting and petty crime as a game in addition to a way of getting things they want.

18   The OECD notes that overall Japanese seniors are relatively well-off compared to their peers in the OECD: "Around 70% of the outlays by social insurance programmes were for elderly persons. Such spending, combined with a relatively high rate of labour force participation of older workers, has helped maintain the income of the elderly at a fairly high level. Indeed, the disposable income of the over 65 age group in Japan is 84% of the 18–65 age group, compared to an OECD average of 76%" (Randall Jones, *Income Inequality, Poverty and Social Spending in Japan*, Paris: OECD, 2007, p. 17). There is, however, greater inequality among the elderly as the Gini coefficient (0 = perfect equality, 100 = perfect inequality) rose from 47.3 in the mid-1980s to 63 by 2000, a 15% increase at a time when the OECD average of inequality for the elderly population remained stable.

19   For an excellent review essay see John Campbell, "Japan's Aging Population: Perspectives of 'Catastrophic Demography'," *Journal of Asian Studies*, Winter 2009, 1401–6.

20   OECD, *Economic Survey*, p. 101. Chapter 4 in this report focuses on healthcare reform.

Chapter 4   Families at Risk

1   Harold Fuess, *Divorce in Japan: Family, Gender and the State, 1600–2000*, Palo Alto, CA: Stanford University Press, 2004.

2   *Japan Labor Review*, Winter 2009, 6 (1), Special Edition, *The Gender Gap in the Japanese Labor Market*: www.jil.go.jp/english/JLR/documents/2009/JLR21_all.pdf.

3   The summary report *Birth: Special Survey of Vital Statistics*, only available in Japanese, can be accessed at the government website: www.mhlw.go.jp/toukei/saikin/hw/jinkou/tokusyu/syussyo-4/index.html.

4   This section draws on Sawako Shirahase, "Age, Change and Poverty: Coping with Social Transformation," *Global Asia*, 2009, 4 (1), 40–4; Chisa Fujiwara, "Single Mothers and Welfare Restructuring in Japan: Gender and Class Dimensions of Income and Employment," *Japan Focus*, January 2, 2008, no. 2623; Naomi Yuzawa, "Single Mothers Urged to Become Financially 'Independent'," *Women's Asia 21, Voices from Japan*, Winter 2007, no. 18.

5   OECD, *Economic Survey of Japan 2006*, Chapter 4, "Income Inequality, Poverty and Social Spending," Paris: OECD, 20 July 2006.

6 See Fujiwara, "Single Mothers."

7 Melinda Rice, "Japan Adopts Tough Domestic Violence Law," *Women's ENews*, December 2, 2001; 2002, 8, 339. For an in-depth assessment of the decades-long campaign by women's advocates to promote women's rights in general and raise awareness about DV in Japan and to lobby the government to act, see Mieko Yoshihama, "The Definitional Process of Domestic Violence in Japan," *Violence Against Women*, March 2002, 8 (3), 339–66.

8 *Asahi*, May 15, 2009.

9 Family members who have lost a loved one to suicide would be incredulous at the notion Japanese culture gives a green light to suicide and accepts it as an honorable exit. Their heart-rending, visceral blogs reflect contemporary attitudes that challenge the romanticized depictions of suicide sometimes evident in Japanese literature and film.

10 The 2009 documentary "Mental" by Kazuhiro Soda features the limitations of the mental healthcare system in Okayama Prefecture.

11 See Shoko Taniguchi, "Suicide Is a Social Not an Individual Problem: Japan in International Perspective," translated and introduced by John Breen, *Japan Focus*, 2007, no. 2507.

Chapter 5   Jobs at Risk

1 Non-standard refers to a variety of contract, indirect, temporary, and part-time work arrangements that may actually involve hours of work similar to full-time employees, but usually at lower pay without standard benefits and job security.

2 These figures understate the true extent of unemployment because an estimated 1.6 million people who have given up searching for a job are excluded (*Asahi/IHT*, May 30–31, 2009, 23).

3 Norma Field, "Commercial Appetite and Human Need: The Accidental and Fated Revival of Kobayashi Takiji's *Cannery Ship*," *The Asia-Pacific Journal*, February 22, 2009, 8-8-09.

4 This tragic incident came on the seventh anniversary of an attack on an Osaka elementary school by a knife-wielding assailant who was later executed for killing eight children in cold blood. Earlier in 2008 there were two high-profile cases involving stabbing sprees in shopping arcades, fueling national anxieties about a wave of violent crime.

5 This sharp contraction of Japan's GDP means that in the dozen years from 1997, Japan's economy only grew a total of 2.3%, an anemic level usually achieved on an annual basis by advanced industrialized nations that puts Japan back into Lost Decade territory.

6 Typically, the media does not give much coverage to demonstrations, possibly because there is concern that this might encourage a destabilizing politics of the street. So demonstrations against the Iraq War, citizens gathering at ports protesting the visit of US warships suspected of having nuclear weapons, marches by various activist groups around Tokyo, or right-wing groups trying to intimidate media organizations, embassies, politicians, or critics, are common but very rarely covered.

7 For in-depth analysis see Toru Shinoda, "Which Side Are You On? *Haken mura* and the Working Poor as a Tipping Point in Japanese Labor Politics," *The Asia-Pacific Journal*, April 4, 2009, 14-3-09.

8 Indirect employment involves companies using employment agencies to recruit contract workers. The worker signs a contract with the employment agency and the hiring company also signs a contract with this intermediary agency that provides the workers. In both cases the contract ensures that the contracting company has no ongoing obligation to the contracted worker, with provisions for early termination of the contract under specified situations.

9 NPOs and citizen volunteers also played a key role in Kobe relief efforts that captured the media's attention and pressured the government to pass legislation in 1998 that in some respects improved the regulatory environment for civil society organizations. This legislation was tacit admission that the government realizes it needs to do more to tap the energy, skills, and capacity of citizens in tackling the challenges facing Japan. See Jeff Kingston, *Japan's Quiet Transformation*, London: Routledge, 2004, pp. 70–94.

10 Non-regular jobs include female part-time workers (7.8 million in 2005), young part-time or casual workers (labeled "arubaito," 3.4 million in 2005), contract workers engaged directly by an employer (2.8 million in 2005), and indirectly hired workers engaged through a dispatching agency (1.1 million in 2005) (Shinoda, "Which Side Are You On?").

11 For statistics on employment in Japan see the Japan Institute for Labor Policy and Training: www.jil.go.jp/english/estatis/databook/2009/04.htm.

12 This is the curious name for government job centers where unemployed workers can sign up for unemployment benefits, enroll in vocational training programs, and get job leads.

13 OECD, *Jobs for Youth–Japan*, Paris: OECD, January 2009. Including students, the figure for non-regular employment of 15–24-year-olds in Japan is 46%.

14 Between 2000 and 2007, the youth unemployment rate in France, Italy, and Spain was nearly 20% or above. In the US, it was 9.3% in 2000, 11.3% in 2005, and 10.5% in 2007 (OECD, *Employment Outlook for 2008*, Paris: OECD, 2008).

15 For a critical appraisal of these programs see OECD, *Jobs for Youth–Japan*.

16 Naomi Kodama, Kazuhiko Odaki, and Yoko Takahashi, "Why Does Employing More Females Increase Corporate Profits? Evidence from Japanese Panel Data," *Japan Labor Review*, Winter 2009, 6 (1), 51–71.

17 According to the Federal Reserve Bank of Dallas, "From 1953 to 2003, each 1 percentage point increase in the cyclical component of the male unemployment rate led to a 5.39 percentage point increase in the cyclical component of the male suicide rate. This effect is 38 times larger for Japan than for the United States" (W. Michael Cox and Jahyeong Koo, "Miracle to Malaise: What's Next for Japan," *Economic Letter–Insights from the Federal Reserve Bank of Dallas*, 2006, 1 (1)).

18 "Rising Poverty in Japan," editorial, *Japan Times*, May 19, 2009.

Chapter 6 Contemporary Politics

1 For analysis of Japan's political economy see Margerita Estevez-Abe, *Welfare and Capitalism in Postwar Japan: Party, Bureaucracy, and Business*, Cambridge: Cambridge University Press, 2008.

2 Chalmers Johnson, *MITI and the Japanese Miracle*, Palo Alto, CA: Stanford University Press, 1982; Sadia Pekkanen, *Picking Winners? From Technology Catch-up to the Space Race in Japan*, Palo Alto, CA: Stanford University Press, 2003.

3 Bruce Bowen, *Japan's Dysfunctional Democracy: The LDP and Structural Corruption*, Armonk, NY: East Gate, 2002.

4 Gerald Curtis, *The Logic of Japanese Politics: Leaders, Institutions and the Limits of Change*, New York: Columbia University Press, 2000.

5 Richard Samuels, *Machiavelli's Children: Leaders and their Legacies in Italy and Japan*, Ithaca, NY: Cornell University, 2003; also see his "Kishi and Corruption: An Anatomy of the 1955 System," JPRI Working Paper no. 83, December 2001.

6 Samuels, *Machiavelli's Children*.

7 *New York Times*, October 9, 1994 and March 4, 1995; *Los Angeles Times*, March 20, 1995.

8 Chalmers Johnson, "Special Report: The CIA and Japanese Politics," JPRI Working Paper no. 11, July 1995.

9 Jeffrey Broadbent, *Environmental Politics in Japan: Networks of Power and Protest*, Cambridge: Cambridge University Press, 1998.

10 See Chapter 5, "Downsizing the Construction State," in Jeff Kingston, *Japan's Quiet Transformation*, London: Routledge, 2004. Postmasters played a key role in mobilizing the vote for the LDP in rural areas.

11 Jacob Schlesinger, *Shadow Shoguns: The Rise and Fall of Japan's Postwar Political Machine*. Palo Alto, CA: Stanford University Press, 1999.

12 Ethan Scheiner, *Democracy Without Competition: Opposition Failure in a One-Party Dominant State*, Cambridge: Cambridge University Press, 2005.

13 Alex Kerr, *Dogs and Demons*, London: Hill and Wang, 2001.

Chapter 7 Security and the Peace Constitution

1 For an excellent analysis about the history of Japan's evolving security policies see Richard Samuels, *Securing Japan: Tokyo's Grand Strategy and the Future of East Asia*, Ithaca, NY: Cornell University Press, 2008.

2 Ichiro Ozawa, *Blueprint for a New Japan*, Tokyo: Kodansha, 1994.

3 For analysis of the government's hairsplitting reconciliation of Article 9 with the SDF beginning in the early 1950s see Richard Samuels, "Politics, Security Policy, and Japan's Cabinet Legislation Bureau: Who Elected These Guys, Anyway?," JPRI Working Paper no. 99, March 2004.

4 The *Asahi Shimbun*, July 1, 2009.

5 Richard Samuels, *Securing Japan*; and "Constitutional Revision in Japan: The Future of Article 9," Presentation at the Brookings Institution, December 15, 2004.

6 MOFA, *The Trust Fund for Human Security: For the "Human-Centered" 21st Century*, 2007.

7 See "Human Security and JICA," in JICA, *Japan International Cooperation Agency*, Tokyo, 2007; also JICA, *JICA Policies: Human Security Overview*, Tokyo, 2007: www.jica.go.jp/english/about/policy/reform/human/index.html.

8 Otto von Feigenblatt, *Japan and Human Security: 21st Century ODA Policy Apologetics and Discursive Co-optation*, Academic Research International, 2007.

9 Gavan McCormack and Haruki Wada, "The Strange Record of 15 Years of Japan–North Korean Negotiations," *Japan Focus*, September 2, 2005, no. 1894.

10 Eric Johnston, "The North Korea Abduction Issue and Its Effect on Japanese Domestic Politics," JPRI Working Paper no. 101, June 2004.

11 Haruki Wada, "Japan–North Korea Diplomatic Normalization and Northeast Asian Peace," *Japan Focus*, 2004, no. 1551 (first appeared in Japanese in the journal *Sekai*, January 2004).

12 Gerald Curtis, "The US in East Asia: Not Architecture, but Action," *Global Asia*, 2007, 2 (2).

Chapter 8 Environmental Issues

1 For a critical assessment see Andrew DeWit, "The G8 Mirage: The Summit and Japan's Environmental Policies," *Asia-Pacific Journal: Japan Focus*, July 3, 2008, no. 2797.

2 Madeleine Brand, "Japan Struggles to Meet Its CO_2 Emissions Limits," National Public Radio (transcript), October 16, 2007.

3 Gavan McCormack, "Japan As a Plutonium Superpower," *Japan Focus*, December 9, 2007, no. 2602. McCormack explains why nuclear energy is not a viable option for solving global energy needs: "To double the nuclear contribution to the global energy, a new reactor would have to be built each week from now to 2075."

4 Eric Johnston, "Japan's Nuclear Nightmare," *Japan Focus*, January 19, 2005, no. 1694.

5 Timothy George, *Minamata: Pollution and the Struggle for Democracy in Postwar Japan*, Cambridge, MA: Harvard University Press, 2002.

6 For background on whaling controversies see Andrew Darby, *Harpoon: Into the Heart of Whaling*, Cambridge, MA: Da Capo, 2008.

7 In the 2008–9 hunt (December–April), the Japanese fleet killed 679 minke whales and 1 fin whale compared to a target of 935 minke whales and 50 fin whales, a shortfall due largely to the *Sea Shepherd*'s hindering operations.

8 Bharti Legro, "Whaling: The Meat of the Matter," *Japan Times*, July 22, 2008.

9 World Wide Fund for Nature, "Sink or Swim: The Economics of Whaling Today," June 2009: www.panda.org/iwc.

10 Peter Hartcher, "Japan's Fading Appetite for a Fight," *Sydney Morning Herald*, November 20, 2008. Also David McNeil, "End Game?," *Number 1 Shimbun*, Foreign Correspondents Club Japan, June 2009, p. 11.

11 For analysis of the politics of whaling and the motivations of actors involved in policy-making see Jun Morikawa, *Whaling in Japan: Power, Politics, and Diplomacy*, London: Hurst, 2009.

12 The town council of Taiji, Wakayama Prefecture, reversed a decision to introduce dolphin meat in school lunches due to concerns about high concentrations of mercury in dolphin meat. A 2009 study of town residents' hair samples indicated mercury concentrations 10 times the national average. This issue was raised in the documentary *The Cove* (2009), which focused on exposing the annual dolphin slaughter in Taiji that provoked an international outcry among animal rights activists. The film makes the point that dolphins, like whales, are cetacean mammals and as such should also be protected.

13 For a more detailed assessment see Chapter 5, "Downsizing the Construction State," in Jeff Kingston, *Japan's Quiet Transformation*, London: Routledge, 2004. Also Alex Kerr, *Dogs and Demons*, London: Hill and Wang, 2001; and Gavan McCormack, *The Emptiness of Japanese Affluence*, Armonk, NY: Sharpe, 1996.

14 Mutsuyoshi Nishimura, "Copenhagen and Japan," Association of Japan Institutes of Strategic Studies, Commentary no. 71, August 2009: www.jiia. or.jp/en_commentary/200908/04-1.html.

Chapter 9 Immigration

1 For an excellent analysis of this discourse and sensible policy proposals, see: Hidenori Sakanaka, *Towards a Japanese-Style Immigration Nation*, Tokyo: Japan Immigration Policy Institute, 2009. May be downloaded at http:// jipi.gr.jp.

2 For further analysis of this exclusionary phenomenon see Debito Arudou, *JAPANESE ONLY: The Otaru Hot Springs Case and Racial Discrimination in Japan*, Tokyo: Akashi Shoten, 2004.

3 Hiroko Tabuchi, "Japan Pays Foreign Workers to Go Home," *New York Times*, April 22, 2009.

4 For a detailed assessment see Junichi Goto, "Latin Americans of Japanese Origin (*nikkeijin*) Working in Japan: A Survey," World Bank Policy Research Paper no. 4203, April 2007.

5 Takeyuji Tsuda, "Japanese-Brazilian Ethnic Return Migration and the Making of Japan's Newest Immigrant Minority," in Michael Weiner (ed.), *Japan's Minorities: The Illusion of Homogeneity*, 2nd edn., London: Routledge, 2009, pp. 206–27.

6 Enrollment in national medical and unemployment insurance is compulsory in Japan for full-time workers, but has often been evaded by members of the foreign community. The workers and their employers can save on not paying the premiums, but this practice leaves them vulnerable. Medical insurance is typically paid together with national pension premiums, but since most *nikkeijin* do not expect to meet the minimum 25 years to collect their pensions, many opt out of both. In Japan, those who do not meet the 25-year minimum lose virtually all of their contributions, making it unattractive for foreigners who know they won't be around long enough to collect. From the late 1990s, the government successfully enrolled most *nikkeijin* in unemployment insurance.

7 Goto, "Latin Americans," p. 49.

8 Tsuda, "Return Migration," pp. 213–18.

9 Gracia Liu-Farrer, "Creating a Transnational Community: Chinese Newcomers in Japan," in Weiner, *Japan's Minorities*, pp. 116–38.

10 Daojiong Zha, "Chinese Migrant Workers in Japan: Policies, Institutions and Civil Society," in Tsuneo Akaha (ed.), *Proceedings, International Seminar: Human Flows across National Borders in Northeast Asia, Monterey, CA, November 2–3, 2001*, Monterey, CA: Center for East Asian Studies, January 20, 2002.

11 Hannah Beech, "Chasing the Japanese Dream," *Time*, December 6, 2007. Also see Pew Foundation Opinion Surveys.

12 For a critical assessment of this program see Satoshi Kamata, "Japan's Internship Training Program for Foreign Workers: Education or Exploitation?," translated and edited by Nobuko Adachi, *Japan Focus*, July 15, 2008.

13 *Japan Times*, August 27, 2008.

14 Ratification of the EPA with the Philippines was delayed so Filipinos began arriving in 2009.
15 NHK, March 11, 2007.
16 Gabriele Vogt, "'Guest Workers' for Japan? Demographic Change and Labor Migration to Japan," *Japan Focus*, September 15, 2007.
17 UN Population Division (UNPD), "Replacement Migration: Is It a Solution to Declining and Aging Populations?," March 21, 2000.
18 Nippon Keidanren (Japan Business Federation), "An Economy and Society That Responds to the Challenges of a Declining Population," October 14, 2008: www.keidanren.or.jp/english/policy/2008/073.html.

Chapter 10 War Memory and Responsibility

1 For a comprehensive rebuttal of such pan-Asian fantasies see Goto Kenichi, *Tensions of Empire*, Athens, OH: Ohio University Press, 2003; also Paul Kratoksa (ed.), *Asian Labor in the Wartime Japanese Empire*, Singapore: Singapore University Press, 2006.
2 For a thoughtful examination of this historical debate see Sven Saaler, *Politics, Memory and Public Opinion: The History Textbook Controversy and Japanese Society*, Munich: Deutsches Institut fur Japanstudien, 2005.
3 Yoshiko Nozaki, *War Memory, Nationalism and History in Japan: Ienaga Saburo and the History Textbook Controversy, 1945–2005*, London: Routledge, 2006; and Takashi Yoshida, *The Making of the "Rape of Nanking": History and Memory in Japan, China and the United States*, New York: Oxford University Press, 2006.
4 In post-Tiananmen Square China, the Communist Party sought to shore up its legitimacy by nurturing patriotic education that emphasized its role in defeating the Japanese and teaching Chinese students in gruesome detail about Japanese wartime atrocities. This nationalistic historical discourse in China had reverberations in Japan where conservatives were angered by this fanning of anti-Japanese sentiments. The emergence of a revisionist historical movement in Japan known as the Society for the Creation of New History Textbooks (Atarashi Rekishi Kyokasho oTsukuru-kai) represents, *inter alia*, a Japanese backlash against this patriotic education in China.
5 Yasuhiro Nakasone, *Japan Times*, September 21, 2006.
6 See Tetsuya Takahashi, "The National Politics of the Yasukuni Shrine," translated by Philip Seaton, *Japan Focus*, no. 2272: www.japanfocus.org. Also, Columbia University's Gerald Curtis in testimony to the US Senate in September 2005 said: "Yasukuni is not simply a shrine to honor the young men who fought and died for their country. Yasukuni honors the ideology and the policies of the government that sent these young men to war" (as quoted in *Japan Times*, August 12, 2006).

7   George Will, "Much To-Do about a Shrine," *Japan Times*, August 22, 2006.

8   Hisahiko Okazaki, "Seiron," *Sankei Shimbun*, August 24, 2006, as cited in Hisahiko Okazaki, "Change Needed at Yasukuni," *Japan Times*, September 5, 2006.

9   Saaler, *Politics*, p. 30 reminds us that Justice Pal may have found the defendants innocent of the charges, but Pal "although questioning the legitimacy of the trial did not doubt that Japan had actually conducted a war of aggression or committed war crimes."

10 Eiji Takemae, *Inside GHQ: The Allied Occupation of Japan and its Legacy*, London: Continuum, 2002, p. 250.

11 For analysis of right-wing politics in Japan see Yoshibumi Wakamiya, *The Postwar Conservative View of Asia*, Tokyo: LTCB International Library Foundation, 1999; and Ken Ruoff, *The People's Emperor: Democracy and the Japanese Monarchy 1945–1995*, Cambridge, MA: Harvard University Press, 2001.

12 After reflecting on the repercussions of his official visit, PM Nakasone has consistently and publicly opposed shrine visits by prime ministers and was an outspoken critic of PM Koizumi's visits. This is because he thinks that the costs of the visits in terms of damaging bilateral relations with China make it not worth going and that the national interest must trump personal agendas. Personal communication, Gerald Curtis, Burgess Professor of Political Science, Columbia University.

13 It is important to note that public support for and opposition to Yasukuni Shrine visits remain fluid and vacillate considerably, suggesting ambivalence among the Japanese people. According to an *Asahi Shimbun* poll conducted in August 2006 regarding whether the next prime minister should visit, 31% agreed and 47% opposed. See Asian opinion polls: www.mansfieldfdn.org/.

14 Ienaga Saburo, *Japan's Past, Japan's Future*, Lanham, MD: Rowman & Littlefield, 2000.

15 *Nihon Keizai Shimbun*, July 20, 2006. *Nikkei Weekly*, July 24, 2006 reported that the emperor "believed Yasukuni Shrine erred when it decided to include Class-A war criminals from WWII on its list of people honored there." Emperor Showa is quoted from the "Tomita memo" saying, "That's why I have not visited the shrine [again] … This is from my heart." Emperor Showa visited Yasukuni Shrine eight times after WWII, but never after the Class-A war criminals were enshrined there in 1978.

16 In the emergency poll conducted by *Asahi Shimbun*, July 22–3, 2006, right after the emperor's reservations were reported, only 20% favored a visit to Yasukuni Shrine by the next prime minister while 60% opposed a visit. See Asian opinion polls: www.mansfieldfdn.org/.

17 For analysis of the Tsukurukai see Gavan McCormack, "The Japanese Movement to 'Correct' History," in Laura Hein and Mark Selden (eds.),

Censoring History: Citizenship and Memory in Japan, Germany, and the United States, Armonk, NY: East Gate, 2000, pp. 53–73.

18 Ikuhiko Hata, "No Organized or Forced Recruitment: Misconceptions about Comfort Women and the Japanese Military," unpublished manuscript, 2007.

19 For further information and analysis see Yuki Tanaka, *Japan's Comfort Women: Sexual Slavery and Prostitution During World War II and the US Occupation*, London: Routledge, 2002; Yoshiaki Yoshimi, *Comfort Women: Sexual Slavery in the Japanese Military During World War II*, New York: Columbia University Press, 2000.

20 C. Sarah Soh, *The Comfort Women: Sexual Violence and Postcolonial Memory in Korea and Japan*, Chicago: University of Chicago Press, 2009.

21 The AWF's work has been preserved in a digital museum: www.awf.or.jp/e-guidemap.htm.

Chapter 11　The Imperial Family

1 Douglas McGray, "Japan's Gross National Cool," *Foreign Policy*, May/June 2002, pp. 44–54.

2 For an excellent assessment of the Japanese monarchy see Kenneth Ruoff, *The People's Emperor: Democracy and the Japanese Monarchy 1945–95*, Cambridge, MA: Harvard University Press, 2002.

3 Norma Fields, *In the Realm of the Dying Emperor: Japan at Century's End*, New York: Vintage, 1993. Crown Prince Akihito experienced the depths of these sentiments during a 1975 visit to Okinawa, narrowly escaping a petrol bomb thrown at him by a local extremist protesting the imperial presence.

4 "Statement of Protest to NHK," VAWW-NET Japan: www1.jca.apc.org/vaww-net-japan/english/backlash/statement_by_vaww.html.

5 Gavan McCormack, "How the History Wars in Japan Left a Black Mark on NHK TV (Their BBC)," February 2005, http://hnn.us/articles/printfriendly/9954.html.

6 "NHK Censored TV Show due to Political Pressure," *Japan Times*, January 14, 2005.

7 *Japan Times*, June 13, 2008.

8 Ben Hills, *Princess Masako: Prisoner of the Chrysanthemum Throne*, Los Angeles: Tarcher, 2006.

9 On invented traditions see Carol Gluck, *Japan's Modern Myths: Ideology in the Meiji Period*, Princeton, NJ: Princeton University Press, 1987.

Chapter 12　Yakuza

1 Jake Adelstein, *Tokyo Vice*, New York: Pantheon, 2009.

2 Taro Greenfield, *Speedtribes: Days and Nights with Japan's Next Generation*, New York: Harper, 1995.

3 Kenneth Szymkowiak, *Sokaiya: Extortion, Protection, and the Japanese Corporation*, Armonk, NY: East Gate, 2002. Also Mark D. West, "Information, Institutions, and Extortion in Japan and the United States: Making Sense of Sōkaiya Racketeers," *Northwestern University Law Review*, 1999, 93 (3), 767–817; Eiko Maruko, "Sokaiya and Japanese Corporations," *Electronic Journal of Contemporary Japanese Studies*, June 25, 2002.

4 Eiko Maruko, "The Underworld Goes Underground," *Harvard Asia Quarterly*, Summer 2002, VI (3).

5 This term was first coined by retired police chief Raisuke Miyawaki in 1992. Velisarios Kattoulas details the role of the yakuza in prolonging Japan's economic woes in the 1990s in "Yakuza Recession," *Far Eastern Economic Review*, January 7, 2002.

6 Robert Whiting, *Tokyo Underworld: The Fast Times and Hard Life of an American Gangster in Japan*, New York: Vintage, 2000. Also Howard Felson, "Closing the Book on Jusen," *Duke Law Journal*, 47 (Dec. 1997), 567–612.

7 Manabu Miyazaki, *Toppomano: Outlaw, Radical, Suspect. My Life in Japan's Underworld*, Tokyo: Kotan, 2005.

8 Peter Hill, "Heisei Yakuza: Burst Bubble and Botaiho," *Social Science Japan Journal*, 2003, 6 (1), 1–18.

9 Peter Hill, *The Japanese Mafia: Yakuza, Law and the State*, London: Oxford University Press, 2003, p. 176.

10 Ibid. Hill introduced the term "lumpen-yakuza" to refer to those on the lower rungs of the yakuza hierarchy.

11 Under this system, six randomly selected citizens and three professional judges preside over serious criminal cases that might involve the death penalty.

12 Albert Alletzhauser, *House of Nomura: The Inside Story of the Legendary Financial Dynasty*, New York: Arcade, 1990. Also Richard Hanson, "Uncharted Territory: Bubble to Bust," *Asia Times*, July 10, 2002.

13 *The Economist*, February 26, 2009.

14 Goto was excommunicated by the mob but has resurfaced as a Buddhist priest, hoping perhaps to discourage mob hits and police arrest while angling for the tax benefits accorded religious organizations.

15 Eiko Maruko Siniawer, *Ruffians, Yakuza, Nationalists: The Violent Politics of Modern Japan, 1860–1960*, Ithaca, NY: Cornell University Press, 2008.

Chapter 13   Prospects

1 Bill Emmott, *The Sun Also Sets: Why Japan Won't Be Number One*, New York: Simon and Shuster, 1989.

Further Reading

Chapter 1   Transformations After World War II

For a general background providing an overview from the Tokugawa era (1603–1868) to the end of the twentieth century, see Andrew Gordon, *A Modern History of Japan*, Oxford: Oxford University Press, 2002.

Two excellent and comprehensive works on the Occupation of Japan are John Dower, *Embracing Defeat*, New York: Norton, 1999; Eiji Takemae, *Inside GHQ*, London: Continuum, 2002. For more on how the Cold War influenced Occupation policies, see Michael Schaller, *The American Occupation of Japan*, Oxford: Oxford University Press, 1985. For more on labor relations during the Occupation, see Theodore Cohen, *Remaking Japan*, New York: Free, 1987.

A participant in writing Japan's Constitution has written an engaging memoir of her experiences: Beate Sirota Gordon, *The Only Woman in the Room*, Tokyo: Kodansha, 2001.

For a critical assessment of the International Military Tribunal for the Far East, see Richard Minear, *Victor's Justice*, Princeton: Princeton University Press, 1971. A more positive interpretation is presented in Timothy Maga, *Judgment at Tokyo*, Lexington, KY: University of Kentucky Press, 2001.

On the exposure to risk and the emergence of an ideology of self-responsibility, see Glenn Hook and Hiroko Takeda, "Self-Responsibility" and the Nature of the Postwar Japanese State: Risk through the Looking Glass," *The Journal of Japanese Studies*, Winter 2007, 33 (1), 93–123. On the subject of risk, see Ulrich Beck, *Risk Society*, translated by Mark Ritter, London: Sage, 1992.

Chapter 2   The Lost Decade

Christopher Wood, *The Bubble Economy*, Tokyo: Tuttle, 1993, is an engaging journalistic account of the Japanese asset bubble and its collapse. A collection of essays edited by Gary Saxonhouse and Robert Stern, *Japan's Lost Decade: Origins, Consequences and Prospects for Recovery*, London: Blackwell, 2004, presents a comprehensive economic analysis.

The policy lessons of the Lost Decade are examined by Richard Koo, *The Holy Grail of Macroeconomics*, New York: Norton, 2009; while Jeff Kingston, *Japan's Quiet Transformation*, London: Routledge, 2004, focuses on the social and political consequences.

Chapter 3   Defusing the Demographic Time Bomb

Florian Coulmas, *Population Decline and Ageing in Japan*, London: Routledge, 2008, provides a succinct assessment of Japan's various demographic challenges. Coulmas has also edited *The Demographic Challenge: A Handbook about Japan*, Leiden: Brill, 2008, a comprehensive tome by a group of international scholars running to almost 1,200 pages.

For health-related issues, see John Campbell and Naoki Ikegami, *The Art of Balance in Health Policy*, Cambridge: Cambridge University Press, 1998. The OECD's *Economic Survey of Japan*, Paris: OECD, 2009, includes an up-to-date assessment of the healthcare-related issues of rapid aging.

For basic information about aging in Japan, see International Longevity Center (Japan), *A Profile of Older Japanese*, Tokyo: ILC, 2009. For a somewhat alarmist perspective about the implications of aging, see Keimi Kaizua and Anne Krueger (eds.), *Tackling Japan's Fiscal Challenges*, New York: Palgrave Macmillan, 2006.

The National Institute of Population and Social Security Research provides data and links to articles concerning demographic trends and social security in Japan: www.ipss.go.jp/index-e.html.

The International Longevity Center–Japan provides data and comparative analysis of aging in Japan: www.ilcjapan.org/english.html. The Ministry of Health, Labour, and Welfare website is www.mhlw.go.jp/english/index.html.

Chapter 4   Families at Risk

Marcus Rebick and Ayumi Takenaka (eds.), *The Changing Japanese Family*, London: Routledge, 2006, is an interdisciplinary collection of essays on the family ranging from anthropology and sociology to economics and demography. Roger Goodman, *Children of the State*, Oxford: Oxford University Press, 2001, focuses on child protection institutions in Japan. Roger Goodman (ed.), *Family and Social Policy in Japan*, Cambridge: Cambridge University Press, 2002, is a collection of essays examining how various government policies affect the family.

On post-WWII trends in abortion, see Tianna Norgen, *Abortion Before Birth Control*, Princeton, NJ: Princeton University Press, 2001. For an intriguing look at law and suicide, see Mark West, *Law in Everyday Japan*, Chicago: University of Chicago Press, 2005. Yuko Kawanishi's *The "Lonely People"*, London: Global Oriental, 2009, examines the consequences of isolation for mental health. On unwed mothers, social policy, and inequality in Japan, see Ektarina Hertog, *Tough Choices*, Palo Alto, CA: Stanford University Press, 2009. Natsuo Kirino, one of contemporary Japan's leading novelists, has written about dysfunctional families in *Grotesque*, New York: Vintage, 2008 and *Real World*, New York: Vintage, 2009.

See a very useful website for educators maintained by Columbia University that has a section devoted to various aspects of the family in Japan among other topics: http://afe.easia.columbia.edu/at_japan_soc/.

Chapter 5 Jobs at Risk

The consequences of job insecurity are examined by Yuji Genda, *A Nagging Sense of Job Insecurity*, Tokyo: International House of Japan, 2005. Growing income disparities and the changing labor market are analyzed by Toshiaki Tachibanaki, *Confronting Income Inequality in Japan*, Boston: MIT Press, 2005. For an excellent description of Japan's secure employment system that anticipates recent changes, see John Beck and Martha Beck, *The Change of a Lifetime*, Honolulu: University of Hawaii, 1993.

The Japan Institute of Labor maintains a website featuring reports in English and various links, including the Japanese Journal of Labour Studies: www.jil.go.jp/english/index.html.

Chapter 6 Contemporary Politics

The best overall introduction is by Gerald Curtis, *The Logic of Japanese Politics*, New York: Columbia, 1999. Also see Louis Hayes, *Introduction to Japanese Politics*, Armonk, NY: Sharpe, 2004. The Koizumi era is analyzed in Steven Reed et al. (eds.), *Political Change in Japan*, Palo Alto, CA: Shorenstein Asia Pacific Research Center, Stanford University, 2009.

Japan's political revolution in 2009 is examined by co-authors Robert Pekkanen and Ellis Krauss, *The Rise and Fall of Japan's LDP: Political Parties as Institutions*, Ithaca, NY: Cornell University Press, 2010. Pekkanen has also authored an excellent book examining the potential and constraints of civil society organizations in Japan, *Japan's Dual Civil Society*, Palo Alto, CA: Stanford, 2006. Richard Samuels probes the history of leadership and scandals in post-WWII Japanese politics in *Machiavelli's Children*, Ithaca, NY: Cornell University Press, 2005.

For analysis of the politics of fiscal crisis, see Jennifer Amyx, *Japan's Financial Crisis*, Princeton, NJ: Princeton University Press, 2006. Stephen Vogel's *Japan Remodeled*, Ithaca, NY: Cornell University Press, 2006, provides an excellent analysis of policy reform and corporate restructuring in contemporary Japan. Leonard Schoppa's *Race for the Exits*, Ithaca, NY: Cornell University Press, 2008, analyzes the political economy of Japan's prolonged recession and the reasons why reform has been slow.

Tobias Harris, a former legislative aid in Japan's Diet, writes up-to-date and very insightful political analysis at www.observingjapan.com/. For links to numerous websites with information on Japanese politics, see http://web-japan.org/links/government/index.html.

Chapter 7   Security and the Peace Constitution

The best introduction to this subject is Richard Samuels, *Securing Japan*, Ithaca, NY: Cornell University Press, 2008. For analysis of contemporary security policy and how it has evolved during the Heisei era, see Andrew Oros, *Normalizing Japan*, Palo Alto, CA: Stanford, 2008.

The prospects for the US–Japan alliance are examined in Michael Green and Hideki Wakabayashi, *The US–Japan Alliance*, Washington, DC: Center for Strategic and International Studies, 2008. For analysis of Japan's post-Cold War foreign policy, see Michael Green, *Japan's Reluctant Realism*, New York: Palgrave Macmillan, 2003. For analysis of controversial plans to expand security cooperation with the US, see Christopher Hughes, *Japan's Security Policy and Ballistic Missile Defense*, London: Routledge, 2011.

Japan's Ministry of Foreign Affairs website is www.mofa.go.jp/. The Defense Ministry website is www.mod.go.jp/e/index.html.

Chapter 8   Environmental Issues

For a comprehensive assessment of Japan's environmental record and its policy miscues and successes, see Hidefumi Imura and Miranda A. Schreurs (eds.), *Environmental Policy in Japan*, Cheltenham, UK: Elgar, 2005. For analysis of current environmental policy, see Andrew DeWit, "Regime Change Short-Circuited: Carbon Emissions and Japan's Feed-in Tariff System," *The Asia-Pacific Journal*, November 9, 2009, 45-4-09 and Iida Tetsunari and Andrew DeWit, "Is Hatoyama Reckless or Realistic? Making the Case for a 25% Cut in Japanese Greenhouse Gases," *The Asia-Pacific Journal*, September 21, 2009, 38-4-09.

Robert Mason examines the environmental movement in Japan at century's end, "Whither Japan's Environmental Movement? An Assessment of Problems and Prospects at the National Level," *Pacific Affairs*, 1999, 72 (2), 187–207.

For an excellent critical assessment of Japan's whaling policy, see Jun Morikawa, *Whaling in Japan: Power, Politics, and Diplomacy*, London: Hurst, 2009. The government-funded organization responsible for promoting whaling is the Institute for Cetacean Research, www.icrwhale.org/eng-index.htm. In the Ministry of Agriculture, whaling is the responsibility of the Fisheries Agency, www.jfa.maff.go.jp/e/whale/index.html.

For more on the problems with Japan's reliance on nuclear energy, see Gavan McCormack, "Japan as a Plutonium Superpower," *Japan Focus*, December 9, 2007, no. 2602. The Ministry of Economy, Trade, and Industry (METI) blueprint for nuclear energy development, *The Challenges and Directions for Nuclear Energy Policy in Japan*, December 2006, is available at www.enecho.meti.go.jp/english/report/rikkoku.pdf. Japan's nuclear plans are further analyzed in Emma Chanlett-Avery and Mary Beth Nikitin, *Japan's Nuclear Future*, Washington, DC: Congressional Research Service, 2009.

Public opinion and nuclear energy is examined in Mindy Kotler and Ian Hillman, *Japanese Nuclear Energy Policy and Public Opinion*, Rice University, 2000, available online at www.rice.edu/energy/publications/docs/JES_NuclearEnergyPolicyPublicOpinion.pdf.

For general information on Japan's environmental policies, see the Ministry of the Environment at www.env.go.jp/en/. Further information is available at the National Institute for Environmental Studies www.nies.go.jp/index.html.

Chapter 9   Immigration

John Lie's *Multiethnic Japan*, Cambridge, MA: Harvard University Press, 2001, presents an interesting exploration of diversity in Japan that is both scholarly and personal. Michael Weiner (ed.), *Japan's Minorities*, London: Routledge, 2008, is an excellent collection of essays on various minorities in Japan that challenges notions of homogeneity and explores the dynamics of diversity.

Joshua Roth, *Brokered Homeland*, Ithaca, NY: Cornell University Press, 2002, focuses on Brazilian migrants in Japan, drawing on the author's ethnographic fieldwork. Ray Ventura's *Underground in Japan*, Manila: Ateneo de Manila University Press, 2008, gives an insider's view into the world of illegal migrant workers in Japan. Glenda Roberts and Mike Douglass (eds.), *Japan and Global Migration*, London: Routledge, 1999, examines the wave of migration during the late 1980s and 1990s and how migrants have coped and how Japanese society has responded.

For a running commentary about life for non-Japanese in Japan by a naturalized citizen originally from the US, see www.debito.org. Debito Arudou has also written an account of his legal struggles against discrimination in *Japanese Only*, Tokyo: Akashi Shoten, 2004.

The Ministry of Justice website is www.moj.go.jp/ENGLISH/index.html. The National Police Agency website is www.npa.go.jp/english/index.htm. For comparative migration policy, see the Migration Policy Institute, www.migrationinformation.org/Feature/display.cfm?id=487.

Chapter 10   War Memory and Responsibility

There is a vast literature on this subject, some of it cited in the footnotes for this chapter. Yoshiko Nozaki's *War Memory, Nationalism and Education in Postwar Japan*, London: Routledge, 2008 focuses on the political controversies over history textbooks and national identity in contemporary Japan. Franziska Seraphim in *War Memory and Social Politics in Japan, 1945–2005*, Cambridge, MA: Harvard, 2006, probes the politics of war memory, refuting assertions that collective amnesia prevails.

Jennifer Lind, *Sorry States*, Ithaca, NY: Cornell University Press, 2008, examines issues of war responsibility, contrition, and reconciliation, comparing Japan and South Korea with France and Germany, and questioning the premises of apology diplomacy. Alexis Dudden's *Troubled Apologies*, New York: Columbia, 2008, is an excellent read, exploring the nexus of politics, war memory, and apology and how it shapes contemporary relations between the US, Japan, and South Korea.

For an insightful overview about the ongoing debate over the Nanjing massacre, see Takashi Yoshida's *The Making of the "Rape of Nanking"*, New York: Columbia, 2006. Forced labor is examined in a series of articles by William Underwood at *Japan Focus*, www.japanfocus.org/. *Japan Focus* is a searchable online journal with an entire section devoted to history and historical events with many relevant articles on war memory.

Also see Paul Kratoska (ed.), *Asian Labor in the Wartime Japanese Empire*, Armonk, NY: Sharpe, 2005. Kenichi Goto, *Tensions of Empire*, Athens, OH: Ohio University Press, 2003, focuses on Japanese aggression in Southeast Asia, arguing that securing natural resources was more important as a motivation than pan-Asian solidarity, a factor emphasized by conservative Japanese scholars. For more on pan-Asianism, see Sven Saaler and J. Victor Koschmann (eds.), *Pan-Asianism in Modern Japanese History*, London: Routledge, 2007.

Yuki Tanaka's *Hidden Horrors*, Boulder, CO: Westview, 1997, and *Japan's Comfort Women*, London: Routledge, 2001, are authoritative accounts of Japanese war crimes.

The National Archives of Japan maintains a website called the Japan Centre for Asian Historical Records, with some English language documents such as transcripts of the International Military Tribunal for the Far East: www.jacar.go.jp/english/index.html.

Chapter 11 The Imperial Family

Herbert Bix won a Pulitzer for *Hirohito*, New York: Harper, 2001, a critical reassessment that challenged the emperor's more benign image that prevailed in the post-WWII era. Ikuhiko Hata's *Hirohito*, London: Global Oriental, 2007, examines critical decisions that defined his reign. Kenneth Ruoff's *The People's Emperor*, Cambridge, MA: Harvard, 2003, is a superb scholarly study of Emperor Akihito and his role in contemporary Japan.

Ben Hill, *Princess Masako*, Los Angeles: Tarcher, 2006, is a fascinating and sympathetic portrait of a troubled royal that stirred controversy and drew considerable criticism in Japan. John Schwartz's novel *The Commoner*, New York: Nan Talese, 2008, presents a captivating portrait of life inside the Imperial cocoon.

The Imperial Household Agency website is www.kunaicho.go.jp/eindex.html.

Chapter 12 Yakuza

The most comprehensive source is David Kaplan and Alec Dubro, *Yakuza*, Berkeley, CA: University of California Press, 2003. Peter Hill, *The Japanese Mafia*, Oxford: Oxford University Press, 2006, is an excellent scholarly study about contemporary developments. Robert Whiting, *Tokyo Underworld*, New York: Vintage, 2000, and Jake Adelstein, *Tokyo Vice*, New York: Pantheon, 2009, are very entertaining and insightful accounts of gangsters in Japan.

Insider perspectives are shared by Funichi Saga, *Confessions of a Yakuza*, Tokyo: Kodansha, 1995; Miyazaki Manabu, *Toppamono*, Tokyo: Kotan, 2005; and the daughter of a yakuza, Shoko Tendo, *Yakuza Moon*, Tokyo: Kodansha, 2009.

Additional Selected Internet Links

www.atimes.com/ (*Asia Times* online).

http://web-japan.org/stat/index.html (government statistics).

www.newsonjapan.com/ (current news on Japan culled from various sources).

www.jcer.or.jp/eng/index.html (Japan Center for Economic Research).

http://fuji.stanford.edu/jguide/ (Stanford University Jguide-Info clearing house).

http://coombs.anu.edu.au/asia-www-monitor.html (Australian Asian Info resources).

www.jpri.org/ (Japan Policy Research Institute).

www.japantoday.com/e/ (*Japan Today* daily news and features).

www.japanfocus.org/ (*Japan Focus*, searchable archive of social science articles on contemporary Japan).

www.japanesestudies.org.uk/ (electronic *Journal of Contemporary Japanese Studies*, searchable archive of social science articles on contemporary Japan).

www.japantimes.co.jp (*Japan Times* daily newspaper).

Index

abductions 135–40, 141–2, 169, 217
Abe, Shinzo 131–2, 133, 137, 140,
    143, 201, 215, 219, 220
abuses 61–2, 74, 75, 176, 199
  institutionalized 201
  systematic 203
  see also child abuse; domestic
    violence
accountability 6, 28, 32, 37, 193, 196,
    217–18
  improved 119
  poison victims' quest for 155–6
  promoting 27, 33, 259
Aegis destroyers 129
Afghanistan 133, 134, 142
Africa 130
aging population 35, 42, 55, 122, 248
  businesses catering to 57
  coping with 49
  healthy 58
  problems due to 62
  rapidly 41, 43, 65, 80, 82, 103, 104,
    121, 182, 231
  see also elderly people
Aiko, Princess 222
air force capabilities 129
Akahata (communist party
    newspaper) 114
Akaishi, Chieko 72
Akihabara 86

Akihito, Emperor of Japan 192, 205,
    209–26
Akishino, Prince 223, 224
Akita 81
alcoholism 68
alien registration cards 180
Alzheimer's 58, 61
amakudari 106, 112, 122, 161, 176,
    259
  citizens' deep misgivings about 31
Amaterasu 213
ANA 113
ancestral blood ties 172
Antarctic Ocean 160, 162
anti-Japanese demonstrations 12, 141,
    186
anti-Korean backlash 169
Anti-Poverty Network 87
anti-whaling activists 158, 160, 161
armed forces 126, 129
  see also Imperial Armed Forces;
    militarism; SDF; US Occupation
Asahara, Shoko 30
Asahi (newspaper) 128, 216, 218
ASDF (Air Self-Defense Force) 126,
    129, 130
Asia Cup (2004) 141
asset bubble 3, 13, 15, 21, 231, 234,
    237, 238, 240, 250, 251, 259
  bursting of 23, 25, 99, 209, 239